Chicago Kid

Chicago Kid

From Whence I Came

29 years a-growing, from cradle to altar, with plenty of humble heroes to guide my ways in the old Bridgeport neighborhood.

Hughie Boy LeVoy

To order additional copies of this book, contact:
Xlibris Corporation
1-888-795-4274
www.Xlibris.com
Orders@Xlibris.com
97256

Contents

to my parents,

Patrick and Margaret LeVoy,

from whence I came.

AUTHOR'S NOTE

Some forty years ago, I was watching the 10:00 PM news in Chicago. The coverage was of President John Kennedy thanking Mayor Richard J. Daley and the Illinois Democrats for his narrow victory in the 1960 Presidential election. Kennedy had won Illinois' 27 electoral votes by a razor-thin margin of 8,858 out of 4,845,000 votes cast. In his remarks, the President referred to Mayor Daley as "my old friend", and to Illinois as "from whence I came, in a sense."

I remember staring at the TV in our front room as Kennedy spoke, listening intently, watching him as a slow grin lit up his face after he said, "in a sense." Then the TV station returned to the news anchorman.

Kennedy's phrase "from whence I came" started to resonate with me immediately. It seemed to be a very unique and indirect way for him to say "Thanks" to the Democratic Party of Illinois for helping to elect him. And it was so subtly delivered, understated, with that characteristic JFK pause before he said it, as though he was letting us into a secret. Instead of gratefully saying "I owe it all to you", or a rousing "You put me over the top," there was this somewhat oblique, classical phrase, "from whence I came." I heard poetic sounds in the phrase, especially with the word, "whence." It brought me back to some distant time when language was not only written but also spoken with structure and rhythm, and most importantly, nuance. "Whence" conjured images in my mind of a single man coming out of the mist, walking in a foreign land.

I tucked "from whence I came" into my memory, hoping that someday I would resurrect the phrase and use it, perhaps in a memoir, or in a poem about my youth in Chicago. And, I continued to follow the Presidency and person of John F. Kennedy, devouring articles from the daily newspapers, reading books like *The Making of the President 1960* by Theodore White, watching coverage on television, and marveling at his speech style and New England accent.

Through my years of college, marriage, grad school, and career in teaching and administration, I would gently nudge the part of my memory that contained John Kennedy and "from whence I came." This was especially evident as I would plunge into the latest biography of the slain President, by now my fallen hero. His sudden, tragic death seemed to add poignancy to this old-world phrase that I was carrying along with me thru wife-loving, child-rearing, career-building, and of course, bill-paying.

When I finally reached the age of memoir-writing, it was obvious "from whence I came" would be in my title, somehow. I had never forgotten seeing and hearing John F. Kennedy say these words, and thought, for sure, that the occasion of his remarks was the Mayor Richard J. Daley Family visit to the White House on his first day in office, January 21, 1961. The Chicago papers made a big deal of the visit, emphasizing Daley's role as kingmaker in electing Kennedy to the Oval Office.

But to use JFK's phrase in my memoir title, I needed to verify where and when he said it, as well as corroborate why he said it, and what the phrase meant. I found the web page for the JFK Library in Boston. After skimming through various screens, I found Popular Quotations of President Kennedy. But, there was no listing for the date, January 21, 1961. However, there was a quotation from a speech that President Kennedy gave at Newport, RI to the crews of the America's Cup race on September 14, 1962. He used the phrase "from whence we came," referring to mankind's origins in the sea.

Next, I contacted Stephen Plotkin, Reference Archivist at the Kennedy Library to see if he could help. I told him of the "whence" phrase and the January 21st date of Kennedy's remarks, as I had remembered, and he searched the Kennedy White House key word index. There was no reference to the "whence" phrase in the index, nor were there any written versions of remarks by President Kennedy to the Daley Family from January 21st.

I checked with the Kennedy Library Senior Archivist, Allan Goodrich, in the Audiovisual Archives Dept. There was no transcript or television newsfilm of the Daley Family visit, he advised me.

I decided to search Kennedy biographies, written before or after his tragic death in November of 1963, to see if the authors covered the Daley Family visit from 1961, and also, perhaps, recorded President Kennedy's cryptic phrase, "from whence I came." The bibliography of JFK biographies that Stephen Plotkin sent to me from the Library shows at least 34 books in English, with quite a few in other languages. I searched at least 12 for the phrase, to no avail.

Doubts started in me as to my memory of hearing President Kennedy say the "whence" phrase 40 years ago. Maybe I imagined that he said it, made it up for some reason because I was such an avid follower of JFK. *He was my hero.* Or worse yet, I was a victim of memory loss while writing my own memoir! Could this have happened even though I had firm recollection of childhood events from as early as 1941? But then I would reassure myself that I had heard and saw him say it. And, it was already documented that he used the phrase "from whence we came" in 1962.

I had three more possibilities to investigate. One was the Daley Family. Even though Mayor Richard J. Daley was not alive, perhaps his son, Richard M. Daley, the current Mayor of Chicago, would have remembered Kennedy's phrase during the White House visit. Maybe Mayor Richard M. Daley would respond to a written inquiry.

Then there are the national television networks. Perhaps they would still have the newsclip in their archives, even though it would be 40 years old.

Finally, I found out accidentally that Theodore Sorenson, Special Counsel to President Kennedy, and also his speech writer, was in a law firm in New York City. I had been reading his book, *Kennedy*, and decided to write to him to see if he remembered the "whence" phrase from his first day of work in the White House.

I continued reading the Kennedy book by Sorenson, especially Chapter XXIV—"The Confrontation in Cuba." At one point in these thirteen critical days of October 16 to 28, 1962, that almost brought the United States and the Soviet Union to nuclear war, President Kennedy flew to Chicago. It was Friday, October 19th, and the Democrats of Illinois, led by Mayor Richard J. Daley, were having a political fund-raiser for the 1962 Democratic candidates for Congress. President Kennedy was to give a political speech to the Party faithful at McCormick Place, promoting the slate.

Much was written by O'Donnell, Powers, and McCarthy in their book, "Johnny, We Hardly Knew Ye," indicating that Kennedy had made a firm promise to Mayor Daley to come to Chicago in October to plug for the Democratic Congressional hopefuls, especially Rep. Sidney Yates, who was running against Sen. Everett Dirksen, the Republican minority leader of the United States Senate. And O'Donnell *et al.* further emphasized in the book that this political trip had to be made by Kennedy to avoid suspicions by reporters and speculation by politicians in Washington that a crisis was looming at the White House. *The quarantine against Russian ships going to Cuba was announced to the nation by President Kennedy on Monday, October 22nd.*

Slowly, something started stirring in my mind as I was reading about the missile crisis with Cuba and Russia. That trip by President Kennedy to Chicago caught my attention, even though I was somewhat captivated by the peril of the brink of nuclear war, and vividly remember listening to Kennedy's somber speech on national television from Monday the 22nd.

What if JFK didn't say "from whence I came" at the White House on January 21st, 1961. Maybe he said it in Chicago on a political trip there to thank Mayor Daley and the Democrats of Illinois for his narrow victory in November of 1960. Perhaps it was on this trip, October 19th, 1962, in McCormick Place on Chicago's lakefront, that Kennedy's political speech was covered by television, and his "whence" phrase was picked up and put on the 10:00 news as a pithy, political remark that would make a good sound bite. Could it be that my memory was all right, after all?

I had a chance to go to the Harold Washington Library in downtown Chicago to read the old newspapers on microfilm from October 20, 1962, the day after the Kennedy visit and speech. On the front page of the Chicago Tribune for that day, I found an article covering the visit and another article by George Tagge about the speech to the Democratic fund-raisers and party faithful.

I skimmed Tagge's article for the phrase "from whence I came," but it wasn't on page 1. I scrolled the microfilm to look at the continuation of the article on page 2, wondering if I would be disappointed again. I was now a little nervous, hoping that I'd find Kennedy's phrase. Quickly, my eyes located a section of the Tagge article that was headed—Introduced by Daley. I slowed down to read everything now! Tagge referred to Kennedy's compliment to Mayor Daley, "my old friend." And there it was, just resting on the screen, waiting for me to read it! Tagge wrote, "The President said of Illinois that it is 'from whence I came, in a sense.'"

WOW! I found it! After five months of searching, and doubts as to its existence, I had uncovered the when and where, the what and why of "from whence I came." My memory was still intact! I had nestled it into my memory that October night from 1962, knowing that I would never forget it, just as I couldn't ever forget the man who brought it into my consciousness, one of the humble heroes from whence I came.

The LeVoy House – 469 West 28th Place.
Remodeled exterior and interior, 1954-55

The LeVoy House gangway- next to Torrise`s House.

28th Place, looking east to Canal St. and then the
Railroad tracks and viaduct. The manhole cover in the
street foreground was homeplate for softball.

28th Place looking west to Normal Ave. and then
St.Anthony de Padua School and Church

1

PAT SEEREY

And somewhere men are laughing, and somewhere children shout,
But there is no joy in Mudville—mighty Casey has struck out

Ernest Lawrence Thayer, 1888, "Casey at the Bat"

Our playground was 28th Place between Canal St and Normal Ave. in the old Chicago neighborhood of Bridgeport. It was the 1940's and we played all kinds of games on the street, on the sidewalks, dirt parkways, yards, and alleys. There was "Chase," a rough game involving a lot of running thru gangways, backyards, and the alleys. "Kick the Can" was always played at night so the kid who was ON couldn't see you sneak up to kick the can off the manhole cover in the middle of the street. "Horses on the Runaway" was a game that girls and guys would play together. One person was ON in the center of 28th Place. When he or she yelled "Horses on the Runaway," we all had to run across from curb to curb. Whoever got tagged was ON with the starter for the next "Runaway."

There were sidewalk games like "Hopscotch" and "Handball," and one of my best, "Bounce or Fly," where the hitter would throw a rubber ball against the front stairs of a house. One or two opponents would have to catch the ball after it went flying, either on one bounce or on the fly. And we used to really work up a sweat with "Runnin' Bases." Two boys with baseball gloves would stand fifteen feet apart and toss a hardball back and forth. The runner in the middle had to get from one base (player) to another *without* gettin' tagged (or getting' hit in the head with the ball).

"Rummy," "War," and "Crazy 8" were card games we'd play on Torrise's front porch when we were tired of runnin' or the weather was bad. Oh the

1

arguments we would have over card games, and all for nothin' because we never had any money to bet. Later on, when we did have money from deliverin' papers, the card game was always "Penny Poker," a penny bet on each card and no more than two raises on the last card.

"Marbles" was another quiet game we would play in someone's backyard or on the parkway. The parkway was a stretch of dirt and sometimes trees about four feet wide that ran the length of the block, from curb to sidewalk. We'd draw a circle about three feet in diameter in the dirt with a stick, ante up three or four marbles, and then lag our Shooters into the circle to see who got to shoot first. Every Shooter was bigger than the other marbles we had, very colorful, and could easily knock out the smaller marbles called pee-wees, when shot into the circle with a flick of the thumb sliding off the fore-finger. *The kid with the biggest Shooter usually won the marbles.*

The first game to have an impact on me was "Piggy in the Hole." I must have been around five years old because Piggy was a safe game for little kids on the block. We were not allowed to play on the street or alleys or around the corner in the empty lot on 29th and Canal. Three or four of us kids would dig a hole in the parkway in front of Mary Regan's house that would be big enough to hold a rubber ball. Then, each player, one at a time, would stand about ten feet away from the hole on the parkway and roll the small rubber ball along the dirt toward the hole. If the ball landed in the hole and stayed there, the player would shout "PIGGY IN THE HOLE," and he would get a point. The winning score was seven points.

One sunny, Sunday afternoon four of us kids had begun to play Piggy. I was standing by the hole as Huck Lynn rolled the ball. He rolled it too hard and it hit a small tree beyond the hole and bounced into the street. I yelled "I got it," and raced over the curb and into the street for the ball. Suddenly there was a loud, screeching sound, like brakes on a car!

The next thing I remember was waking up in the kitchen of our 2nd floor flat, with my father looking at me, my worried mother, my brothers and sisters, and this strange man. I was sitting in my father's kitchen chair and they were standing by the old, iron kitchen stove and the ice box.

"How are you?" my father asked as he rubbed my head. (He always would rub the kids' heads when he came home from work, with a big smile on his face).

"Wha . . . What happened," I whispered.

"You were hit in the rear end by this man's car," Daddy said.

"I didn't mean to," the strange man said nervously. "You ran out so fast, I couldn't stop in time. I just bumped you a little in your backside. Are you O.K.?"

I cried and dropped my head. I still didn't understand what happened.

He'll be all right," said Daddy. "But no more Piggy in the Hole for Hughie Boy."

*

Every Fall there was "Touch Football" in the street, or "Tackle" in Mary Regan's backyard. She was the only one on the block to have grass in her yard. We'd always sneak into her yard from the alley, hoping that she wasn't home. Mary would yell from her second floor windows if she saw us playing Tackle. She didn't like all the noise we'd make, and the arguing from the game.

One day, tall Jimmie Allen took the kickoff by the alley fence and came running straight toward me. I got down low to tackle him, so he tried to hurtle me, figurin' he could easily get over this little kid. But I came up slightly in my stance, just caught his shoes with my hands as he was flying over my head. What a crash he made as he hit the grass, head first. He rolled over, and got up with this crazy look on his face.

"You dummy, yer tryin' to kill me! Yer not s'posed to do that," he screamed at me and came real close, staring down at me.

I couldn't help but smile at him. "We're playin' tackle, ain't it!"

If we were playin' Football on the street, it was always Touch, not Tackle. No blocking either. The end zones were the manhole covers and the curbs were the out of bounds lines. We'd use that old football until the pigskin was all worn off the ends and the inner tube started to pop like a balloon. No amount of tape could keep those little black bubbles inside the cover.

I used to listen to the Chicago Bears football games on Sunday afternoons after church in Grandma Bosak's parlor. She had a small white radio on one of her end tables by the sofa. She owned the two-flat where we lived. We were on the 2nd floor and Grandma lived on the 1st. She was not really our Grandma. Her daughters and grandchildren lived in Nevada and Arizona. But she really liked it when we called her Grandma.

Our radio upstairs did not work very well and Grandma always liked the company I provided when I came down to listen to the football games and read the National Geographic magazine that she would get each month. She was Hungarian from the "old country." She told me once that she knew the groundskeeper, Mr. Doerr, at Wrigley Field, where the Bears played their home games. She also knew that George Halas, the Bears owner was Hungarian. One late Fall day I said jokingly to her, "Grandma, our football just busted and can't be fixed. Can you ask your friend Mr. Doerr to get a football from Mr. Halas? Even a used one would be good."

Three days later, Grandma called me to her front door as I was coming home from school at St. Anthony's. She reached behind her for something. "Yah, vy na' sure, Mr. Halas sent this to me for his little Bear fan."

I couldn't believe it! Here was a genuine Chicago Bears football. Real leather with the National Football League printed on it. I hugged Grandma. She was all smiles as I tossed it from hand to hand, getting the feel of the new ball. I even put it to my nose to pick up that new, leathery smell. Wow!

All of a sudden, I was the most popular kid on the block. All the guys wanted to feel and toss around the new ball.

"Man, what a football. I betcha I can throw it thirty yards. It's Johnny Lujack fadin' back to pass," shouted one of the older guys who usually was a captain and played quarterback on our street games. He stopped fading and threw a perfect spiral to Carl who had started running down the street for a pass.

Carl caught the ball in mid-stride and then did some fancy zigs and zags to avoid the imaginary tacklers in his way. When he got to the manhole cover, he turned around, took two long strides and then we heard a dull POP sound as he punted the ball back to us.

Did that ball soar, going over our heads, landing about twenty feet from the corner, and then tumbling end over end toward the intersection.

But the best game, the game we never got tired of, the game that required so much thinking, scorekeeping, arguing Foul or Fair, Safe or Out, Ball or Strike, the game that we would talk about endlessly, memorize players and statistics in the paper, the game that I was always "hungry" for was *Baseball*.

And of all the guys on that block of 28th Place; Jimmie Allen, my brother Patrick, Carl Torrise, Richie Johnson, Frank Schicke, Huck Lynn, and Johnny Stephens, I was the one who would fall under Baseball's spell, live and die for the game, and devote my youth to the sport and to my team, the Chicago White Sox.

*

I turned the dial slowly on the old console radio in the living room between the two front windows, but I couldn't find the ballgame. It was supposed to be on WGN. But all I could get was static from this old thing as the lighted numbers inside the little window in the center showed 100, 90, 80. Finally, I could hear what sounded like a crowd, and cheering, and an announcer.

"Hank Greenberg comes striding up to the plate. It was his homerun in the 8th inning that tied up this ballgame at 7 and 7. And the hopes of the Detroit fans ride right now on the broad shoulders of Big Hank Greenberg as he strides up to the plate. He's hit a couple of homeruns in this World Series. He hit one down in Briggs Stadium and he's hit one here. He's batted in 5 runs, 6 runs for the Detroit Tigers. Borowy curves him carefully under the knees for ball one. One out, Kramer on at first in the top half of the 10th inning. Hank Greenberg at the plate now. Holds that bat high off of his right shoulder.

Borowy checks his runner at first and delivers to the plate. *And Greenberg swings and misses. He really swung!"*

It was October 8th, 1945. I was seven years old, listening to my first World Series game. The Cubs were battling the Tigers at Wrigley Field, with Big Al Helfer doing the play-by-play and Bill Corum, the color and highlights. I could hear the kids outside the house, playing on the sidewalk, but I, I had to listen to this game. I was glued to that old radio for every pitch, every hit, comment, cheer, you name it. It didn't matter that the sun was shining outside and the kids on the block were having fun. I was captivated by the words of that announcer telling me of the drama at Clark and Addison Streets on the north side of Chicago.

It was now the bottom of the 12th inning. Bill Slater took over the play-by-play for the Gillette Cavalcade of Sports. "Fordham" Hank Borowy had held the Tigers scoreless for four innings. Billy Schuster was on first, pinchrunning for Frank Secory who had singled to center for the Cubs. Stan Hack was coming to bat.

"There's a called strike that Trout puts in on him. Fast one just above the knees and on the inside corner. There's a tremendous hole between center and right field. Schuster has a long lead off first. Trout delivers to the plate. Schuster goes back to first and that is strike two on Mr. Hack. Hack was backing away from it but it nipped the inside corner on him . . . . *And Charlie Grimm comes charging in from third, shouting like a bull . . . .* Now Jolly Charlie goes back into the box. Takes off his hat. Two strikes is the count on Hack. Two outs. Game winning run is at first. *Here's the pitch.* Outside, ball one. One and two on Stanley Camfield Hack. One of the greatest third basemen in the history of baseball. 36 years old. Knows a lotta ball. *There's a throw over to first and Schuster has to dive in on his stomach.* He was traveling right in there on the pit of his stomach, sliding and reaching for that bag. *Trout's throw over to York was fast . . . .* Here's the pitch to Hack. It's fouled off as Schuster was breaking for second . . . . Hack busted his bat on that. The count on him is one ball, two strikes. And Hack goes trotting over to the Cub dugout, which is just out of the third base, to get a new bat. And he's going to pick out the one that he himself personally selects. Little Jimmy Shilekas, the batboy for the Cubs finds one for him. Hack looks at it and says it's all right. Now he's beating the handle end of it on the ground just to make sure it rings true. 'Cause I doubt if Hack has ever been up to bat in a more important spot than this one right here . . . . Billy Schuster is leading down first there. He's a Buffalo boy, born, bred, and lives there. And Hack up here with a count of one ball and two strikes on him, and two outs. *Now Schuster is breaking. Hack hits it. It's a clean hit out into left field. And it bounces over Greenberg's head and is rolling towards the wall and Schuster's rounding third and Schuster comes in to score, and the Cubs win."*

I continued to listen as the cheers went on and on from the Cub fans. Bill Corum was raving about the exciting finish to this 6th Game, and telling all the listeners that the showdown 7th game would be on Wednesday, right here at Wrigley Field. I was flushed with excitement myself, and didn't even feel my mother poking me and telling me to go outside and get some fresh air.

*

I could see my Dad's car as it turned the corner on 28th and Normal, heading for home after a days work at the Wabash Railroad. It was the summer of '46 and he was driving a 1938 Plymouth, 4-door sedan. Patrick and I and our friends stood on the parkway between the curb and sidewalk waiting for him to park. I was especially anxious to see him because the White Sox had a night game. He smiled as he got out of the car, and we all waited for him to come on the parkway.

I blurted out, "Dad, can we go to see the Sox tonight. Whitey Platt is playing left field. I just know he's going to hit a homer. Please, Dad. We can sit in left field and catch the ball. We've got plenty of time because it starts at 8:30."

I don't know if my voice sounded like begging, but I would just about do anything to see the Sox play. And my father knew how much I wanted to go to Comiskey Park. All I ever did at home when I wasn't in school was listen to the Sox on radio. Bob Elson, the Commander, was the announcer on WJJD. I would do all my chores in such a way that I could listen and work. It was funny too because the Sox home games were announced live from Comiskey Park, but the road games were by ticker tape. Elson would read the ticker tape in the Chicago studio of WJJD, and then make up part of the play-by-play. I could always tell when a hitter was going to hit a double or triple or home run, because Elson would drag out the "and here comes the pitch," so I was tense waiting to hear what happened.

We didn't go to the Sox game that July night in '46. My father had some work to do after supper in the basement, and he never said, "Let's go." Perhaps he was tired, with five kids and one on the way, working part-time as a carpenter on his days off from the Railroad, as well as being the handyman for Grandma Bosak. More than likely, he didn't have the money for the game. Even in the 40's, before the GO GO SOX, it cost to go to a major league baseball game.

I played Bounce or Fly outside that night after supper, and as dusk started coming around 8:30, I started to drift from the game we were playing and imagined I was in the left field stands at Comiskey Park. Whitey Platt was moving into the batter's box. I stood up in front of my seat and yelled, "C'mon Whitey, show 'em where you live. Hit one out here! C'mon Whitey, you can do it." And in my twilight reverie, Whitey pulled a fastball from the St.Louis Brown's lefty on the mound and lined it toward me. All the fans in left field stood up, cheering. I jumped on my seat to see better. The ball was coming closer, arching down, straight at me. I reached out with both hands, hoping the shock of catching that hardball would not sting too much!

"Whadda ya doin' Hughie Boy," my Bounce or Fly teammate yelled. "Get yer head in the game" as the rubber ball went flying past me and rolled across the street.

The Left Field fantasy was broken. I was still on 28th, chasing some kid's home run.

Whitey Platt was my first baseball hero. I don't know why. He only played one full season with the Sox., 1946. He hit just three homers that year in 247 at bats. Why Whitey? Maybe because he played left field and that's where my father liked to sit. Perhaps it was his nickname, Whitey. (His full name was Mizell George Platt).

My father's older brother, Uncle Johnny was "Whitey." And Whitey has been a baseball nickname. Whitey Kurowski—St.Louis Cardinals in the 40's. Whitey Lockman—New York Giants in the 40's and 50's. Whitey Ford—New York Yankees in the 50's and 60's. And Whitey Herzog—Kansas City Royals in the 70's and 80's.

Maybe it was simpler than that. Whitey was my hero because he batted and threw right-handed, *just like me.* And he was big, 6'1 and ½" and 190lbs, *not like me!*

My addiction to the White Sox continued. I *had* to listen to every game (154 games in a season), or find out how they did when I got home from school. My hunger was not satisfied with hot dogs and peanuts, but with the food of Sox action. The more they lost, 6th Place in 1945, 5th Place in 1946, the more I continued to follow them on the radio and in the papers. I was in 3rd Grade and gobbled up everything about them in the *Herald-American* sports pages. My older sister Mag was now deliverin' papers after school, and I would take our family copy as soon as her bundle was delivered in the early afternoon to our porch. I'd read about "Luscious" Luke Appling, Joe Haynes, Bob Kennedy, Casimir (Cass) Michaels. And my favorite baseball player name, Dario Lodigiani (DAR ee o Lo de gee AHN ee).

By October of 1946, our family was complete, three girls; Mag, Kate, and now Maureen. And three boys; Patrick, Hugh, and Fred. Patrick later became "Jake." He got the nickname at the end of 8th grade in 1950 when he had a fistfight with Little Red right in front of Schmidt's Grocery Store on the corner. One of my brother's classmates at St.Anthony's, Nickie Spata, liked the way my brother was fighting, and called him "Jake" after the reigning middleweight champion, Jake LaMotta. The nickname stuck!

Once in a while my mother liked to go downtown with the kids to shop at Sears on State and VanBuren Streets for clothes, and walk down to the basement to Hillmans for some smoked fish—my father's favorite—and for pigs' feet—not the kid's favorite. She would always park Jake, Fred and I by the big magazine rack on the first floor. We had to stay there and amuse ourselves with the magazines until she finished shopping. Needless to say, Jake and I sampled every Sports and Car magazine on the rack, and Fred looked at the comic books. We would be there over an hour and never lost interest or were bored, waiting for Mommy. The old man who was behind the counter for tobacco and magazines would give us dirty looks, because he knew we were killing time, but we didn't care. Our mother had told us to stay by the magazines until she came back.

One Saturday morning in October of 1947, we were again taking the Racine Downtown streetcar to shop at Sears. The trolley stopped at 29th & Canal for passengers and then make a quick turn to Canal St. Mommy lurched as she was giving her nickel to the conductor, while holding Maureen. We kids moved around the rear compartment, past the conductor to get to the seat section of the streetcar. I didn't like the hard, wicker seats, but was hypnotized by the sights of Chicago and the sounds of grinding of the iron wheels on the rails, the bell that signaled the motorman to move ahead, and the frequent flashes of sparks as the trolley arm rode along the overhead wire, sending electricity to the motors.

As soon as we got to Sears, I asked Mommy if I could go upstairs to the new television section on the third floor, instead of going to the magazine stand. She looked surprised even though we didn't have a TV at home. I told her that the World Series was on TV, and I wanted to see the Yankees play the Dodgers, especially see Yogi Berra and Jackie Robinson.

When Jake and Fred and I made it to the 3rd floor on the elevator, the television sales area was right in front of us, along a wide walkway down the center of the floor.

"WOW! Look at all those TVs," I yelled to my brothers. There must have been twenty of them on each side of the aisle. It was hard to find one TV that didn't have four or five boys and men in front, watching the start of the game.

"Good Afternoon, folks. This is Mel Allen, bringing you the 5th game of the 1947 World Series between the New York Yankees and the Brooklyn Dodgers. *What a matchup we have today!* For the Yankees, it's Spec Shea, the burly righthander, 'The Naugatuck Nugget.' Shea won Game 1 of the Series over Ralph Branca. And for the Dodgers, it's Rex Barney, the tall righthander from Omaha."

My brothers and I found a good spot to stand by one of the TVs. The salesman didn't know whether to feel good about all the interest in the television sets, or to get mad because all the viewers were men and boys looking at the game. Then a woman came along and started asking him questions about the sets. You could see the smile on his face as he sized up his next sale.

I was totally captivated by the game. It was like watching magic. The World Series! Ebbetts Field! DiMaggio, Berra, Heinrich, Rizzuto. And on the other side, Jackie Robinson, PeeWee Reese, Carl Furillo, and one of my new baseball heroes, relief pitcher Hugh Casey! I was completely oblivious to anyone around me as the game went on. I watched each pitch to see how Spec Shea rotated on the pitching rubber and followed thru to home plate with the ball, and how Yogi Berra would come out of his catcher's stance like a bolt if some Dodger—Robinson or Reese or Stanky—was on first and tried to steal second. I was totally intent when Joe Di stepped to the plate the first time and took that nice full stride as he swung at Barney's pitch. I could see the crowd and hear them and wished I was out there. The October sun was shining in Brooklyn and the shadows already were creeping up the home plate umpire's back as they moved forward to the pitcher's mound, engulfing the batter in darkness while the pitcher was in light.

I didn't even notice my brother Jake poking me. "C'mon, let's go. Mommy's here."

I looked around and saw her in the middle of the aisle with the girls. She had this knowing smile on her face, like, "you're just so crazy about baseball. How can I ever get you away from a game?"

I protested to Jake and to her, "Wait for the next batter. DiMaggio's up again."

All of a sudden I heard Mel Allen raise his twangy voice. *"And there's a long one to left. Hermanski goes back, back. It's going, going, gone. Home Run! Joe DiMaggio belts it over the fence and high up into the crowd! Yankees 2 Dodgers 0"*

I smiled. "Thataway, Joe," and hurried to catch up to my mother who was stepping into the elevator with the other kids.

During that summer of '47 all the boys on the block played softball in the street. Home plate was the manhole cover in the middle of the street. First base was a piece of cardboard along the curb on the other side of the street. The next manhole cover was second, and third base was another piece of cardboard on our side of the street. We played from 9 AM to noon, had some lunch, and then went out again for an hour until it was time to deliver papers. Our dugout was the curb under the tall trees in front of Torrise's house, next to ours at 465 W. 28th Place. We were truly the "Boys of Summer," playing ball all day long.

Fair territory was basically the street because if someone hit a ball into a front yard, he was Out. Also, we had to learn to hit line drives and straight away, because every house had front windows. We couldn't afford to pay for a broken window. We always played Pitcher's Mitts are Out, if we didn't have enough guys to have a first baseman. The best way to hit was "down and hard." Drive that softball down onto the street so that it started bouncing, and no one could field it cleanly and throw to the pitcher for the Out. Pop Ups were easy Outs, along with Fly Balls.

We never had to worry about hitting cars because all the men took their cars to work during the day,. There would be an occasional car that came down the street (I'd move to the curb, remembering Piggy in the Hole), or a truck with a delivery. We used to ask our milkman, Herb Martin, not to park in fair territory, even though his delivery of milk and cream to our house would put his truck in front of third base.

The softball was called a sixteen-incher. That was the circumference. It was hard and white when brand new, but pretty soon it softened as the guys would hit it. You didn't want to *ever* catch a line drive when the ball was new because it would sting your hands something fierce. We really liked to get a Clincher softball because the seams were better than a softball with string seams. The Clincher would last forever (or at least a month).

My hunger for softball was heightened each morning as the guys on the block got together to choose teams. They were all one or two years older than me, so I was either picked last to play on a side, or was told to sit on the curb until another kid showed up to make even sides. I knew I could play as good as the older guys, but I was small. Nobody wanted the little kid on their team. "He can't hit it past the pitcher!" was the complaint. So, sometimes I'd sit on the curb with my head down, kicking the street with my shoe, dropping deeper within myself, half-listening to the sounds of the game, and half-trying to avoid the hurt of not being picked, not playing the game I loved.

I'd tell myself that I can hit, and field too. And I'm faster on the bases than any of these big guys, even Jimmie Allen. They'll see. When I get in the game I'll catch every pop up in my hands, not my gut! And I'll pick up those grounders and throw to the pitcher. These guys'll find out how good I am. They'll see!

THUMP brought me back to the game as Carl hit a solid fly ball to center field. CLANG went his bat as it bounced on the asphalt and rolled toward my feet and the curb.

"I got it," yelled the outfielder on my brother's team.

"Run Carl. He's gonna drop it," shouted the other team.

Sure enough, he did drop it!

"You dummy, why didn't you catch it in your gut?"

"Aw, shut up. It was too high. If you're so good, you play center field"

There never was a quiet, friendly game!

And then at night, after a day of chores at home, softball on the street, deliverin' papers in the neighborhood, and games of Chase and Kick the

Can before dark, five or six of us kids would settle down to the bottom steps of my porch, lettin' the sweat roll down our cheeks, waitin' for any kind of breeze to come along the sidewalk and cool our foreheads. My parents were above us, sittin' on the second floor stoop, talkin' quietly, enjoyin' the flavor of the summer night, watchin' the northern skyline and lights of Chicago, and catchin' a better wind off nearby Lake Michigan.

I'd be happy because I was part of the gang, the kids on the block. There were no worries at night among us because everyone on the block knew each other. We were neighbors, families, guys, girls, teammates, classmates, friends. We belonged here. We were bonded and bounded by this Bridgeport block of 28th Place. It was our street, our alley. These buildings were our houses, gangways, yards and sidewalks. The asphalt and manhole covers and curbs were our "stadium" where the dreams of play and competition were carried out in all seasons, not just summer.

As if by magic, like Cinderella's warning to be home by midnight, our interlude would be broken each night at 10 PM with calls by parents for their kids to come home to go to bed. Starting with stern Mr. Johnson from the second floor porch, two doors east of us, we'd hear "Dick, Shirl, Carol." Then from other front porches came "Frankie," and "Carlo," and "Johnny." And finally, I'd hear my father above us, with a slight tone of sadness, "It's time to go in." Another summer day slides into darkness and sleep. 28th Place is quiet now, except for a lonely car passing on Canal Street.

By the summer of '48, the guys on the block were old enough to go beyond to play ball, walk to the Salvation Army gym on 31st for basketball, see the movies at the Wallace Theatre, go swimming at Mark White Square Park on Halsted St., and hike to Sox Park on our own. One of our favorite games was to play Fast Pitchin' in the small empty lot around the corner on 29th & Canal. We would draw a strike zone on the side of the brick building that was next to the empty lot, bring along a piece of wood for home plate, and play pitcher vs. batter with balls and strikes, hits, pop ups, etc. The pitcher would start his windup about thirty feet from the batter and give him his best fastball on every pitch. If the batter took the pitch, or swung and missed, the rubber ball would bounce off the building and roll back to the pitcher. Pretty soon, some of the guys could really time the fastball, so we started fooling around with a curve ball and the change. Since the ball we used was hard rubber with seams, a pitcher's mistake would be hit all the way up the railroad tracks on Canal for a round tripper.

Spats Field was on the "other side" of those tracks at 28th Place. We had to walk under the tracks thru the viaduct to get to the other side. This field was our favorite place to play "Hardball" or "League" as some of the guys called it. Spats Field was a vacant lot where a big, three-story building had been torn down some years before. The "Field" was full of small bricks, pieces of plaster, weeds, and some dirt. But it was great for Hardball because there was only one house we had to worry about, and that was down the 3ʳᵈ base line. Right field was short, with Stewart Ave. and the massive wall of the train tracks looming fifteen feet high. A shot over this wall was *not* a homer. It was the end of the game because we only had one ball. It took half an hour to go back under the viaduct to the Canal St. side of the tracks, climb up the short wall, watch out for the railroad dicks, look forever down the tracks both ways to see if any trains were coming, then run across twenty pairs of tracks, and finally look for the baseball.

But when we did play at Spats, it was always the Sox vs. the Yanks. The two captains would use a bat and take alternate hand grips on the bat to see who had first pick and got to be the Sox for the game. If there were six guys playing, each side would have a pitcher, an infielder, and an outfielder, and Pitcher's Mitts are Out. All ground balls had to be fielded and thrown to the pitcher before the batter reached first base. If there were eight players, we'd add a first baseman, and play First Base Out. Defensive positions rotated every inning so we all had a chance to pitch. A piece of cardboard was our scorecard, or a piece of old plaster used for a pencil on a slab of rock.

"I'm Snuffy Stirnweiss," said Little Red as he stepped up to be the first Yankee hitter.

"Yah, yer goin' to see a Howie Judson fastball," said Frankie as he wound up, taking a double rotation of his arm before he pivoted and fired the pitch.

"C'mon Howie, get 'em," I'd be yellin' from my infield position. "Show those Yankees who's boss."

The best part of playing at Spats Field for right-handed hitters was that you could blast away with the bat and see how far you could pull the ball. Center field was just a continuation of Stewart Ave. and the massive tracks wall. Left field was almost one half block long. No one ever hit one into the left field street.

The worst part of Spats Field was the infield. The dumbest move an infielder could make on a ground ball hit hard to him was to get in front of it. So many tricky hops could happen to that ball with stones and weeds, that no one *ever* played grounders in front of them, unless they were slowly hit. One day, Johnny got in front of a shot off the bat of Carl that bounced once. Johnny thought he had the ball all the way, but it took another short hop and came up on him right into—you know where! (Now, we never wore jock straps or cups, never even heard of 'em.) Poor Johnny gave a cry of agony and crumpled in pain to the ground. We ran to his aid but all we really could do was loosen his belt. When the hurt finally subsided, Johnny returned to his position, sporting a new, falsetto voice.

One afternoon, we were sitting around the corner on Canal, between Fast Pitchin' games, just lookin' at those railroad tracks. One of the guys said, "Ya know, if we walk the tracks from here to 33rd, we can hangdrop on the other side and go see the Sox play."

Pretty soon we were doin' it, but with a whole lot of fear. Up on the tracks, we usually walked along the Canal St. side because we could drop off the tracks easily since the wall was not as high as the Stewart side. We had to constantly listen for trains however. One of the guys said that if a fast train went by and you were on the side of the tracks, it would suck you into the wheels and you'd be ground up like hamburger. *Ooh! No one wanted to get close to a train to test that!*

The real physical part of "walkin' the tracks" was the hang drop at 33rd by the Sox parking lot. Fifteen feet is a lot to drop, even though we were hanging down from the edge with our height of 3'6" or 4'. The guys who were good at hang drops said to land on your toes so it wouldn't be such a shock for your feet. But the first time I did a hang drop from the tracks' wall, my feet were tingling in pain and shock after I hit the dirt. I had to tiptoe across the parking lot to get to the Park.

We used to get to Sox Park at least an hour and a half before the game started, 12:00 noon for a day game, or 7:00 for a Night Game. It was easy to get into the Park because trucks would be delivering concessions, and no ushers were by the pass gates that early. Or if someone was there at the delivery gate, we would go to the collapsible gates at 35th and squirm under and run like heck to the left field stands.

Left field was our favorite hangout. Usually the visiting team was having batting practice and we'd sit in the first row, eat our sandwiches, and keep an eye out for ushers or cops. We knew all of the players in the American League. There were only eight teams and each team had twenty five players. It was easy to see who was out in left field shagging balls, doing wind sprints, or catching fly balls hit by the coach. We'd yell down to a player we recognized, "Hey Dom, you gonna get some hits tonight?" Dominic DiMaggio from the Red Sox would smile through those thick glasses and wave to us. "Wow! There's Teddy. Look how tall he is." Teddy Williams, all of 6'3" would glide over to catch a long flyball from the hitter in the batting cage.

One night in late June of '48, we were settled in our favorite seats in left field, first row along the wall, midway between the foul line and center field. The Sox were taking batting practice. Every once in a while a hitter would drive the ball to left and it would roll to the wall, unattended. We were leaning over the concrete wall in front of our seats watching the ball roll over the grass, over the stones on the warning track and gently hit the green wall right below us. We watched intently but *no* Sox player came for that ball. We all had the same idea. "Let's get that ball."

Jimmy was the tallest, so he said, "It's only nine or ten feet from the top of the wall to the track. That's an easy hang drop. I'm gonna drop down and grab that ball. I'll throw it up to you guys and then you reach down and pull me up."

It worked! In a matter of ten seconds we were sitting and passing around the new ball that Jimmy got from the field for us. It wasn't really new because it had four or five scuffs on it. But it was a lot better than the white-taped ball we were using at Spats Field. We were all flush with our success because no one; ushers, cops, or Sox players noticed what we had done.

So, then the guys looked at me and said, "You're next."

I gulped and protested. "Me? What if Seerey comes over and stops me?" By now, Pat Seerey, the stocky left-fielder for the Sox was shagging balls in front of us.

"Don't worry, you're the fastest kid here! You can outrun him. He's real slow. Just run toward the stands if we can't hoist you up in time," one of the guys said.

The Sox got Seerey in June from the Indians for Bob Kennedy. They wanted home run power for their lineup. Pat was 5'10" and 200 lbs and could wallop the ball.

Well, a minute later another batted ball rolled to the wall about fifteen feet closer to the foul line. The guys all looked at me and said, "GO." I hang dropped the wall easily and landed on my toes on the stone warning track—no pain this time. I started running right away to that ball, not even looking at the players in the field. Fifteen feet! That's all! I could see the guys running along the first row to get to the spot where I'd grab the ball and they would boost me up the wall to the stands.

But I could also hear a growl behind me, "Hey kid, whadda ya doin'?" I turned around to see Pat Seerey bearing down on me. He had this huge wad of tobacco in his left jaw, with juice rolling down the side of his mouth. He looked mean like he was going to throw me around for stealing a ball.

I grabbed the ball in my left hand and reached up the wall for help with my right. Jimmy was reaching down with the others but they couldn't grip my fingers. I was on my toes and jumping as high as I could, but still I was too short! Their fingers were just missing mine as I jumped up and swung my right hand.

Seerey grabbed me by the shoulders. "Whadda ya doin' with that ball, kid," he bellowed at me.

I started to cry. "Pat, they made me do it. They made me get the ball. Those guys up there. I'm sorry. I won't do it again."

He started to grin a little, and said, "Don't worry kid. You can keep the ball." Then he put his strong hands under my armpits and hoisted me up the wall. The guys could now grab me easily, and pull me up and over the wall.

I continued to cry a little, but still clutched that baseball. We looked down and there was Pat smiling at us with tobacco juice still running down the side of his mouth. "Thanks, Pat. I won't forget you. You're goin' hit one tonight. I know it," I yelled down to him. He gave me the thumbs up sign, and then trotted back to left field to shag balls.

My new left field hero hit 19 homers in '48 and one warm day in Philadelphia's Shibe Park he set a White Sox record with four home runs in one game. But just like Whitey Platt, he was gone from the Sox the next year. And "my" baseball did not survive the obstacles of Spats Field and the blasting of our bats, gradually losing its cover and finally finding rest on the train tracks near Stewart Ave.

Left field was also my mother's favorite place to watch the Sox play. When she and my Dad and the kids went to Comiskey Park for a Ladies Day game, she would insist on the left field seats. Little did we kids know that she would purposely wait for the Boston Red Sox to come into town, and then cheer for their left-fielder, Teddy Williams. My father would get upset with her because he did *not* like "The Splendid Splinter," as Teddy was called by the sportswriters. Daddy booed Teddy when he came to bat, and yelled at Williams when he was playing left field. But my mother would smile and cheer for Teddy, especially if he stroked a drive into the right field stands. The kids got a big kick out of her little show of female independence, even though it was only the late 1940s.

If the guys on the block were not playing baseball, or hangin' on the block, or doin' house chores, we were probably at Sox Park with the players, watching the game. In the late 1940s, the Sox relief pitchers used to sit along the low wall down the 3rd baseline on a green bench, waiting to be called to warm-up to go into the game. They would sit on an angle facing the infield because they were down the line from 3rd at least 50 feet. The two warm-up rubbers were just ahead of them towards the White Sox dugout. One August afternoon in 1948, the Sox were losing, as usual. The starting pitcher was long gone and a reliefer was in there. The crowd was very small for that weekday game, so we snuck down to the Sox bullpen to talk to the pitchers. I found my favorite, Joe Haynes, sitting on the end of the bench, facing the game. "Hi Joe, are you gonna pitch today?" The score was 6-1 in favor of the Senators.

"Hi kid," Joe said. "Maybe I'll get in there yet, if Grove has any trouble."

"I'm gonna get you ready, Joe," I said. His right arm was resting on the green concrete wall that separated the stands from the foul territory. "Here we go, Joe," as I began to massage his shoulder and upper right arm. "Yer gonna have a good fastball and curve today."

Joe looked at me, a kid of 10 years old, who was working his arm into shape. He just had this "pleased as hell" smile on his face from one side to the other.

One of the other pitchers near Joe was Frank Papish. "Hey kid, what about my rubdown. I'm goin' in there next. They'll need a lefthander to get these Senators out."

My dreams and fantasies were coming true. I was playing baseball every day, reading the sports pages, and now being with the team's players. I looked at Joe Haynes smiling while I rubbed his pitching shoulder and thought, "When will I be on the other side of this wall, shagging flies, fielding grounders, warming up, taking batting practice, signing autographs." My baseball world was right in front of me.

Who cares that the White Sox were in last place. They won only 51 games out of 152 in 1948. Who cares that they hadn't a winning record since 1943. It didn't matter that the only .300 hitter on the team was Luscious Luke Appling, or that every pitcher, even Joe Haynes, had a losing record. I didn't care that they would usually lose when the guys snuck in to see them. It didn't bother me that the stands were never filled, even when DiMaggio or Williams were playing. I was *always* hungry for baseball and the Sox, win or lose. I was *so* hungry that during the 1949 season I saw close to 50 games at Sox Park, and didn't pay for one of them.

I internalized all of these minuses, like the pain from not getting picked for a softball game, and like my father had done before me with the Sox teams he followed in the 20's and 30's. During those two decades, after the disgrace of the Black Sox of 1919, he *only* saw six winning teams in twenty years of baseball. And *none* of the six teams ever won a pennant. "Damn Yankees" was a common epithet from his mouth, especially when we would sit on the front porch at night during the summer heat and talk about his youth. Little did I realize that I too would become a Yankee hater in the 50's

Being raised so close to Comiskey Park at 30th & Shields, in the shadow of left field, my father lived *and* died with the Sox from 1914 on. He followed the family tradition as a die-hard Sox fan just like his father, Grandpa Hugh LeVoy, and his brothers. Grandpa was born and raised at 31st & Halsted—within the "extended" shadows of the third base line. Grandpa actually became a White Stockings fan in 1900. When the team joined the new American League of baseball in 1901, the White Stockings became the White Sox. They played at South Side Park at 39th & Wentworth. Then Charles Comiskey, the Old Roman, built a brand new stadium, called White Sox Park in 1909. Grandpa and his first two sons, John (Whitey) and Hugh (Red) went to the first game played there on July 1, 1910. All together, by the year 1985, seventy-five years later, four generations of LeVoys rooted for the Sox each year at the Park, which later was named Comiskey Park. Our family entered White Sox history on July 2nd, 1985 when Uncle Hugh, at the age of 81, was honored as one of 11 "original" Sox fans who had attended the first Sox game at Comiskey in 1910.

Daddy would tell me about all the old-timers he'd seen play; Ty Cobb, Honus Wagner, Walter Johnson, and of course, Shoeless Joe Jackson. I used to pester him, "Tell me what Ruth was like. Did all the fans at Sox Park cheer when he came up to bat, just like they say?"

He'd smile and say, "The Babe was really something. He was bigger than life itself. He'd sneak up to home plate with those bird-like steps and casually swing the bat a couple of times. Then he'd settle into the batter's box and take a tremendous cut at the first pitch. If he missed, the crowd would go wild, although everyone was rootin' for him to hit one. And when he got ahold of one, it'd go way up in the air and then drop into the right field stands. Another souvenir from The Babe."

No matter what players and years we talked about, my father would always come back to Ted Lyons, his favorite Sox pitcher from the 20's to the 40's. He said, "Everytime I went out to see Teddy pitch, it would be against the Yanks or Indians, or Tigers. Teddy would match the other guy pitch for pitch, but the other team would always have more hitters than the Sox. Eventually it would come down to the seventh or eighth inning. The other team would have a man on, a tie score, and their best hitter up to bat. Lyons would be working carefully to get the third Out and keep the game tied. But that third strike, third Out never came. Usually it was a double or triple that would beat Teddy."

My father would add, "It would tear the heart out of me to see Teddy lose another one." (Teddy Lyons pitched for the White Sox from 1923 to 1946, with three years in the Service. For most of those twenty-one years, the Sox were a sub-500 team, losing more than they won. But Teddy's lifetime record was 260 wins and 230 losses.

I began to absorb the self-pity that engulfed my father and most of the Southsiders in Chicago. I understood without ever hearing it spoken or see it in print the meaning of "diehard Sox fan." So I turned inward again. My fantasies as a kid were of games that the Sox would play and win. I had every player, position, and lineup in the American League memorized, and I would mentally play the whole game thru, pitch by pitch, batter by batter, inning after inning. And the Sox would *always win* 4-3, or 8-6, or 1-0. *It was my game, my outcome, my deliverance from losing, on my field of dreams.*

By the Spring of 1949, I was eleven years old. I was finishing 6th Grade at St. Anthony de Padua School and was old enough to get around the Bridgeport neighborhood, especially when I had to pay for my newspapers on Saturday afternoon at the *Herald-American* branch office at 32nd & Halsted.

All the Sox fans had high hopes for the '49 season. Not only was a talented rookie coming to play center field, Jerry Scala, but also a big guy named Gus Zernial from Beaumont, Texas, nicknamed Ozark Ike, was doing well in spring training.

I was all excited as the season approached. The Sox started with a lot of attention to Scala and Zernial. Scala got off to a slow start, but Zernial was burning up the opposing pitching. He was batting well over .300, hitting extra bases and the occasional homerun. More importantly, he was driving in runs, something the Sox hadn't seen since Zeke Bonura in the late 30s. The press was saying that Gus would lead the Sox out of the 2nd division where they had been for so long.

There was a tavern on my paper route that had a subscription to the *Herald-American*. Every afternoon I'd stop with the paper. The Sox or Cubs game would be on Channel 9 with Jack Brickhouse and Harry Creighton. I'd ask the bartender if I could watch part of the game. He'd usually say "Yes" because the bar was hardly full, and most of the action was by telephone with him writing little slips of paper with horses' names.

So I had lots of chances to watch Scala and Zernial play. And Gus was truly awesome. What a hitter! A short, compact swing. And Scala was a gazelle in center field, tracking down everything. "The next DiMaggio," the papers printed in the sports section.

But then, one sunny, summer day, Zernial came running in from left field to snag a low line drive. He dove straight forward to catch the ball, hit the ground hard, and rolled over, lying on the grass in pain. There went the Sox season, a broken clavicle. Gus didn't come back that year, and Scala was sent down to the minor leagues because he couldn't hit. As Yogi Berra said later, when he managed the Mets, "It's *déjà vu* all over again."

It seemed as though the curse of 1919 was at it again. In 1934, Monte Stratton came to the Sox as a tall, lanky right handed pitcher. He was 22 yrs old, 6'5", 180lbs. He not only had a sweeping curveball, but also a trick pitch called a gander. He had no record in '34, one win and two losses in '35, five and seven in '36. But in 1937, with a winning team made up of Jimmy Dykes, Zeke Bonura, Luke Appling and Mike Kreevich to name some of the Sox stars, Stratton posted a fifteen and five record, and helped the Sox to a third place finish. And in 1938, the year of my birth, Monte won fifteen games again and lost nine. The curse of '19 caught up to him in the Fall. Monte shattered his right knee in a hunting accident. The leg had to be amputated and it appeared that he was through as a major league pitcher. He was fitted for a prosthesis, but he never could regain his pitching ability, especially when hitters would bunt on him. He just couldn't run fast enough off the mound to field the bunt.

As a kid, I never knew about the Black Sox of 1919 until my father sadly told me one summer night when we were sitting on the front porch. He just raved about that team. Joe Jackson. Eddie Collins. Buck Weaver. Ed Cicotte. They had hitting, pitching and defense. Daddy was eleven years old the year of the scandal that hit the World Series between the Sox and the Cincinnati

Reds. With a grave voice he explained to me how the gamblers got to nine of the Sox players to lose games. He talked on and on about Jackson, the star outfielder who hit and fielded better than anyone in the league. Shoeless Joe, they called him. Joe was such a great hitter that years after he and the other eight were banished from baseball in 1920, Joe was still hitting .300 while over 40 years old, and playing under an assumed name for a semi-pro team. What a ballplayer!

Whether there was a curse on the Sox, or whether it was just bad luck, my father, and now I, had this loser mentality about our team. His sadness from years of rootin' for a weak team was absorbed by me. Another generation of LeVoys had succumbed to the lure of a losing team. Our White Sox had no money, no hitters, a pitcher or two, but never a pennant.

*

But there were no losers or curses when it came to Fall in Chicago and professional football. Each September, as the days started to cool off and the trees began to change, I'd grab my Bears football. It was showing some wear, especially at the ends from hitting the street so much. But, it still had a lot of touchdowns in it. I'd squeeze it into my right elbow and chest, and imagine that I was running for the goal line with one man to beat. I stuck out my left arm, pushed his head and arms away and ran into the end zone. Touchdown!

The White Sox were going nowhere, so my interest would turn to the Chicago Bears football team. They were a perennial powerhouse in the National Football League, winning championships in the 30's and early 40's. I would listen to their games on Sunday afternoons, and root for Sid Luckman and Hugh Gallarneau and George McAfee. George Halas was their owner and head coach. But, I couldn't get to see them play because they played their home games at Wrigley Field on the North Side. (And we couldn't afford the tickets).

On the other side of the city, where we lived in Bridgeport, we had the Chicago Cardinals football team. They were the champions of the NFL in 1947 and runner-up to the Philadelphia Eagles in 1948. The Cardinals had two great runners, Charley Trippi and Pat Harder, and a smart quarterback named Paul Christman. They also had a big lineman, Chet Bulger, who later, after his pro career was finished, coached at DeLaSalle High School, down the street from the Cardinals home at Comiskey Park.

Each season the Bears and Cardinals would square off twice, once at Wrigley and once at Comiskey. These games were the grudge matches of pro football because both teams were from Chicago, and both were winners. It was the Northside vs. the Southside.

As the 1949 football season approached, I began to collect photos from the newspaper of current Bear players into a scrapbook. I had Johnny Lujack throwing a pass, George Gulyanics running thru the line, fierce Bulldog Turner centering the ball, tough George Connor playing defense, and lean Ken Kavanaugh catching a long, Lujack pass.

Another kid from our school, Nick Spata, who was in my brother Jake's class at St.Anthony's, was the only other kid I knew in Bridgeport who was a Bear fan like me. Everybody else, including my father, were Cardinal fans. Nick had been working on a Bears' scrapbook too, and even had a photo of the Bears' rookie quarterback and place kicker, George Blanda.

Nick and I knew that the first Bears-Cardinals game of the '49 season would be at Comiskey Park in early October. It would be the second game of the season for both teams, and each team would be pointing to it as a big game. The Bears and the Cardinals each won their opening games of the season, so the showdown was coming.

On the morning of Sunday, October 2nd, after the 9:00 Mass, Nick and I got together on my front steps to look at our Bears' scrapbooks. While we were sharing photos, I said to Nick, "Why don't we take our scrapbooks to Sox Park this morning and get some autographs before the game."

"Yeah," Nick said, "maybe we'll see Johnny Lujack. We should take our bikes because we can get there faster."

By 11:15, we were standing outside the players' entrance to Sox Park on Shields Ave. We had put our bikes against the high iron fence that surrounded the players' parking lot.

After five minutes of waiting in the October sun, we could see two husky men drive up to the lot and park. When they got out of the car, I recognized George Gulyanics. Nickie saw them too.

"Nick, who's the other guy with Gulyanics?" I said.

"It looks like Blanda," Nick answered me.

Sure enough, there were the two Georges coming toward us. George Gulyanics, the Bears' halfback and punter, and George Blanda, the rookie quarterback and place kicker.

"Hey Georges, can we get your autographs in our scrapbooks," I yelled to them as I held up the scrapbook.

Both players looked a little surprised that we had called them by name, and were actually looking for autographs of Bears' players at Comiskey Park, the home of the Cardinals.

Gulyanics and Blanda came up to us smiling. "Sure kids, we'd be glad to sign your books," said Blanda.

I opened my book and gave it to Gulyanics, showing the picture of him running thru the Detroit Lions defense last year. "Hey," Gulyanics brightened,

"I remember that run. Nice moves, eh," as he signed his name on top of the photo.

Nickie was showing Blanda his picture that the Bears had given to all the papers in the summer. "Good lookin' guy, eh George," Blanda joked as he showed the photo to Gulyanics. They both laughed as Blanda signed the picture.

There seemed to be a pause in the conversation so I just said, off the top of my head, "Hey Georges, this is a big game today and we're rootin' for the Bears to win. We know that you can beat those Cards. We don't have any tickets for the game. Is there any chance you guys have extras?"

Blanda looked at Gulyanics and smiled, kind of shaking his shoulders like, "Why not help these kids get into the game!"

'C'mon kids, you're goin' in with us," Blanda said.

I was shocked they took me serious. I couldn't believe we'd really see the big game!

'But what about our bikes," Nickie blurted out as he pointed to the two bikes against the iron fence.

"Don't worry," Gulyanics said. "C'mon."

The four of us walked to the Pass Gate, Blanda and Gulyanics leading the way and Nick and I trailing as we pushed our bikes. When we got to the Andy Frain usher at the gate, he had seen us coming and already had a puzzled look on his face.

Blanda told him in an authoritative voice as both players showed their team passes, "These kids are with us," The usher looked surprised and somewhat resigned as he surveyed Nick and I. Then his eyes fixed on our bikes.

"And take care of their bikes too," Blanda ordered.

We followed the two Georges into the Park, pushing our bicycles past the disappointed usher. "Gee, thanks guys. We know you're goin' have a great game today, and beat up those Cards," I gushed with a big smile on my face.

"Yeah, thanks for the autographs too," Nickie chimed in.

"Anytime," Gulyanics said as they patted us on the shoulders and took off for the locker room.

The Bears beat the Cardinals that day, 17-7. The Bears defense stopped Trippi and Harder, the two Cardinals threats to score. George Blanda kicked a field goal and Gulyanics ran well.

Fall and football gave way to Winter, but neither the Bears nor the Cardinals won the championship that year. So, now the familiar "Wait 'til next year" was in my head as the cold days of January & February continued, ushering in the new decade of the 1950's. There always was the Hot Stove League that was covered by Bob Elson, the White Sox announcer. He had a winter radio show from the Pump Room to keep all the diehard Sox fans informed about off-season baseball news.

*

By the time I reached eighth grade in September of 1950, I was the shortest boy in the class, and only one girl, Jackie Sheppard was shorter than me. The reason for this occurred in Kindergarten. When I started the half-day Kindergarten program at the nearby Mark Sheridan Public School, I was beginning to read. By April of my Kindergarten year, the teacher was urging my parents to put me into second grade at our Parish School, St.Anthony de Padua. Sister Henry in the second grade agreed that I should move up after testing me.

So, I skipped first grade the following September, making a double promotion. I was a six-year old boy going into a class with seven-year olds. The age difference didn't seem to matter much in the early and middle grades. I did very well with my subjects, read every cowboy and Indian book in our school library, was an altar boy, a patrol boy, and played sports at recess with the guys from my grade. (I sure could've used an extra year's growth when Pat Seerey was chasing me to the left field wall and the guys couldn't reach down to hoist me up).

Even though I was the smallest boy, Fr. Laske, our Assistant Pastor and 7th & 8th Grades Coach, picked me to be the 8th Grade football team quarterback. I think that Father wanted me at quarterback because he knew if I handed the ball off to the running backs, I wouldn't get clobbered because of my size. I was too small to see over the linemen if we wanted to pass the ball downfield. So our team kept the ball on the ground.

Arthur "Bucky" Barrett was our fullback, and he was huge for eighth Grade. He had to be at least 5'9" and weighed around 150lbs. The offensive line never had to worry about opening a hole for Bucky to run thru because when I called his number 32 BUCK or 33 BUCK, he would hit that space between right or left guard and center and just push everyone forward for yardage. It took three or four tacklers to bring him down to the ground.

One day, Bucky smashed into the #2 hole between center and right guard and popped out of the pile of players about seven yards downfield. Everyone could see his clear path to the endzone except Bucky whose nose was bleeding and broken. Nobody was paying attention to the defensive lineman who had hit Bucky and was now lying on the field, "out like a light."

I still have an eighth Grade graduation photo of myself, Jane Weller, and George Schramm in front of my house. George was as tall as Bucky Barrett. And Jane came up to his chin in height. Here I am at the end of the photo, only as tall as Jane's eyes, and barely in line with George's chest. I looked like their 6th grade cousin.

But, I was not depressed about my size, even though my mother would keep pushing the vitamins on me every day, and some people would call me, Little Hughie. After all, I was elected 8th Grade vice-president, and continued to get real good marks. I was still deliverin' papers and making money for high school. I was planning to go to St. Patrick Academy, downtown at Adams and DesPlaines, where Jake was a freshman. I was playin' ball and hangin' with Jake's neighborhood gang, the Chi-Annies. Since I was smaller and younger, they would only let me play second base or right field when they needed another kid.

We now had a television at home, a used 14" table model made by Garod. And finally DELIVERANCE had come to the Comiskey Park in Chicago. Hallelujah!

Our God, the God of Abraham, Isaac, and Teddy Lyons, had finally heard the wailing and "waiting 'til next year" from his people on the Southside who had gone so long—32 years—without a champion. He decided to relieve the despair of White Sox fans. On April 30, 1951 He sent a new Moses to lead the Sox out of the desert of the second division of the American League. The modern-day Moses was Saturnino Orestes Armas Minoso, a.k.a. MINNIE. And to help Minnie with his message of hope to Sox fans (he only spoke Spanish) God sent a new Aaron, Paul Rapier Richards, the new Sox manager. These two men and other baseball players; Jacob Nelson "Nellie" Fox, Alfonso "Chico" Carrasquel, and William Walter "Billy" Pierce would now, in the season of 1951 lead the reborn White Sox to the Promised Land of big crowds, exciting games, stolen bases, tight defense, tough pitching, close wins, and the first division of the American League. My team was now called the GO GO SOX.

The Sox actually had a Moses and Aaron on the team in the 40's, although not at the same time. Wally Moses played outfield for the Sox from 1942-46, hitting around .260 and stealing a few bases. Aaron Robinson played the 1948 season as a catcher and only hit .252 with 8 homers and 39 runs batted in.

Through the '50s, my teenage years, I continued to follow the Sox like a religion. I had to "attend" every game, whether by radio or TV or in person. And they did well. The Sox placed fourth in 1951 and then third in 1952 in the American League. They combined pitching, defense, running, and timely hitting to win close ballgames. Going to their home games was exciting as huge crowds filled Comiskey Park, especially when Casey Stengel's Yankees came to town for a weekend series. The Yanks had stars like Yogi Berra, Mickey Mantle, and Whitey Ford. The attendance for a weekend matchup;

Friday night, Saturday afternoon, and a double-header on Sunday would be over 160,000 fans. The Sox were now the "talk of the town" and the "hottest ticket."

And for me, every game was a life and death drama. If the Sox won, my life was bright and cheerful. If they lost, I was dejected. Each game was them vs. us, the good guys against the bad guys, for "all the marbles." Life was either sweet or sour, up or down, all dependent upon the final score.

It was so black & white, this winning and losing. So simple that I couldn't think of any shade of color or off-white. I couldn't believe that the other team were really persons, with hopes and fears, tears & cheers. Even the uniforms verified this with the Sox in white, and the opposing team in gray or dark colors.

How clear it all was to me. Life was a baseball game. There were winners and losers. People had smiles or tears. Every game ended with a victory and a loss. I never saw a tie game in baseball. You play until someone wins, even if it means 18 innings. And if it goes extra innings, or if the game is decided in the last at bat, the win is that much sweeter, or so much more depressing to lose.

I was hooked into this madness. I had left the real world and entered the zone of heroes, play by play, the ballpark, World Series. I had become mesmorized by uniforms, action, and pennant fever. *Why me? What didn't I have, or what did I crave inside that drew me like a magnet to baseball? Was it imagination?* I could listen, visualize, feel, sense, anticipate, become totally absorbed in a TV or radio account of the baseball antics of 18 men. And at the Park, I was totally absorbed in every pitch, hit, and play.

Maybe it was all about heroes! Was that my problem? Did I need a hero? Why was it so important that I have someone to look up to? Someone to root for. To take after. To be like. Did I need a model? A person who was doing what I wanted to do. A player who was getting the attention that I craved for.

Once the Sox started winning and the fans coming, the guys in the neighborhood found that we couldn't sneak into the park as easily as when we were younger kids. Every gate seemed to be covered with an usher, and there were all kinds of police and security in and outside the Park. So, we would save some money and go to the Bleachers ticket booth in centerfield and pay 60 cents to get in for the game. Even though we could see the pitches real well from the bleachers because we were right behind the pitcher, especially the curve balls, I was lonesome for my favorite seats in left field, waiting for a homerun from Minnie Minoso or Sherm Lollar.

One July night in 1956, the Yanks were in town for a 3-game, showdown series for first place with the Sox. Since 1951, the Sox would chase the New York Yankees and the Cleveland Indians each baseball season from April 'til September for the pennant. And come the World Series in October, it would always be the Damn Yankees playing against the National League winner. The Indians, with their stars; Larry Doby, Al Rosen, Roberto Avila, and Early Wynn had to settle for second place, except in 1954 when their great team won an outstanding 111 games. And for each of these years, my White Sox would end up third, too short in hitting and runs batted in, but long on speed and excitement. I was cheering and crying at the same time!

The first showdown night game with the Yanks was getting so much publicity that a bunch of us guys just had to go to the game. I was 18 years old, and had money for a ticket in the grandstand. When we got to the Park at 7:30 PM, there were large crowds of people at 35th and Shields, waiting to get in or picking up their tickets from Will Call. No tickets were available because even the Standing Room Only tickets had been sold. We walked around the Park, asking if any of the fans coming to the park had tickets to sell. Nothing! We started to get desperate, and Buzzy said, "Let's split up and see if we can sneak in. Maybe we'll see each other inside the Park."

Everyone agreed that was a good idea. I decided to go with Buzzy. We weren't far from the front gates, so we both went to the closed end gates that weren't being used for entry by fans. Sure enough, there was just enough space under the collapsible iron gate for a teenager to squeeze under and get in. It would be tight, but Buzzy and I thought we could do it, one at a time.

We looked around to see if there were any cops or security inside the closed gate. No one! Everybody was further down where the fans were filing in and handing their tickets to the ushers. We checked behind us, but with the huge crowd of people outside on 35th, we had a perfect cover from the cops on the corner.

"I'm goin' first," Buzzy tapped my arm. "As soon as I get under, I'm runnin' up that ramp"—he pointed to the end of the ramp we could see about ten feet inside the closed gate—"I'll meet you in left field, under the lower deck seats."

Buzzy laid down on the concrete and began wigglin' under the bottom of the gate. When he was almost under, with just his feet to go, I laid down and started to squirm thru. I was halfway under and I could hear Buzzy was up and runnin' to the ramp.

"Hey you, come back here," came a shout from the ramp. I got scared but kept squirming under the gate. It was impossible to squirm backwards to get out. I was just picking myself off the concrete, ready to run to the ramp when I heard the same voice, "Stop! Right there!"

I froze as I looked up at a Security Guard with a bright, yellow jacket coming to grab me. There wasn't anywhere to go to escape, so I just stood there, waiting for him. Afraid!

I was taken to a Security Room under the lower deck stands behind home plate. All the while that the guard and I were walking to the room, he had his strong hand locked on my arm, and he was preaching to me about stealing from the White Sox by sneaking in the Park. I was told to stand in the corner of this small room. While he was taking my personal information, I could hear the roar from the crowd as the Sox took the field and the National Anthem was announced,

When I told the guard that I was eighteen, he got really serious and said that I was an adult, and I would be arrested for theft. Sneakin' in the Park is a criminal offense and I'd have to go to Court. As he was telling me all of this, another Security Guard came in, "escorting" a black kid about fifteen.

"What'd he do?" asked the Guard that was handling my case.

"He stole a case of beer from a vendors' locker in the upper deck on the third base side. We got him after he had one of the beers," answered the other Guard casually.

"Well, get his name and address and birthdate, and then escort him outta' the Park."

I couldn't believe what I was hearin'. This kid steals a case of beer and all he gets is kicked outta' the Park. And I'm sittin' here waitin' to go to jail for sneakin' in.

In the meantime, I could hear the crowd roar it seemed for every pitch. *Oh how I wish I could see the game. See the Sox beat those Damn Yankees!* Why did I have to be second under that gate. If I had gone first, I'd be sittin' in left field now cheering for the Sox, followin' every pitch, feelin' the tension in the crowd. Getting' caught up in all the action. Yeah!

After twenty more minutes, or so it seemed, the Guard that had nabbed me sneakin' in, told me to go with him. I thought, "Here we go to the police." But he didn't take me by the arm like he did when we walked to the Security Room, so as we were walking toward the front gates, I momentarily thought about runnin' for it.

When we got to the only front gate that was still open, the Guard looked at me and said brusquely, "Get lost!" He motioned for me to leave the Park.

While I walked thru the gate to the outside, I could hear the noise from the crowd erupt as though the Sox hit a homer. "Darn it. I'm missin' all the action!. Why can't I be in there!" I said to myself.

Just then, one of my friends, Billy, who had split from Buzzy and I, came up to me.

After we exchanged stories about tryin' to sneak in, I noticed two business men leaving the Park thru that same front gate.

"C'mon," I said to Billy, "let's see if they still have their tickets."

Sure enough, they did, and were happy to give them to us so we could watch the game. (They must've been Sox fans! And yes, the Sox were winning)

So Billy and I calmly marched over to the open gate, presented "our" tickets to the Andy Frain usher and walked in. I looked around to see if any Security were nearby. None! As Billy and I strode toward the steps to the lower deck seats behind home plate, I glanced at my ticket. *Lower Deck Boxes!* A big smile came on my face as we went up the steps. In front of us were the box seats, the big screen for foul balls, the field, the home plate umpire, Yogi Berra, the catcher, Whitey Ford winding up, and Minnie Minoso cocking his bat for the swing. THIS IS IT!

For 1957 and '58, it was strictly the Sox and the Yankees in the race for the Pennant. But again, it was always that little something that would put the Yankees in the lead. The Sox were now managed by Al Lopez, the same skipper who led the Indians to 111 victories in 1954. He was instrumental in the winter of 1957 to trade Minnie Minoso and Fred Hatfield for Early Wynn and Al Smith. These two players proved to be the big difference a year later, 1959.

There had been eight years of the GO GO SOX, and they had improved from 6th Place in 1950 to 2nd Place in 1958. But it seemed like every year it was the Yankees standing between the Sox and 1st Place. It was going on forty years since the Sox had won a pennant. Did they have to be "in the desert" for those forty years before God would reward them with the Promised Land of baseball, a championship?

Ironically, it wasn't the Yankees who would stand in the Sox' way in 1959, but the Cleveland Indians, with Minnie Minoso on their team now. The Sox were in first place for most of the season, especially in the spring months and after July. The season was exciting as the Sox won a lot of close games, forty in number. It all came down to the night of September 22nd. The magic number was ONE! One more Sox win or Cleveland loss would do it! And the Sox were playing the Indians in Cleveland. A win for the Sox meant the pennant. A loss would bring the Indians closer to tieing for first place.

My father and mother and three of us kids were in the living room, watching that game. It was a hot, steamy night in Chicago, even though it was late September. We sat, glued to the TV as the Sox had put together a 4-2 lead going into the last of the 9th inning. But then the Indians loaded the bases with one out. The Cleveland crowd of over 54,000 fans were on their feet, cheering for a comeback victory.

Vic Power, the good-hitting first baseman stepped to the plate. Gerry Staley, the reliable, relief pitcher for the Sox, had just been called in to pitch. He usually made the hitters ground his sinkerball to one of the infielders. I was really nervous, figuring that Power would easily hit the ball hard and it would go thru the infield, scoring two runs and tieing the game. I could feel the curse of 1919!

On the very first pitch by Staley, Power swung and hit a hard, three-hop ground ball toward center field. "Oh no," I yelled at the TV, "It's goin' thru."

The TV camera followed the ball as it quickly went past the pitcher, heading for center field. Instantly, out of the left of the screen came "Little Looie" Aparicio, the Sox shortstop. Moving quickly, like a cat, he scooped up the ball, stepped on second base for one out, and threw to the first baseman, Earl Torgeson, for the double play.

"SOX WIN! SOX WIN! HEY! HEY! HEY! HEY! Jack Brickhouse was yelling into the WGN Channel 9 microphone.

The whole family cheered loudly in that living room. "They did it," my father yelled as he clapped his hands together. My mother was smiling and clapping too. Fred was cheering and looking at the Sox celebration on the field as all the Sox players were huggin' each other and smilin', wavin' their caps.

I couldn't believe the game was over. After I saw Looie turn that final double play, I yelled "Yeah! Yeah!" Then I shook my father's hand, and Fred's too! Finally, we had a winner. The Sox did it! They did it! The monkey was off their back. They won the American League pennant. Deliverance after 40 years. The curse was gone!

There was so much "joy in Mudville" on that muggy night that someone turned on the city's air raid sirens. Our first reaction at home to the wails from the sirens was that the Russians were coming. *Was it finally going to happen? What we've been afraid of since the Cold War began.* We went out to the front porch and looked up into the Chicago night sky? Were there Communist planes overhead? Or worse yet, did they fire the ICBMs.

Deep inside though, all the Sox fans who saw that last play by Little Looie knew that the sirens were really a trumpet blare of triumph for our team, the Chicago White Sox. *They* were coming back to Chicago with the American League championship.

Minnie Minoso

Hugh LeVoy (left), 81, was one of 11 fans honored last night for attending Comiskey Park's first game in 1910. Here he chats with Charles Comiskey.

Eleven 'original' Sox fans honored at Comiskey

Eleven persons who attended the opening game of Comiskey Park July 1, 1910, were honored last night before the White Sox game:

Edward Carlson, 78, now living in McHenry County, former supervisor for Swift & Co.

Ann Marie Briesch, 79, Chicago, was housewife until age 52, then worked at comptroller's office in City Hall for 25 years.

Hugh LeVoy, 81, Chicago Ridge, was marble mason most of his life, but worked 5 years in shipyards for George Steinbrenner's father's company.

Gardner Stern, 81, Chicago, currently chairman of board of Stop 'n' Shop (great grandfather was close friend of Charles Comiskey Sr.)

Maurice "Buster" Meade, 81, Cicero, former truck driver for Joseph T. Ryan Freight Co.; still attends almost every Sox home game.

Sheldon Gordon, 86, Oak Lawn, started the automobile business in 1922; once played pro soccer in Chicago.

Frank Bentivegna, 88, Chicago, was professional musician (played drums with Benny Goodman and Louis Armstrong).

Edward Saltiel, 88, Chicago, was state senator from 1935-55; practiced law for 66 years.

William Trow, 92, Crystal Lake, former salesman for a Chicago gas stove company.

Jesse Iser, 95, Oak Lawn, retired self-employed contractor.

Art Wheeler, 95, Midlothian, worked in Chicago stockyards for 40 years.

2

FATHER RICHARD LASKE

Lead me along the right path
Show me the way.

Anonymous Prayer

The first time I was "called" was on a cold, windy Sunday afternoon on March 6th, 1938. We were all, except one, in the vestibule of St. Anthony de Padua Catholic Church in Chicago. The parishioners had left from the 12:00 Mass. The ushers were checking the pews for discarded bulletins or anything else left behind. And the organist was turning off the large organ above our heads in the loft

"Where is he? It's almost one o'clock." My Dad said to my Mom.

"I don't know. It's probably the drink again." sadly answered my Mother.

They both looked around. There were Beatrice Curley, my godmother-to-be, my Aunt Mary, Aunt Catherine, Mag and Patrick, my sister and brother, but no Uncle Stephan Flanagan.

"Mr. & Mrs. LeVoy, are you ready?" said Father Martin Schmidt, the parish administrator, as he entered the vestibule from the Church. He had just finished saying the 12:00 Mass, but was now wearing a white surplice over his cassock and a gold stole instead of the Mass vestments.

"No, Father, we don't have the godfather yet." Slowly and quietly said my Dad.

"Well, is he coming, or is there someone nearby you can get to replace him now?" questioned Fr. Schmidt in a slightly upset tone.

"I know," my father said quickly, "maybe we can get Emil Beyer. He's just down the street."

My mother looked nervous. She glanced at her sister, Mary. *Why did we pick my brother Stephan to be Hughie's godfather, she was thinking. He's been trouble since he came in 1930 with Mary from Roscommon, Ireland.*

I started to squirm inside the blankets because the cold, damp vestibule air was beginning to settle in, and a gush of frigid air hit us as my Father went out the front door of the church to go the half-block down Wallace St. to get Emil. My brother Patrick was being held by his godmother, Aunt Mary, but he was beginning to fuss, sensing the tension in her. His bright, curly, red hair was breaking out of his little cap and Aunt Mary was playing with it, trying to calm him. Only my sister Mag seemed settled as she stood next to Aunt Catherine, looking at Father Schmidt as he rocked nervously from one foot to the other.

"I'll get an usher to stand in as a proxy," said Father Schmidt to my mother, "just in case your husband can't get Emil Beyer. It's getting late."

Then he went into the church and we could hear his footsteps going down the marble aisle all the way to the altar. My mother made a face, pursing her lips because she didn't like this commotion, and all because of her brother.

Just as Father Schmidt came back to the vestibule with an usher, Patrick DeVitt, whom my mother had seen in church before, the front door opened again with a loud rush of cold, north wind. My father came in hurriedly with a red face under his fedora. "Emil's not feeling well. He can't come now, but said we could count on him to be Hughie's godfather," haltingly said my father, half out of breath.

"Then let us begin," Father Schmidt stated abruptly. "Peace be with you." He started the ceremony. "What name do you give your child?" he then asked solemnly to my upset parents, as he continued the Rite of Baptism.

"Hugh Edward," they both responded to the priest.

"And what do you ask of God's Church?" said Father as he lifted his voice at the end of the question.

"Faith," answered my parents in somewhat calmer voices. I started to kick a little inside the blankets and make some noises. My mother started to rock me slowly in her arms to calm me from starting to cry. Patrick was now squirming to get out of Aunt Mary's arms and stand on the cold, marble floor.

"You have asked to have your child baptized. In doing so you are accepting the responsibility of training Hugh in the practice of the faith. It will be your duty to bring him up to keep God's Commandments as Christ taught us, by loving God and our neighbor. Do you clearly understand what you are undertaking?"

"We do," answered my parents, more confidently. I was calm now, but Patrick was now trying to slide down from Aunt Mary so that he could stand on the floor. Mag was stretching her arms to him, hoping he would go to her.

Fr. Schmidt now moved slightly to indicate he was directing a question to Beatrice and the proxy godfather, Patrick DeVitt. "Are you ready to help the parents of this child, Hugh, in their duty as Christian parents?"

"We are," responded Patrick, slightly ahead of Beatrice's Irish brogue, "We are."

There were no responses from me that Sunday afternoon, except a messy diaper when we got home afterwards at 3007 South Normal Ave. I could not answer the "call" of Baptism at that time because I was an infant of just two weeks. But, there would be quite a few occasions in the future when I would be "called" again, and my responses varied from understanding and acceptance, to guilt and rationalizing and rejection.

And perhaps, my Baptism was *not* the first "call" from God, just as it was *not* for Mag or Patrick before me, and Kate, Fred and Maureen afterwards.

*

My mother, Margaret Mary Flanagan, was born in 1906 in Kilroddan, Loughglynn, County Roscommon, Ireland. Her parents were Michael Flanagan and Catherine Giblin, both of Loughglynn, a small town in western Ireland. In fact, they were next-door neighbors. The Giblins and Flanagans owned small farms of less than ten acres. Margaret was the first girl in the family after nine boys; John, the oldest, born in 1892, James, Tom, Michael, Dominic, Packy, Harry, Edward, and William. After the turn of the century, the family enlarged to fourteen children with Stephan, Mary, Catherine, and Luke, the last child, who was born in 1914.

The Flanagan family survived on the food raised on nine acres of Irish countryside that was partly bog, which yielded the peat or turf for burning in the fireplace. Things were so difficult that the boys had to leave home at age ten to work in England in the coal mines and be off on their own. Only the oldest son could count on getting the farm when he married. The younger sons' departure was always signaled by a pair of shoes they would receive from their father, with his stern admonition, "Start walking."

The Irish weather was damp and chilly, with little heat in the old cottage. There were no shoes for the kids, and a diet of milk, cabbage, and potatoes. My mother contracted rheumatic fever and St. Vitus Dance when she was a young girl. She had the Dance so bad that once she fell into the turf fire in the kitchen fireplace. Her brothers, Mick and Packy made a special pilgrimage to the Knock Monastery in County Mayo to ask for the prayers of the monks, when the rheumatic fever overcame her.

When she came to the United States in 1924, my mother had regained her health, although she always needed daily rest in the afternoon. She and my father married on August 18, 1934. Their plans were that God would bless them with children. They were both good, faithful Catholics. And my father came from a large family of seven, being raised in the Bridgeport neighborhood of Chicago.

She became pregnant with Mag in the Fall of 1934. The first doctor's visit was fine until he examined her heart. It was weak from the rheumatic fever in the poor conditions of Ireland. The doctor concluded that this pregnancy might be too much for her heart, unless she took special care to rest. The damage to her heart was irreversible, in fact, she was fortunate to be alive, having emigrated across the Atlantic Ocean, traveling steerage in a steamship called The Baltic with her brother, Packy. Rheumatic fever resulted in many deaths, especially in Ireland. Even if she survived this pregnancy, the doctor warned her that she should *not* get pregnant again, for that surely would be fatal. He advised that she and my father should be happy with the one child, and not try for a larger family.

But, my mother and father answered this serious news with prayer and faith that God would take care of her. He would see them through this pregnancy, and bless them with a child. As I grew up later, I used to see her in the bedroom off the kitchen, lying in my parents bed in the afternoon, working the Rosary beads and then reading the prayer cards before she would nod off for a nap.

Was it meant to be, ordained by Providence, that she would bear six healthy children? Was God calling my brothers and sisters and me even before we were born? Was He saying that medically we couldn't be conceived and carried full term and be born, but both He and my parents believed that we *should* be born? Were these decisions by my parents, and support by God another miracle of the power of Faith over human conditions?

*

One of the first Religion lessons that I learned in St.Anthony de Padua School was that babies had to be baptized as soon as possible after birth. That is why the Catholic Church promoted infant Baptism, even though there are no references in Scripture to infants or children being baptized. And we know that both Jesus and his followers, the Apostles and Disciples, were not only baptized as adults, but Jesus instructed the Apostles, "Go, baptize all nations."

But I learned in school that if an infant was *not* baptized and the baby died, this little baby would go to Limbo. The theological reasoning was that the baby could not go to heaven because he/she still had original sin. Only the Sacrament of Baptism washes away original sin. And the baby could not be sent to Hell because he/she was too young to commit any sins, even though the baby did *not* die in the state of Grace.

So, where is Limbo, I thought as a young student in the Catholic faith. Since I was an avid reader and radio listener, I was developing a terrific imagination as to places I had read about or someone told me of, or I heard on the radio, even though I had not been there. I had mental pictures of all the American League parks; Yankee Stadium, Fenway Park in Boston, the "Wigwam" in Cleveland, and Briggs Stadium in Detroit from listening to the White Sox games. Going thru my mind as a young child when I heard the word Limbo, was a scene from outer space with thousands of dead babies with diapers on, floating aimlessly. Red-haired babies, black babies, Chinese babies, babies with no hair, but all with eyes closed, and no expression on their faces. Just floating thru space!

I used to always pray after this image of Limbo came to me, to thank my parents for having me baptized even though it was very cold that March Sunday afternoon, and I was only sixteen days old, and Uncle Stephan didn't come. My fearful imagination would always conjure a scene at St. Anthony's baptistery where Father Schmidt had cancelled my Baptism because there was no godfather. Then my mother and father would have taken me back home still in the state of original sin. On the way home, I got cold from the north wintry wind, got sick that night, and died in my crib. And then I went to Limbo to float for all eternity.

The second Religion lesson I learned is that I am a sinner, and if I get hit by a car while going to church on Sunday, and I die, I'll go straight to Hell. Why? Because I am not in the state of Grace. And how do I get into the state of Grace? Go to Confession! Now later on, in the intermediate grades, I did learn that if I only committed venial sins, and I got hit by that same imaginary car that drives around Chicago, I would go to Purgatory and serve some time there, kinda like a prison sentence.

So, early in my childhood, I became aware of and somewhat comfortable with the legalese of the Catholic Church. Later on in the seminary, I would hear this referred to as Canon Law. Anyway, I memorized the list of mortal and venial sins that were available to commit, the Ten Commandments, and the proper form and contrite voice for the confessional box. I also checked each time I came to a street corner, not only to look both ways, but also to see if there were any mortal sins on my soul. Up to the age of seven I didn't have to worry about mortal sins, because I hadn't reached the age of Reason yet. In second grade I was only six years old. I was learning about the Sacrament of Penance, but wasn't old enough to make my First Confession, in preparation for First Communion.

Putting aside the humor and guilt and fuzzy theology, it was a grand day on Sunday, October 7th, 1945 when all the third grade boys and girls assembled in St. Anthony's School at 8:30 AM for the 9:00 First Communion Mass. I was wearing the traditional dark blue suit—double breasted—with a white shirt and white tie. I had my First Communion pin in the lapel of the jacket, the Rosary in my jacket pocket, and my First Communion prayer book. The little boys and girls must have looked great as we marched from the School down the sidewalk in front of the Rectory to the front of Church on Wallace St. and then slowly down the center aisle to our pews, boys on the right and girls on the left.

It felt good to be the center of attention in the family, with my parents there, looking at me as I went past them with folded hands, my "real" godfather, Emil Beyer and his family, my godmother, Beatrice Curley, my Aunts Mary and Catherine, and Mag, Patrick, Kate and Fred. And, just as if it was planned, when I received my First Communion at the Communion rail from Father Schmidt, the host stuck to the roof of my mouth! For the next ten minutes as I walked back to my pew place and kneeled to pray, my only thoughts were how to get the host unstuck so that I could swallow it.

Sister Ponciana had preached endlessly to us about Communion being the Body of Christ, so we should reverence it. And here am I pushing my tongue up in my mouth to try and get under Jesus to unstick him from the roof.

God's next call to me came on the night of September 30th, 1947, again in St. Anthony de Padua Church. All of the fourth and fifth grades confirmandi were assembled with their sponsors and parents and family for the biennial Confirmation at our parish. Presiding and confirming was the gentle, smiling Samuel Cardinal Stritch, the Archbishop of Chicago. Also on the altar were the pastor, Father Martin Schmidt who was starting to slip a little with his memory, and Father Austin Graff, the assistant pastor.

Father Graff was tall and soft-spoken. Whenever I talked to him it seemed as though his eyes penetrated my eyes, going directly to my brain, and from there searched throughout me until finding my soul. I was always affected by his quiet, clear voice and the feeling of holiness he personified.

Sister Mary Ignatius had been working with us for months in preparation for the Sacrament of Confirmation. We memorized what a Sacrament is as well as the names and understanding of each Sacrament. They were, in order of reception for most Catholics; Baptism, Penance, Holy Communion, Confirmation, Matrimony, and Extreme Unction. The seventh Sacrament was received by men who became priests. It was called Holy Orders.

We could recite the seven gifts of the Holy Ghost and the ten Commandments. Sister kept telling us that Cardinal Stritch would ask us questions about our faith, *before* he would confirm us. She also got particular delight when she warned us that part of the actual Confirmation was the "slap in the face" by the Cardinal after he anointed us with the oil of Confirmation.

That slap was supposed to prepare us to be "soldiers of Christ" who would go into the world and defend the Faith.

On that night in '47, as I was nine and a half years old, in fifth grade, and had practiced and memorized all the answers to the possible questions we would be asked by the Cardinal, and with all of the Church's lights on, with many candles burning, finally Cardinal Stritch walked from his throne seat on the right-hand side of the sanctuary to a stand-up microphone right of center. I was in the third row exactly in line with the Cardinal. My sponsor, Don Page, was sitting to my right, in the pew for sponsors.

"Now boys and girls, I know that you have prayed and studied with your teachers, the wonderful sisters of St. Anthony de Padua School, to understand the Sacrament of Confirmation. And all of you have already received First Communion, and have gone to Confession, and are now in the state of Grace. I have some questions to test your Faith," began Cardinal Stritch. He looked closely at the sixty-five boys and girls that were seated in front of him on both sides of the main aisle, and he was smiling broadly.

"Who can tell me what a Sacrament is?" asked the Cardinal.

My right hand shot up as he began the word "Sacrament." Other hands started to raise and pretty soon the Cardinal had to choose someone to answer his first question. I was hoping he would call on me because I had the answer memorized.

Slowly he scanned the children. Then he settled his eyes on me, and he said, "Young man. You had your hand up first. Tell me what a Sacrament is."

I stood up and in a loud, clear voice, proclaimed, "A Sacrament is an outward sign instituted by Christ to give Grace."

The Cardinal's face beamed as he heard the definition. "Very Good. You have said that perfectly."

I sat down with a big smile.

"Now tell me, boys and girls, what is asked of you when you are confirmed?" continued the Cardinal.

I raised my hand and arm again, and waited to see the others respond to the Cardinal's second question. I couldn't see any boy or girl raise their hands. Cardinal Stritch looked at me again and said, "Well, tell us what we must do with the Sacrament of Confirmation when we receive it."

Again, I stood up and spoke loudly and clearly. "With the Sacrament of Confirmation, we receive the Holy Ghost. Our head is anointed with oil. We receive a slap on the face. These make us soldiers of Christ so that we can go out to the world and defend our Faith."

I sat down and looked at my sponsor, Don Page. He was smiling broadly and giving me a Congratulations sign with his hand. In the meantime, my parents were feeling so proud that I had answered the Cardinal's questions.

"I have another question for all of you. Can you give me the names of the seven gifts of the Holy Ghost?" asked the Cardinal.

There was silence in the Church. Not a single hand of any of the boys and girls shot up. I was sitting in my pew waiting and hoping that someone would raise his or her hand to answer the Cardinal's question. Seconds and longer seemed to go by, but no response. I looked around to my classmates, but no one seemed to want to answer. I glanced back to Sister. Her face had a tense smile like she was not happy but had to smile.

Finally, I raised my hand. Cardinal Stritch, the priests, and the nuns seemed relieved. "Can you tell me the seven gifts of the Holy Ghost?" repeated the Cardinal.

"Yes, your Excellency. They are Prudence, Justice, Fortitude, Understanding, Counsel, Piety, and Wisdom."

There was a stir amongst my classmates and the people. Some murmuring was clearly audible. Cardinal Stritch looked at me with his wide smile and a knowing look on his face. "Wonderful. Wonderful," he said.

I thoroughly enjoyed the notoriety of this moment as my fellow students in fifth grade smiled at me, and the nearby sponsors were silently congratulatory. Don Page was really beaming now, feeling proud that he was the sponsor of a boy who knew his Faith, at least Confirmation.

The Cardinal asked two more questions which were answered by my classmates.

For the actual Confirmation, we had to kneel at the old Communion rail with our sponsors standing behind us, with their right hands on our right shoulders. Since the fifth grade sat on the right side of the aisle, we knelt on the right half of the rail, and would be the first to receive Confirmation from the Cardinal. I had wondered all the way thru the ceremony what the Cardinal was going to do when he came to confirm me. As I was kneeling on the rail, he kept coming closer, confirming the fifth graders from my right to left on the rail, one student at a time. Each of these Confirmations were friendly, with a gentle smile on his face.

When he walked to me, he saw my Confirmation name of Lawrence. He started to smile very broadly now and just stood for a moment and looked at me. I looked back and the recognition from both of us was clear. The Cardinal then went thru the anointing with Holy Chrism on my forehead, reciting the prayer formula, smiling all the time. As it came time for the slap, he paused ever so momentarily, and then gave me a good crack on the face, again with those twinkling eyes and knowing smile.

*

"In nomine Patris, et Filii, et Spiritus Sancti. Amen. Introibo ad altare Dei." intoned Father Schmidt in Latin, as he stood before the three steps to the altar.

Ray Fendler and I responded, *"Ad Deum qui laetificat juventutem meam."*

Father continued, *"Adjutorium nostrum in nominee Domini."*

We answered him, *"Qui fecit caelum et terram."*

After the Confiteor and other opening prayers to Mass, Fr. Schmidt ascended the steps to the altar. Ray looked at me as we settled into kneeling on the first step, each of us on the end of the step, away from the center of the altar. Ray smiled, and I started to laugh slightly. I could *never* keep a straight face as a server in Church, especially with Ray.

Father Schmidt interrupted our light moment with, *"et omnium sanctorum: ut indulgere digneris omnia peccata mea. Amen."* as he kissed the altar.

It was 8:00 AM on this weekday morning in the Fall of 1947. We were now in fifth grade and Confirmed and old enough to be altar boys. Sister Mary Magna had come into our fourth grade room at the end of last school year and began the call for Mass servers. She said that it was part of our responsibility as Catholics to serve the Church. She would teach us the proper procedures, how to vest in a cassock and surplice, the lighting of candles, incense, and torches as well as the Latin responses to the priest, which had to be memorized. At the end of her little pitch, she wagged a finger at us, "Any boy who wants to serve just to fool around, or just to get out of school, will *not* be put on the list of servers."

Since my brother Patrick was already serving, and my parents expected me to serve, I told Sister Magna, "Yes," when she looked at me. Actually, serving Mass and other Church events like Benediction, Stations of the Cross, Weddings, Funerals, and High Masses proved to be fun, interesting, and full of Grace. I really can't say that I earned that much Grace for my efforts because I wasn't very devout, what with my inability to look at another server without smiling or giggling. But, sitting on chairs next to the priest's throne when he read the Gospel and then preached at the pulpit, I felt a sense of importance as I glanced out at the parishioners, looking for someone I could smile at or possibly wink.

One morning, Ray Fendler and I had to serve Father Schmidt's Mass. We were happy to get him for the Mass because he was fast. He had set the Papal record for a Sunday Mass once. *Twenty minutes.* Father Schmidt spoke quickly and did not have a lot to say for the sermon. All the men in the parish tried to get to his Mass on Sundays to fulfill their Sunday obligation in the shortest amount of time.

On this particular morning, it was getting close to the Offertory of the Mass and Ray and I were wondering if we had a chance today. It was usually at the 7:00 AM Mass that Father Schmidt would not be awake enough to know how much wine he was taking. Ray and I went to get both the water and wine for Father. We stood at the end of the altar and waited for him to finish the Offertory prayer. He came over to us with his chalice, and he looked half-asleep. I poured just a little wine into the chalice and Ray followed quickly with some water. No notice was given by Father. We both smiled at each other, Ray and I. Over half of the wine cruet was still filled with Sauterne. And Father Schmidt never asked for more wine after Communion. He didn't notice after Mass when we innocently brought the leftover wine to the servers' side of the sacristy, and helped ourselves.

One of the more mysterious server assignments was the 6:00 AM daily Mass in the Convent. For me, it was just a half-block walk at 5:40 AM to the convent at the northwest corner of 28th Place and Normal Ave. The steps leading to the front door were numerous and very steep, and I had to be very careful, especially in the winter with snow and ice. I feared getting' to the top step, trippin' on the ice, tumblin' down fifteen steps, hittin' my head on the way down, and layin' on the sidewalk freezin' to death because no one was around at that time of the mornin'.

I'd ring the doorbell and about twenty seconds later, the door would open and a nun would nod to me. I'd go into the foyer, leave my coat and hat on the chair, and turn slightly right into a long, dark hall that ran the length of the convent. There was silence everywhere. After a few steps down the hall, I'd turn left and go up the creaky stairs to the second floor. The Convent chapel was straight ahead from the top of the stairs.

Sisters would be moving silently through the halls. It seemed to be a sin for me to make any kind of noise. So I found myself tiptoeing instead of walking. As I entered the chapel, Father Graff or Father Schmidt, or later on Father Laske would be vesting. The priest said nothing, just nodded to me. After putting on my cassock and surplice, I would hear the soft steps of the nuns and the slight swishing of their habits as they came devoutly into the chapel for Mass. It took me two years of serving in that convent to find out that the Sisters have to keep the Magnum Silentium from evening prayers the night before to breakfast the next morning. The Big Silence!

Some of my classmates who weren't servers would ask me, "What's it like in the convent?"

I'd respond, "It's dark, and mysterious, and all the Sisters walk around in silence. They don't even talk to Father. And he doesn't say anything to me."

"Do they really have hair under those veils?" I'd be asked by the guys.

But all I could answer was, "I never saw a nun with her veil off her head."

*

One of the privileges of serving and being in the sacristy of the Church before Mass would start, was to help ring the Church bells in the tower. The caretaker of the bells and church doors was an old man called Frankie. He was about sixty five years old, just under four and a half feet tall, with a little hump in his back on the left side. He knew we liked to go up to the bell tower and help him ring the bells before Sunday Mass at 9:00 AM or at noon. But he also had a good memory about which kids in the neighborhood would make fun of him when he was walking between Church and his home. The kids would see him walking down the sidewalk on Wallace Street and yell out, "Quasimodo, go ring the bells. Quasimodo." And then they would run because Frankie would turn around trying to get a glimpse of who was taunting him.

The trip with Frankie up the bell tower at St. Anthony's was like a scene from The Hunchback of Notre Dame. We had to climb this dark, musty, winding staircase that began at the south end of the vestibule right next to the Baptistry. When we got up to the choir loft, we then had to hand and foot climb this eight foot, wooden ladder that was fastened to the wall. Once we made it to the top of the ladder, we would push open the trap door and climb into the bell rope room.

Inside this room we could feel the air from the outside because as we looked up, there were the bells with the open tower spaces next to them. We'd hear the flutter of the pigeons as they scrambled because of our sounds down below them.

And then we saw it! *It* was the bull rope that Frankie used to ring the bells, hanging some forty or fifty feet down from the bell housing in the tower. To ring the bells, we had to jump up, grab onto the rope and let our weight and gravity drag the rope down. Slowly, we would hear the mechanical action above our heads and then the "Gong, Gong" of the bells. At the same time, if we held onto the rope, it would rewind itself above and we would go for a little ride up the tower for about ten feet.

*

Father Richard Laske came to St. Anthony's Parish in July of 1948. He had been ordained in May, so we were his first assignment. Besides saying Mass, hearing confessions, working with the Ladies Sodality, and visiting the sick for Communion calls, Father had to visit the School regularly, coach the seventh and eighth grades boys sports teams, and encourage vocations to the priesthood. As I had already been "called" five times by God; birth, Baptism, First Communion, Confirmation, and altar boy, it wasn't long before Father was talking to me about Quigley Preparatory Seminary on the near northside of Chicago. He would arrange for trips to St. Mary of the Lake, the major seminary at Mundelein for small groups of seventh and eighth grades boys who might have a interest in studying for the priesthood. That interest might just turn into a vocation to serve God. (It took me thirty-five years to discover that *everyone* has a vocation in life, but the only persons who use the word are priests, brothers, and nuns).

At first, during seventh grade, I didn't pick up on Father Laske's inquiries about the high school I might be going to, or the suggestions for me to consider Quigley, or even the long, car trips to the seminary. It just didn't dawn on me that he felt I had a vocation. I was missing his call altogether. I was totally involved in baseball, and making money with the paper route, and now, girls!

When Sister Mary Roger announced one Spring, Friday morning in 1951 to her eighth grade class that today the boys would learn how to dance, and the girls would show them, I laughed and clapped my hands. Hooray for Sister!

Sure enough, at 1:00 PM she had Arthur Barrett and George Schramm carry the record player and the forty five RPM records that the girls had brought, to the School basement. We helped move the tables out of the center, positioned the chairs so that they were around the perimeter of the dance floor, and began the music.

The first song was a slow one, and Janie Weller, my next door neighbor on 28th Place, came up and asked *me* to dance. "After all," she said, "this is what Sister Roger wants." There were quite a few laughs as Little Hughie joined arms with Tall Jane to dance. But all of the other boys were soon paired with girls and the lessons began, much to the delight of Sister.

Before the end of the afternoon was over and I had to put on my patrol belt and go to my station at 28th Place and Normal Ave., I had already learned the Jitter Bug from Jeannette Hadley, and the waltz from Jane Weller. I never realized my legs could be so coordinated for something other than sports. Sister's dance lesson was a lot of fun. What a great afternoon!

Although Father Laske kept trying to get me to study at Quigley for high school and to consider the priesthood, I avoided his call, and developed plans to go to St.Patrick Academy where my brother was a freshman. I did have guilt feelings about turning down Father because we had learned from the nuns and priests that there was no higher calling on earth than the religious life. In fact, if we had any thought at all about a life of holiness, we should follow it. It was bad to turn down God's call, my conscience kept telling me.

But Father Laske was understanding and not pushy. He was a quiet man, not given to high pressure or an inflated sense of himself. I did recognize that I had the makings to study for the priesthood, and Father Laske was a very good role model for me, just like Father Graff before him. I certainly couldn't ask for two better priests to follow. Both were the kinda men I'd like to be.

But, I just couldn't make that decision in eighth grade. I just started living, coming out from within myself as a boy, from the shell of self-pity and small size. I looked forward to a regular high school, even though St. Pats was all-male. (St.Pats Girls High School was right next door)

It was too much to give up, especially as I was moving into teenager time. There was so much happening in the "real" world. It was the Fabulous Fifties! Television. Girls. Dancing. Money. Clothes. Baseball. Cars. Cigarettes. The Gang. *I couldn't walk away from all that to spend hours on my knees in church. I just wasn't ready for the religious life, for "the path less traveled."*

Mommy and Hughie in back yard, 1938.

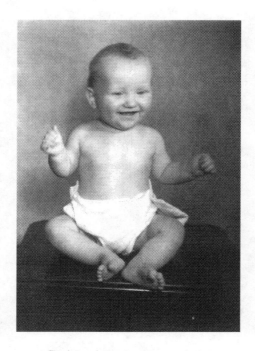

Patrick at home in summer of 1937.

Mommy and Hughie at McGuane Park, 1938.

Mag, Hughie, and Patrick, 1939.

Hughie on Wallace St., 1944.

Daddy and the first 5 kids, Cedar Lake, 1944.

Mommy and the first 5, 1945.

The LeVoy Boys, Hughie, Fred, Patrick.

The Servers, Patrick and Hughie, 1947

The Alley house with tunnel.

Mommy in the backyard.

All 8 LeVoys at Regan's House, 1947

Hughie and Patrick at the
Victory Garden, 1945.
Hughie's First Communion

The Graduates; George Schramm, Jane Weller,
Hughie – In front of the house- June, 1951

REV. RICHARD LASKE

St.Anthony de Padua School and Convent

Herald CHICAGO American

AN AMERICAN PAPER FOR THE AMERICAN PEOPLE

MONDAY—JUNE 26—1950

E UN CR

KOREA V

ETINS

e 25.—(AP)—The UN Security
a fire in Korea and demanded a
ders

RGENCY STRATEGY PARLEY
e 25.—(INS)—Gen. MacArthur
munition to South Korea and Presi-

Record Hunt On for Lost Airliner

Hope for the 58 persons
aboard the missing Northwest

Atta Fat

WASHINGTO
action tonight des
serious" and a pr
with a fateful test.
Gen. Omar N,
of Staff, declined

3

MARY GALVIN

When once again the bowl was filled, but not in mirth or joy.
'Twas mingled by a mother's hand to cheer her parting boy.

Oliver Wendell Holmes, "On Lending a Punch-Bowl"

"Paper boy, collect!" I announced after knocking on the Galvin's door at 2938 S. Union Ave. It was a cool, sunny, Saturday morning in October of 1950. The kind of day that always made me feel good. The door opened and Mr. Galvin stood there looking at me. I handed him the Saturday *Herald-American* and repeated, "Collect. It's 45 cents."

"Mary, it's the paper boy and the bill is 45 cents," Mr. Galvin yelled to his wife who was in another room, probably the bedroom.

"Give him 75 cents," I could hear Mary yell back from the bedroom. "He deserves a tip for delivering the paper between the two doors every day," she added.

Mr.Galvin reached into his left pants pocket and came out with three quarters. He didn't smile as he handed them to me, but said, "Here."

I had a big grin on my face. "Thanks a lot."

I left that first floor rear apartment very happy that I had received a 30 cents tip. Mrs. Galvin was always kind and friendly to me and always gave me a good tip each week. She was one of the big reasons I stayed with the paper route. She was my best customer, always complimenting me on my delivery and being generous.

I had started deliverin' papers in the summer of 1947 when I was going into 5th grade at St. Anthony's. My sister Mag started deliverin' papers two years before that in 1945, and my brother Pat started in 1946. Each of us delivered for the *Herald-American*, and we all had routes close to home, within walking distance of our house. My route was from 29th to 31st on Union Ave., and from 31st to 29th on Emerald Ave., with one delivery at the lumber yard on 30th & Halsted. I had 54 daily customers who received the paper from Monday thru Saturday, and 35 Sunday customers. The News Agency would bring out bundles of papers to our house at 469 West 28th Place, and put them on Grandma Bosak's first floor porch. One bundle for Mag, one for Pat, and one for me. When we got home from St.Anthony's School each day, we would change clothes, fold a bunch of our papers on the porch, and be on route by 3:15 PM. My route was only five minutes walk from the house.

At first we used the heavy canvas, *Herald-American* bag to carry our papers. That was a load for a kid, especially on Sundays with 35 copies. But later, Daddy built carts that had a large box in front on two wheels and a rod nailed to the box for pushing and steering. The box was large enough and deep so that it could hold all of the papers, either laid flat in the box, or folded. The paper cart was a real labor-saver, and it even rolled in the snow.

Only the daily papers could be folded because there were usually only three or four sections; the News, Business, Sports, and Local/Classified. A newspaper was folded by taking the loose, ragged ends and folding a section, about two inches, over and again. Now the paper had a seam end into which those three folded sections were tucked. The result was a paper that resembled a flat missile and could be thrown onto the porch of a house, or up to a 2nd floor landing, or even up and over a 3rd floor banister—my favorite was the 3rd floor delivery inside the hall at 3029 South Union. If the paper didn't loop over the banister when I first threw it upwards, the paper would come tumbling down to the 2nd floor banister, hit that and then come tumbling down to me. Sometimes I would try five or six times to toss that paper over the third floor banister instead of just walking up the two flights of stairs and saving the wear and tear on the paper and banister. *I just hadda prove to myself that I could loop it over.*

Most customers wanted their paper between the front door and the screen door, or if there was no screen door, then tucked into the space between the door knob and door jamb. Some wanted me to slide the paper under the door because there was some space between the door sill and the bottom of the door. And then there were others who wanted the paper put into the mailbox. And just a few, a very few, gave me a specific request to hand deliver the paper to them after knocking on the door. The biggest fear that we and the customers had was to have an unfolded paper blow apart from the wind or get soggy from the rain or snow.

The whole route took one hour, unless I stopped to watch a Sox or Cubs game at the tavern on 30th and Union, or the weather was bad with snow or rain and everything took longer. On days when there was a St.Anthony's baseball or football game after school, I would use my bicycle and rush thru the route in 45 minutes, and then take the short ride to 29ᵗʰ & Halsted to Mark White Square Park.

One of my first lessons in job responsibility came one winter day when I couldn't find my mittens after school and it was time to deliver the papers. I searched everywhere but the mittens couldn't be found. Our closet. My dresser drawers, Under the bed. In the basement. In Fred's jacket. They were nowhere to be found. So I pleaded with my mother to help me with the paper deliveries, but she couldn't because of the young ones at home, Kate and Fred and Maureen. She said that I had to deliver those papers, gloves or not. I just couldn't face the task of doing the paper route with bare hands.

Reluctantly, I went downstairs and took my cart from the gangway, came around to the front, folded some papers, and packed the rest into the cart. My hands were already cold because the temperature was in the 20s. Alternately I would blow on one hand and then the other as I pushed the cart. I would push first with the right hand and have the left hand in the deep pocket of my Navy jacket. Then the right hand would start to freeze and I would bring the left hand out, push, blow on the right hand, and plunge it deep into the right pocket. For the next hour and fifteen minutes, this was the only solution to fighting the freezing of my hands. *I kept thinking of the warm stove in our kitchen and my frozen hands over it, thawing out.*

When I finally got home after the deliveries, my mother realized how cold my hands were and made a cup of tea for me. It was so good to be in that warm kitchen with my freezing hands wrapped around the hot cup of tea—a cup of "cheer" for the returning boy—although my fingers were painful as they began to thaw. I had to "wring" them to reduce the tingling running thru my fingers, as the nerve ends kept crying for heat and comfort.

I never delivered papers again in the winter or shoveled snow, or did any outside activity without mittens or gloves. To this day, in fact, my hands always are sensitive to the cold in winter. Even with gloves, the finger tips get cold quickly and act like they're frozen.

*

Ray, the delivery manager, sat behind the large counter in the News Agency at 3238 S. Halsted. It was Saturday afternoon, and time for me to pay for my papers that I had delivered and collected from customers for Sunday thru Saturday. "Well, let's see what you owe us," he said. "You had 54 daily papers for six days. That's 324 papers times four cents a paper. That's $12.96. Then you delivered 35 Sundays, times twelve cents. That comes to $4.20. So your total bill for this week is $17.16."

I put all of my change from my left hand front pocket on the counter and all of the dollar bills from my wallet also. Slowly, I stacked the quarters into piles of four and the dimes into piles of ten, and also the nickels into stacks of ten. There were eight single dollar bills, five piles of quarters, three stacks of dimes, and twenty three nickels. I needed a penny to make the $17.16 for Ray. As I was reaching to push a penny from the rest of the change, Ray said that I could keep the penny from the 16 cents. For Good Luck! He laughed as he scooped all of the stacked change into his cash drawer under the counter and put the singles in there also. Then he gave me a receipt for my payment. Sitting on the counter in front of me were the coins that represented my work and tips for the week. My pay!

All of my customers had paid their bills on time and it was a good week. I pocketed the change that was left on the counter and made a mental note that I would count it at home on the kitchen table with my mother. On the way back home, I stopped at David's Restaurant at 31ˢᵗ & Halsted to look at the new paperback books on display, as well as the sports magazines. The magazine rack was as large as the one at Sears, and even had *The Sporting News*, the baseball newspaper.

Paperboys in 1950 received a penny for each daily paper delivered, and three cents for each Sunday. Since I delivered 324 daily papers a week, I could count on $3.24 as my share of the customer's bills. I would get three cents for each Sunday, and that amounted to $1.05. Finally, since the weekly bill for most customers was 30 cents for the six daily papers and 15 cents for the Sunday, a lot of people would give me two quarters when I came to collect, and say, "Keep the change," since the bill was 45 cents. My tips usually were around $2.00 per week. When I sat down at home on Saturday afternoon, I usually would count around $6.50 that I had earned.

My mother would get $5.50 of my paper route money each week. I would put the pennies and nickels into my piggy bank in our bedroom, and keep the dimes and a quarter for spending. The $5.50 to Mommy was called my "Room and Board." It was part of our responsibilities as we became old enough to deliver papers, or eventually work downtown during high school, or even after that, if we were working, living at home, and not married.

My mother was a housewife. She had to take care of the children, the food, the laundry, the apartment, as well as the bills. Each of the kids went to Catholic grammar and high school. We had to work to earn our tuition, and pay for our books. In addition, money was needed for our clothes, and carfare for high school. Hopefully, there would be some spending money left over.

We lived in a Cash Economy in the late '40s and early '50s. All of our purchases and bills were paid with cash. Each month Grandma Bosak received $40 in cash for the monthly rent of our six room apartment. The electric, gas, and telephone bills were paid at the bank on 31ˢᵗ and Wallace in cash by my mother. The cash had to be "on hand" in Mommy's hidden bank drawer *before* a purchase could be made or a bill paid. The milkman, Herb Martin, collected each week from my mother for two quarts he delivered each day except Sunday. My mother would take about $50 with her when she went to the A & P on 31st for the week's groceries. The tuition at St. Anthony's was $1.00 per month per child. In 1948, there were five LeVoy children paying tuition; Mag in 8th grade, Pat in 7th, Hugh in 6th, Kate in 3rd, and Fred in 1st.

Even the Metropolitan insurance man would take cash for the monthly premiums that my mother paid for our small life insurance policies. He would walk up the steep back stairs to our flat carrying a thick, black book that had all of the insured names on his route, along with a ledger page for each person's payment record. Sitting at the end of our kitchen table, he would take the cash and coins that my mother would give him, and record the date and amount of payment in very fine numbers on the ledger side of the big book. He'd chat socially with my mother as some of the kids stood by, watching him. He'd always ask us about school. When it came time for him to leave, I could hear his change from all his collections jingle in his pocket as he got up from the chair and walked down the back stairs again. *I would wonder if he had as much change as I did when I collected from my route*

One payday my father was in a playful mood after receiving his check from the Wabash Railroad, and having a few "boilermakers" at Down's Tavern on the corner of 29th & Wallace. The tavern would cash payroll checks for the men if they had a drink or two or were regular customers—the wives of the neighborhood were always fearful on paydays that the stop at Down's meant more than a quick shot and beer. Maybe a good chunk of the check would be gone before the husband got home.

Daddy brought home the cash one late afternoon and gave it to Mommy with an admonition to be careful with the cash because there was a $50 bill in with the $20s and other bills.

She took all of the cash and put it into her secret drawer because she was mad that he was late for dinner and we were waiting for him. The boiled potatoes were overcooked and beginning to fall apart. They looked soggy instead of firm.

In fact, my mother would sometimes send Pat or I on payday afternoons to fetch my father from Down's if it was suppertime and he wasn't home. When I would go, I always had mixed feelings because the tavern was full of men who were drinking at the bar and laughing over the fantastic stories being told, slapping each other on the back. I'd come into the bar and look around for my father, but it always seemed dark in there. I couldn't see where my father was sitting at the bar.

Some "regular" would spot me and say in a loud voice, "Paddy me boy, one of yer kids is here. It's time to drink up and be on yer way home now."

And then there'd be a howl of laughter in the place. My father would finally see me at the door and call me over to him.

Anyway, my mother had time the next day to go to her hidden bank in her bedroom dresser and take out the cash to count it. She laid out the bills on her bed and suddenly became very nervous. She spread the bills into singles, fivers, tens, and twenties. There was *no* fifty dollar bill!

Was the fifty still in her drawer in the envelope? She checked and couldn't find it. Did it fall on the floor as she carried the bills to the bed? No. Did it fly under the bed? She bent down but couldn't see it. She even got the broom and swept under the bed. Where was the $50? She finally decided to bring all of the bills to the kitchen table, one bill at a time. Still no fifty showed up. By this time she was very worried. *Somehow she had lost $50 from my father's pay! What could she do? How would she pay the bills if we were short that amount of money? What happened?*

All throughout the rest of the morning and early afternoon she fretted and was agitated, as she took care of Fred and Maureen. Then Mag, Pat, Kate and I came home from school. Mommy didn't look good and when we asked, she started crying, saying she lost $50. She brought out all of the bills again from her dresser, and had us watch as she went thru each bill. Still there wasn't a $50 bill.

We didn't know what to do other than offer comfort. We knew that Daddy had to be told and $50 out of the budget would make things difficult for awhile.

Finally, he came home from work that day and was whistling as he came up the front stairs. Before he could set the lunch pail down on the sink in the kitchen, with all of us sitting at our assigned spots at the table, Mommy blurted out that she could not find the $50 bill he had brought home yesterday with his pay.

We expected an explosion from him, but instead there was a wide smile on his face. "There was no fifty in my pay! I was feeling good and playing around," he announced.

My mother felt the stress she had gone through with his joke, and turned slowly and tearfully to the pot of Chili on the stove in front of her. Slowly she stirred it, not knowing what else to do. The kids looked at Daddy with blank stares.

My father realized that he had made a very poor joke, a big mistake. The smile had vanished from his face. He went over to Mommy and put his arms around her and said, "Aw Mar'gret, I'm sorry. I didn't know you'd take me serious. I won't fool around with the pay again."

Daddy had worked at the Wabash Railroad since 1935, the year that Mag was born. He was officially known as a freight clerk who checked freight as it came into Chicago in boxcars to be unloaded and sent to various companies in the area. He didn't make a lot of money, and there wasn't much overtime with time and a half pay. So, he would supplement his income by taking remodeling and home improvement jobs in the neighborhood during his days off from the Railroad on Wednesdays and Thursdays. Carpentry was his real love, his avocation, and he was good at it. He had the patience and skill to work with wood.

But even with the extra income, the family with six kids and my mother as homemaker couldn't make ends meet, keep the children in Catholic Schools, without us kids working and paying Room and Board.

There was no shame in the low wages my father received from the Railroad, or the fact that we all had to work. We recognized early on in life that economic necessities had to be met. And that meant work. There was no credit at the time, although the department stores had lay-a-way for larger items like furniture and appliances. We didn't have a television until the early '50s, and that was a used, eleven inch Garod. My father drove an early model Plymouth for many, many years, and did not purchase a new car until all of the children were pretty well raised in 1959. But, we did rent an old cottage every summer in August for two weeks at Cedar Lake, Indiana to get away. It was a must that our family would go away from Chicago to the country for swimming, boating, and fishing. We had to get out of the city heat.

Most importantly for me, the experience of delivering newspapers daily, collecting weekly bills from the customers, paying my Saturday paper bill at the News Agency, making my Room and Board, and saving and spending money, gave me early experiences that developed life-long skills, habits, and values.

Perhaps most significantly, I was my best *Herald-American* customer. I would devour the Sports pages in five minutes before I would fold any papers to get ready for delivery. I was such an avid sports fan at an early age,that I had to know what was happening in all of the major sports, no matter what season of the year. I followed basketball, golf, tennis, horse racing, auto racing, hockey, and college sports as well as baseball and football.

Jerome (Guts) McCarthy, one of my classmates from St. Anthony's, used to have contests with me to see which of us could "stump" the other one on ballplayers in the Major Leagues. He would name the team and player position and I would have to name the ballplayer who played there. Then we'd switch, and I'd give the team and position. Neither of us rarely won because we both knew every player's name on each of the sixteen teams in baseball, even the Cubs. No self-respecting Sox fan would ever admit knowing "anything" about the Cubs, not even where Wrigley Field is located.

I would also look thru the front section of the paper, especially at the photos. I recall being afraid when the North Koreans invaded South Korea on June 25th, 1950 and the United States became involved. I got real nervous when I saw the headline on my papers. All of a sudden I was reading and becoming familiar at the age of twelve with the horrors of war, as well as the geography of the Korean Peninsula, China, and the continent of Asia.

Each day I would study the map of the Korean Peninsula on page 1 to see where the battles were fought and whether we were advancing or losing the war. American troop attacks were shown in bold, black arrows around the 38th Parallel.

And at home in Bridgeport, some of the older guys from the neighborhood club called the DOBS on 28th Place & Normal had been drafted and were fighting in these battles. These were the same guys I'd see in front of the clubhouse when I walked to Wallace or went to St.Anthony's.

The Room and Board requirements at home made it a lot easier for me to accept and fulfill my responsibility to deliver papers every day. There were no excuses, no Off days, no counting on Mommy or my older brother or sister to do my route. I *had* to complete my route every afternoon and Sunday morning, no matter how I felt or what was happening after school or on Sunday. It also was a lot easier for me because I was in very good health—except for toothaches from cavities because I didn't brush regularly.

I remember one brutal night, lying in bed, tossin' & turnin' with the pain in my lower molars. No matter what position I took on the pillow, the throbs continued. Finally, I went cryin' to my mother for help. She put that god-awful-tasting pain killer on the teeth so that I could sleep. That's if I could somehow swallow the terrible taste in my mouth.

Actually, Mag, Pat, and I had perfect attendance at St.Anthony's from 1941 to 1951. Mommy saw to it that we got up each morning, had breakfast, put together our books and homework, and went off to Mass and School. Short of a heart attack, we could use no excuse with her to stay home from school or work. This LeVoy attendance record stood until Kate broke her arm in 4th grade and had to miss a couple of days.

I learned early on with the delivery of papers that the customer has to be pleased, both with the time that the paper arrives to them, and where it is placed by me. When I first started the route in 1947, I asked the customers where they wanted the paper put, and whether they wanted it folded. Except for an occasional detour at the tavern on 30th & Union to watch the ballgame, the papers were regularly delivered between 3:15 to 4:15 PM, in time for the customers when they came home from work. All of this customer attention, of course, was aimed at making the collection of the paper bill on Saturdays a painless event, and perhaps a tip added to the bill by the customer.

I also began to learn how to plan my time around the paper route. There were always "pickup" baseball and football games after school on 28th

Place in front of our house. These would start around 3:30 PM and last until suppertime. If I wanted to play, especially if the older guys were playing and they needed another kid, I had to get my route completed in quick time. One October afternoon, I brought out my Bears football because the older guys—three or four years older—wanted to see and toss it around. Pretty soon they had a pickup game going, without me playing. When I started to complain, my mother heard me and came out of our flat. She stood on the small porch and yelled at the older guys for taking my football. All of a sudden, I was patted on the back by Eddie Rentz, the quarterback for one team, and put on his team. But, he never passed the football to me, even though I was wide-open on every play.

And then in the 7th and 8th grades, we started playing organized baseball and football and basketball for St. Anthony's under the leadership of Fr. Laske. We played the other Catholic grammar schools in the Bridgeport area at Mark White Square. I was counted on as an important part of the teams because we just had enough boys to fill the teams. One kid absent would mean a forfeit. I had to be at the park by 3:45 PM to suit up and be ready for the start of the game at 4:00. Not too many of my classmates were delivering papers, so I had to put the deliveries in high gear to get to those games.

Each afternoon, after I had read the paper and folded some papers, and loaded my cart, I would walk to my route down 29th St., past Parnell Ave. to Wallace St. The city planners in the late 19th Century must have been at a St.Patrick's Day party on the day before they set up the streets in this part of the neighborhood because Canal St. and Normal Ave. had jogs to the east as they reached 29th St. going southbound. The jog was no more than 125 feet, the length of one lot. But it made travel difficult because of the two quick turns in the street, first a left and then immediately a right. We could always hear the screeching of tires as cars made the zig-zag turns. And tucked in between Normal and Wallace was an extra street named Parnell Ave., beginning at 29th and going to 33rd, like Canal. Parnell Ave. was probably named for Charles Stewart Parnell, an Irish statesman from the 19th Century because the Bridgeport area was originally settled by Irish immigrants who were building the Illinois-Michigan Canal. (Being an avid baseball fan, I always thought that the street was named after Mel Parnell, a great lefthanded pitcher for the Boston Red Sox in the 40's and 50's).

Wallace St. was a combination of businesses and housing with the old Pharmacy on the southeast corner, Tommy Weingartner's gas station on the northeast corner—the only place nearby where kids could get air for their bike tires—a grocery store on the southwest corner, and the infamous Down's Tavern on the northwest corner.

Down's Tavern was so popular with the men of the neighborhood that there was always a line of them waiting for the bar to open at 7:00 AM each morning. It was always said that the "boys" needed a wee shot of whiskey early to chase away the shakes from too much the night before. I would always conjure in my mind the scene from the Western movie when the old prospector would take the whiskey glass in his shaking hand, down the drink into his belly, and then vibrate his head and upper body with, "I needed that."

And it was also said many times over, from the wives and their drinking husbands, that Frank Downs made so much money from the Tavern that he made a trip every summer to the "Old Country." Going Home to Ireland, as the Irish would say.

As I came to this intersection of 29th and Wallace with my papers and cart, I would be extra careful because of all the traffic, even though the corner was covered with Stop signs. The old, red streetcar came down 29th to this corner and then turned south, grinding its iron wheels on the tracks as it turned. Cars and trucks used Wallace because it was a thru street all the way from 26th to 47th, cutting thru the hearts of Bridgeport and Canaryville.

West of Wallace was Lowe Ave., a transition block with a mixture of nice brick bungalows and two-story frame or brick buildings. There were many homes with front yards at street level and grass in these yards, and both trees and grass in the parkways, scenes we didn't have on 28th Place. But, I would pass the "Dirty Kitchen" candy store on the corner and peer thru the dusty plate glass windows to see whether there really was candy for sale. The big windows looked as though they had never been washed since the day they were installed in the early 1900s.

Finally, I would get to the beginning of my route at 29th & Union, with deliveries to both 3-story, corner buildings on each side of Union. There was always a feeling I would have when delivering papers, especially on sunny days, that I was in a different neighborhood than 28th Place, even though I was only five minutes walk from my block and house. All of the buildings on Union and Emerald Avenues were brick or stone. There was an assortment of bungalows, two story buildings, and tall, three story apartment buildings. For the most part there was grass on the parkways and lots of trees lining the streets with tall branches overlapping the sidewalks. There were three-feet wide gangways between the buildings just as in my block, and some lots had sunken front yards below street grade.

The smell of some hallways in the two and three-story walkup apartment buildings was warm and mild, especially on cool or cold fall and winter days. I would bring the paper into the hall and toss it up to the 2nd floor landing or place it next to the interior door of the 1st floor apartment.

Then I would stop and just stand there, listening to the silence of this attractive hallway, rubbing my fingers along the nicely stained and varnished banister leading to the 2nd floor. No one was usually home in any of the apartments, so I could linger. The hall was dimly lit with some outside light coming thru the front door panes of glass, as well as a hall window at the 2nd landing.

It was always peaceful in these hallways. Unless I was in a hurry to play a game, I would stand still, look around, and be calm. I didn't have to rush thru deliveries today. The world would stop for me. The faint sounds of car traffic outside were ignored. It was almost as if this moment was owned by me, and no one could take it from me, except by opening the door. I waited, but no one came to spoil my meditation.

"I'd like to live in this building," I said to myself. I'd imagine coming "home" to the 2nd floor apartment, picking up the mail that had been pushed thru the outside slot, softly walking up the carpeted stairs, turning at the top, and heading for "my" front door.

And then there was my dream house at 3019 S. Emerald Ave. It was a black, brick bungalow on two city lots. The 2nd lot was covered with the greenest grass I had ever seen. There was a two-car, detached garage visible in the back of the lot that was black brick also. The front porch had a small portico around it for shelter from the rain and snow, and the front door showed glass along with two sidelights. The three, front windows were wide and together so that the front room admitted western light and sunsets. There was an attic, back porch, basement windows, and a clay tile roof.

Surrounding the property at the edge of the front yard was a three-feet black iron fence. The family that lived here did not subscribe to the *Herald-American*, so I never had a chance to go up the portico steps and deliver a paper.

I would linger here too, on the sidewalk, trying to be non-chalant about my stares at the home where I'd like to live someday.

It was becoming silently, slowly clear to me that I was developing tastes, designs, and future values of both how and where I wanted to live. These homes and buildings and yards were much more attractive than my two-story, frame building on 28th Place with the old, gray siding, wooden porches and exterior stairs. I kept imagining buying one of these buildings on my paper route when I grew up, after I had a job, was married and had kids. As children, we had very little experience with other neighborhoods except for the times we went to visit our uncles and aunts on the Westside or Southside of Chicago, and to Aunt Mary's apartment on the Northside.

These trips did bring us to "better" neighborhoods, as some people would say, but my real longing seemed to focus on the homes and buildings on my paper route. I kept imagining that after I became the starting 2nd baseman for the White Sox at age 20, I would buy this house on Emerald and "stay" in the neighborhood as a loyal Bridgeporter, instead of moving to that "better" neighborhood on the Southside.

But then, my paper route offered some unpleasant experiences also. Between the two brick buildings that stood on the NW corner of 31st and Union and Blake-Lamb Funeral Home, there stood two old, shabby two-flats with a garbage strewn, empty lot in between. I had deliveries in both of these run-down buildings, and I was always a little uneasy with the customers. In the summer the kids would be running in and out of the 1st floor apartments, or yelling and jumping into the vacant lot onto old tires and mattresses. There were no screens in the front windows, and these were open, with the flimsy curtains tied into a knot and hanging inside the windows, blowing in the breeze.

When I delivered the paper, I'd put the folded paper inside the dingy hallway and get out as soon as I could. There was no lingering here because the smell of burnt food and dank, unwashed halls and rooms was overpowering. Unfortunately, these buildings were known throughout the neighborhood as "Hillbilly Haven."

Farther along the route on 29th & Emerald was a three-story building that had seen a lot of transiency. It was probably a good example of an absentee landlord because the building and windows, doors and halls, looked like they hadn't received any attention or paint in some time.

An Irish-American family with quite a few children lived on the 1st floor front apartment. The children were always playing outside with the front and side doors to the apartment usually opened in the summer. The place didn't have very nice curtains in the front windows (definitely not lace), and when I went inside to deliver the paper, I could see the living room strewn with newspapers, old furniture, cigarette butts in overflowing ashtrays, and pop and beer bottles on the floor. Again, I would be edgy if I had to spend too much time there delivering or collecting because of the awful sights and smells. I had a sense of what I was seeing was the "Shanty Irish" that my mother and father would use occasionally to describe some people.

There were times when I was collecting the weekly bill that I would get an answer, "My husband doesn't get paid till next week. Come back then." I usually wondered about this response from a customer, especially if the bill was 30 cents. *Did she really not have the 30 cents to pay the bill? Was she trying to string me along? Did I come at the wrong time?* It was sometimes hard to be understanding of some customers, especially if I saw large bottles of soda and chips on the kitchen table as I was standing by the open door. Not enough money for the paper bill, but more than enough for chips and soda!

There was an occasional family that would go two or three weeks without paying. I would feel embarrassed about persistently knocking on the door to collect, but it seemed that the only way I was going to collect these bills was by wearing the mother down.

One time, I happened to catch the husband at home. After I told him that the paper bill was overdue and was now 90 cents for three weeks, he acted very surprised, and slightly embarrassed. He whipped out a wad of bills from his left, front pocket, peeled off a single $1.00, and with a sense of non-chalance he said, "Keep the change, kid."

As I walked away from the door, I thought, "The last of the big spenders."

What also developed gradually in me after a year on the paper route was a strong sense of independence. At the age of ten, I could walk the neighborhood to deliver papers and collect and pay my News Agency bill. It was no big deal to walk anywhere from Archer Ave. to 35th St., North to South and from Canal St. to Morgan St., East to West.

The only area that was a problem was "the other side of the tracks." Once in a while, trouble erupted between the boys on Princeton Ave.—the wrong side of the tracks—and our boys on the right side of the tracks. You could always count on rock and bottle throwing encounters under the viaducts on 28th Place, and once in a while on 29th. There never were any decent lights in these block-long tunnels under the railroad tracks, so it was great for each gang to assemble on their end and fling rocks and bottles at the other gang.

We never seemed to hit each other, but it was great fun to hear the sounds of breaking glass on the street under the viaduct. The tunnel magnified these sounds so well, we couldn't resist. Each gang never had a good look at the other because it was so dark and we were more than 100 feet apart. All we could see were figures running and throwing against the background of the light at the end of the viaduct.

The battles were not ethnic or racial either because both sides of the tracks had a mix of Italian, Irish, German, and Croatian families. The conflict was territorial, and the huge tracks were "no man's land" between the two gangs. What made it all the more ridiculous was that some of us had relatives on "the other side."

Occasionally I would encounter a lone kid who would try to bother me as I walked the paper route, or went to Halsted St., or was in the park. He was more the loudmouth bully who was looking for someone to yell at or shove around. I never had anyone try to take money from me on the route, or use a knife to hold me up, or shake me down for a dime or quarter. Sometimes on Saturday afternoon, I would have between $23 to $25 from the collections.

The consistency of making money as a paper boy helped me not only to contribute to the family with Room and Board, but also gave me a chance to save and budget. I could plan on money for high school at St. Pat's and not worry if my parents couldn't afford the tuition. Tuition at St. Patrick's Academy for the 1951-52 school year was $100 and the books were $25. Carfare was 50 cents a day, with a transfer.

I could count on money to buy snacks and paperback books. I had money for the Wallace Theatre movies, or the Milda Theatre where they offered three WWII movies for a dime. And the fancy show, the Ramova on 35th and Halsted featured all the latest movies after they showed downtown. I had money to buy my parents a gift for their birthdays and anniversary, and for Christmas. And, I forgot. I had enough cash to buy *two* pairs of mittens for winter. You never know what will turn up missing!

By the time of my 8th grade graduation from St. Anthony's on June 7th, 1951, I was completing four years as a paper boy. I had traversed the neighborhood of Bridgeport many times, saw homes and buildings that were run down, and others that were so appealing I said I would buy one when I got rich.

I had made and saved lots of money, and developed skills of pleasing the customer, collecting funds, paying bills, and meeting the daily responsibility of work, rain or shine, warm or cold. I'd be reminded daily on the route just how important people like Mary Galvin and other good customers were to my success. Their smiles, friendly greetings, and weekly tips made so much difference in my work.

It was now time to go to high school, to move beyond Bridgeport, to see and walk in other parts of Chicago. It was time to test my growing independence in a new environment.

*

Eugene Heinis, my classmate from St. Anthony's, called me during the Spring of 1952 when I was completing my Freshman year at St. Patrick Academy on the western edge of the Loop. He told me that he was leaving Chemists Supply, an old-fashioned drugstore, downtown on the eastern end at Wabash & Madison where he had been working part-time.

He wondered if I wanted to replace him since he knew I needed to work for tuition. The job paid 85 cents an hour. I would work two and a half hours after school every day, and from 9 AM to 2 PM on Saturdays. What was also attractive was the job was year-round, and I could work full-time in the summer. The part-time hours during the school year would be 17 per week, amounting to $13.45, less taxes. Wow! That was twice the money I was getting from the paper route.

I had quit the paper route at the end of the summer of '51 because Father Ackerman, the pastor of St. Anthony's Parish, offered me a job after school. I had to sweep the classrooms at the School, the School I just had left, for one hour a day. My pay would be $6 per week. I took this lonely job because it fit in with the late afternoon hours I would get back from high school, too late to continue with delivering papers.

The job at Chemists Supply involved delivering drugs to various offices, stores, and factories downtown. Each afternoon I would have to bring the parcel post drug orders to the Old Post Office on Adams and Dearborn Streets. And when I wasn't out on the streets of the Loop, I would be helping in the pharmacy counting pills, filling capsules, and storing drugs and chemicals on the shelves.

Since Gene was leaving in the summer, I could begin in August after he gave me on-the-job training. I told all of this to my parents, and they smiled. They said that I should take this job because the tuition and fees at De La Salle Institute, where Jake and I were headed for the Fall of '52, was $160, higher than it was for St.Pat's.

Come September, Jake and I had to leave old St. Pat's because the Christian Brothers were completing a new St. Pat's on the northwest side. This new high school would be much too far from Bridgeport. Even though it would not be ready until September, 1953, it would be better for us to transfer now, since Jake was a Junior and I was a Sophomore.

De La Salle, or "D" as everyone called the school, was located at 34th & Wabash, just east of Bridgeport. It was an easy ride from our home, with one bus transfer at 35th & Wallace. Many of the guys from the neighborhood went there, more than had gone to old St.Pat's.

The Christian Brothers both administered and taught at "D", the same order that was at St.Pat's. The principal did not recommend that the boys from Bridgeport walk to "D" even though it was only a mile away. The neighborhood around "D" was black, and the Brothers were afraid of fights and hold ups because of the differences in races and income. The neighborhood changed from white to black right around Wentworth Ave. which was a half a block east of Comiskey Park

This potential conflict proved to be a danger for me during the first year I was at "D". Instead of taking the 35th St. bus back to Bridgeport each afternoon, and then catching the Racine Downtown bus, I would walk to the El at 35th, between Wabash Ave. and State St. The Howard Street Rapid Transit line ran here. It took passengers downtown to State and Monroe in 10 minutes, where it was a short walk for me to my after school job at Chemists Supply.

If I left "D" on time in the afternoon with the other students, there always were a number of students taking the El either south to Garfield Blvd. or a smaller number who were going downtown to part-time jobs, like me. So there was safety in numbers in case some of the neighborhood black kids wanted to start something or were looking for money. Also, the Brothers, especially big Brother Josephus, would be supervising the boarding of the 35th St. buses going west, and the Michigan Ave. buses going south. And they would keep an eye on the guys that were walking the half block to the El. Since there was so much activity around the school, with so many Brothers and students, nothing much happened from the gangs in the neighborhood.

One afternoon, however, I had to stay late to speak to one of the teachers about grades. It was about fifteen to twenty minutes after all of the 35th St. buses had taken off and Brother Josephus and the other supervising Brothers had returned to "D". I remembered what the warnings were about the danger when walking alone, but I figured I only had to walk one block to the El to go downtown.

As I crossed the intersection of 35th & Wabash, I looked ahead but did not see anybody. There were no guys hanging by the El structure, and no one walking on the sidewalk. The coast looked clear.

I walked swiftly toward the El station, keeping my eyes in front of me, when out of the alley that was the street level for the El station structure came two black teenagers straight towards me.

The bigger guy, who was almost a head taller than me, looked around and seeing no one on the sidewalk or across the street, reached into his jacket pocket and pulled out a switchblade. He advanced slowly to me, kind of swaggerin', followed by his buddy, a shorter black kid with a nervous smile on his face.

"Yo money o yo life," the bigger guy said to me in a slow, cocky voice as he clicked the knife to open the blade, and moved it in a circle toward my chest. He kept glancing around to see if anyone was coming down the sidewalk or across the street.

I looked past these two guys and thought instantly of trying to run to the El steps, and get up before they could catch me. But the path was blocked by them. I'd somehow have to run around them. I checked with a slight head movement to see if there was help nearby from anyone, but no one was in sight, not even cars going down 35th. I had heard from the other guys who had been "held up" that it wasn't smart to run or yell or especially try to fight a guy with a knife. *Just play it "cool", stay calm, and give the guy what he wants. He doesn't want to knife you. He's only looking for money. You can always replace the stolen money, but you can't get back your life if your throat is slashed.*

I was very nervous now, realizing I had no way out. *Panic started! Why had I stayed so late at school?* I quickly reached into my pocket, fingered the two quarters that I had for carfare to downtown, and from the job to home at 6 PM. The two teenagers were getting a little jumpy, jostling their feet. I kept concentrating on the knife as it moved in a circle about two feet from my chest. I brought out the two quarters and reluctantly offered them to the bigger guy. "That's all I have. It's my carfare," I blurted.

The bigger guy looked disgusted at me as he grabbed the two quarters with his left hand. But right away he said to his friend, "Less go!"

They both started running down the same alley they had come from because someone was walking down the sidewalk toward us from Wabash Ave.

I didn't know what to do next, still in shock from that knife. Soon I realized that I couldn't get downtown without a quarter. So there was no sense in running up the stairs to the El. I turned around and went back to "D" to see Brother Josephus.

He yelled at me for leaving late and walking alone to the El. One of his big responsibilities at school was to insure that students got to school safely and went home in the same manner. If there was trouble, he became upset easily. But, with all of his ranting, he did give me a quarter, and personally escorted me all the way across Wabash, and up the El stairs to the cashier's booth. And he waited until I boarded the next Howard train and was safely headed downtown to my job.

Working at Chemists Supply after school and on Saturdays was easy, interesting, but very dated. The store had two entrances, one on 67 E. Madison St., with a large customer area with chairs for persons who were waiting for prescriptions. And a large counter where customers would stand for business.

There was also a side entrance from the lobby of the Mallers Building at 5 S. Wabash Ave. This had a much smaller customer area with a sofa for customer waiting and a small counter.

The interior rooms to the business were dark and dusty because the store had not really been cleaned or even remodeled for quite a while. The first room inside the larger customer area was a small room where Mr. Brady, the pharmacist, filled prescriptions. He would get help from his 81-year old apprentice, Mr. Wickman, who would count pills and mix ointments or pour bottles of cough medicine with Codeine.

Sometimes, if Mr. Wickman was absent, I would be told to work in this room with Mr. Brady, helping to fill prescriptions—not long after I started at the drugstore, I applied to the State of Illinois for an Apprentice Pharmacist license and received it. This gave me the opportunity to count pills, fill capsules, and pour all kinds of elixirs, syrups, etc. from large two-gallon containers into prescription bottles.(That was always a balancing act).

The rest of the business space had the same dark, old, dusty rooms with metal—constructed shelving, that held all of the chemicals and pharmaceuticals. I had to check these shelves daily to see what was out and had to be stocked from the supplies in the large, spooky basement.

The store manager was Mr. Novak. He was responsible for much of the bookwork, payroll, and packaging of Loop office orders and parcel post orders. He'd prepare the deliveries each day and wrap them so that I could take these boxes to various offices or companies in the Loop.

This was the best part of the job because I had a chance to get out of that old, stuffy store—I was the only person working in the store who was under the age of 60, except for the part-time bookkeeper. The deliveries brought me into the fresh air, as well as see people walking around. The delivery locations always presented a challenge to me. I wanted to minimize my steps around the Loop, and line up the lobbies of buildings that I could walk thru and thus not face the cold in Winter, or rain in Spring or Fall.

I found after awhile that the independence of moving thru the downtown streets was liberating and self-satisfying. I was on my own, and getting paid for it too! I felt confident that no matter where the delivery had to go, if a new customer had ordered some drugs, I could easily find the place and put it into my delivery route. There was always a sense of accomplishment when I completed my deliveries to 4 or 5 customers and was at the far, northwest corner of the Loop.

Once I learned the streets and buildings, my attention would turn to observing pedestrians, especially the well-dressed men. Suits, shirts, ties, and shoes. I'd look closely to see if the shirt on the man walking next to me had French cuffs with nice cufflinks. That was a sign of real taste in men's clothes. And did the tie have a neat Windsor knot with a tiepin pulling the two collar ends together?

My brother Jake had developed a fashion for dressing nicely. He had quite a few shirts with French cuffs, both white-on-white and the new pastels. He'd wear them to "D" with a real sharp tie because he wanted to be one of the best dressers in the school. But, he *never* wore yellow on Thursday. The common wisdom was Gay *only* on that day.

Sometimes on my downtown jaunts, I'd stop by the men's store windows in Field's or Carson's and look at the displays of suits, shirts, ties, and shoes on the manikins. I'd just stand there and admire the way the suit fit so nicely, snug in the shoulders with just the right arm length. How the shirts and ties matched colors so well with grey or brown suits. *And look at those silver cufflinks on the powder blue shirt and navy, blue suit with black, wing-tipped shoes. Someday I'll dress like that!. Pedestrians will be looking at me then.*

Besides stocking shelves and counting pills and pouring cough syrup, I also had to fill capsules with soya lecithin for bulk purchases by customers. Each afternoon I would go to my little cubby hole which was just alongside the Mallers Building entrance to the store. This little workroom was about eight feet long and three feet wide, and had just enough room for a stool to set up against a long counter that was the top work area, with many drawers below. Like the rest of the drugstore, the room was not well lit with overhead lights because it had no ceiling, being an add-on to the side service area of the store.

The soya lecithin was a yellowish powder that came in bulk quantities, made up by Mr. Brady, when he wasn't filling prescriptions. I would spread about four to six ounces of the powder on a wide, flat piece of pharmacist's marble slab, and then take each small, red, empty capsule, pull the two pieces apart, fill the large end first with the soya, then the small end, and finally put the two pieces together to make one capsule of soya lecithin. I had a quota of 1000 capsules each week, because this protein supplement was a big seller. I was constantly pushing to get the capsules done each week, so I was not too happy when I was called into the pharmacist's room to replace an absent Mr. Wickman.

Filling the capsules for an hour each day was very boring, so I'd find myself listening to the sounds of the store. A lady in the front was trying to tell Bob, the salesman, that she was ahead of the older man who was being waited on instead of her. Bob's response was familiar, "I'm sorry. I thought that he was ahead of you. I'm doing the best I can. I'm the only one here today." Mr. Foreman, the part-owner, who usually took care of customers also, was probably out of the store having a late lunch.

I'd hear Mr. Brady raise his throaty voice to tell Mr. Wickman, who was hard of hearing at age 81, "No, Mr. Wickman, count the pills for her prescription now."

Mr. Novak, who was constantly clearing his throat and slightly coughing, especially when he was ready to say something, did it again for the fifth time in the last minute.

And then I heard the side door to the store open and someone come in. There was about a five to ten second pause, and I heard a woman's voice. "Hello, is anyone here? Hello."

I waited to see if Mr. Novak would respond from his little work area which was out of sight from the side service area, but within hearing distance. The only salesman that day, Bob, was taking care of customers in the front. Mr. Parks, who worked in the same area as Mr. Novak, never did take care of customers, no matter how many were waiting, because his job involved working with the receiving and storage of large boxes of chemicals and drugs.

I was not supposed to wait on customers because I wasn't 21, so if no one came to the lady's rescue, I would go out from my cubby hole and capsules and assure her that someone would come to wait on her. Of course, I used my best smile to calm her!

Working downtown every day introduced me to other experiences as well. There was the time that I was making an early morning Saturday delivery on Michigan Ave. I was heading south from Madison St. towards Monroe when I could see ahead a group of men walking very quickly towards me. The man in the middle was leading the pack. He was short and stocky, middle aged, with a bright blue suit, and the pinkest face I had ever seen. I noticed that pedestrians on the sidewalk were greeting him, and he was waving or nodding towards them as they approached him. The other men in his entourage were struggling to keep up because he was walking quickly.

When I got within 20 feet of this walker, I began to recognize him and understand what was happening. I could see now his familiar jowls were moving slightly, both as he walked briskly and smiled to people on the sidewalk. I was heading in the line that was directly to him, so either he would have to move over or I had to. I concentrated on that face and kept walking, but slowly moved to the outside of the sidewalk as most of the people were doing. As we came within ten feet of each other, his eyes met mine, and mine his.

"Good Mornin' Mr. Mayor," I said, raising my voice for the occasion.

He smiled and moved his right hand slightly as he replied, "Good Marnin," in a jovial Irish voice. I stopped walking as he passed me and turned to watch him. His bodyguards kept struggling to keep up the pace as Richard J. Daley kept striding north on Michigan Ave.

Another experience of a far, different sort occurred one afternoon on Wabash Ave. near Jackson Blvd. in Rose Record Store. I was coming back from some deliveries around 4:45 PM, and decided to stop and see if the latest Bill Haley record was in the store. I had been in this music store before, since it was so close to Chemists Supply. This store advertised to have any record or album, and at the lowest price in Chicago. I was always a little leery though in coming here because one of the salesmen who helped customers with record searches, was a little funny with his eyes and gestures when I had asked him about a Johnny Mathis record sometime before. I was hoping that he would be busy or not there, so I wouldn't feel uncomfortable.

But, sure enough, as soon as I walked into Rose's, there he was, eyeing me and moving toward me. "Can I help you with something," he spoke slowly in a very familiar and inviting voice.

I felt trapped, regretting my stop at the store. But, I was here so I answered him. "I'm looking for the latest Bill Haley and His Comets single."

"Yes, we have it," he smiled. "Come back here and I'll get it for you from the shelf."

I should have known not to go back behind the counter with him. Something in the back of my mind said, "Watch Out!"

As soon as we came around to the back side of the counter, which was about three feet high, he went to a certain shelf, found the record and came close to me. "Is this the Bill Haley record you're looking for?" he said as he handed the record to me. When I took the disc from him, his hand, hidden by the counter to others in the store, came around my waist and started patting my rear end.

I said to myself, "Oh no!" My face flushed. I was shocked. How could I be so stupid. I should have known better. I handed the record back, didn't even look at this queer. I turned and walked out of the store. *No more with Rose Records. Never again.*

My initiation into the big city adult world continued on the bus I rode home each night from Chemists Supply. Mr. Novak would prepare all of the drug orders that were going parcel post by 5:30 PM. I would take them to the Old Post Office on Adams & Dearborn and have them weighed, posted, and put into the proper mail bags.

Then, around 6 PM I would catch the Racine 87 bus at State and Adams by the Fair Store and go home. Usually the bus was crowded with executives, lawyers, secretaries, and some store people riding home, so I normally had to stand. This was preferable to me because I always felt guilty if I was sitting on the bus and a woman was standing in the narrow aisle, groping with the starts and stops and turns of the bus, while holding her purse in one hand and the overhead handbar in the other. The rule that I learned from my parents was to offer my seat to a lady. I never could figure out though how old the lady had to be before I would offer my seat. Obviously, the old lady with a shopping bag and stooped shoulders should get my seat. And of course, if the lady had a baby, that was automatic.

But what if the lady was twenty-one and really sharp lookin'? If I looked up at her, as she held onto the grabbar in front of me, and I smiled and said, "Would you like a seat?" she might think that I was tryin' to flatter her, tryin' some move, even though I was fifteen years old. If she said "Yes," then she'd be seated and I'd be standin', lookin' down at her. That might be more uncomfortable for her than standing and hanging onto the grabbar.

What was a real eye opener for me each night on the bus ride home was the block between VanBuren and Congress on State St. This block, on its west side, had a number of adult arcades, a loan shop, tattoo parlor, military surplus store, a short order restaurant that looked greasy, and of course a burlesque follies theater with live dancers. There were numerous pictures of *"femmes fatales"* on the windows of the theater, in various enticing poses, with lotsa skin showing, and large, bold letters on the marquee. The flashing lights around the marquee and the edge of the theater were light bulbs that were constantly going off & on as the tide of light moved around the edge, drawing my attention.

Now I had learned in St. Anthony's that these places on South State St. were occasions of sin—occasions of sin usually lead to sin, and practically everything on this block was definitely leading to mortal sin. God forbid that

I should *ever* walk down this street and look at all these enticements, or if I was on the bus going home at 6 PM, peer thru the windows each night to get a glimpse of unclad women. I could have easily stood on the bus so that I would be facing the other way, which was the Sears Store, as the bus moved down this infamous block. Then I never would be tempted by the sexy sights.

But alas and alack, I was a teenager, and the hormones were stirring in my blood stream, so I would always get a view of the sights each evening, especially if I had a seat against the window on the "right" side of the bus. And, if I sat next to the window, it was very difficult to give up my seat to a woman because there was a person sitting next to me on the aisle that I would have to climb over.

One evening in 1953, as I was viewing the female beauty that was advertised at Minsky's Rialto Theater on VanBuren and State, I noticed on the large marquee, "Come and see Mae West with her $100,000 Treasure Chest." And plastered on the glass next to the theater entrance were huge pictures of Mae with her amply endowed chest. *Tres Magnifique!* Mae was the star who used to get on the radio and purr with her signature line, "Hey Big Boy. Why don't you come up and see me sometime."

I rode the Racine 87 bus from 1952 to 1955 while working at Chemists Supply during high school. And never was I tempted to look at the bargains in the Sears Store windows. *C'est la vie!*

REV. RAYMOND
ACKERMAN
REV. RICHARD
LASKE

1. RAYMOND   HUGH   THOMAS   THOMAS   FRANK   JOSEPH   JOANNE   EDWARD   SR. MARY
   FENDLER   LEVOY   JESSE   DONOVAN RIZZO   RICARDO MCCARTHY FRANCIS ROGER

2. LAWRENCE STEVENS JACQUES   JOHN   CHARLES   HELENE   CAROL   CAROL   DOMINIC
   STUBITSCH CASCA   SHEPPARD CARL   KURFERST KIEGNOWSK MARTIN   BRUNA   EDZZO

3. NANCY   JANMARIS DARLENE DARING   CAROL   JANE   MARY   MARIE
   KEATING   HADLEY   AKERMAN ROLANDO WARNKE   WELLER   INGVINA SCHEIBER

4. ROBERT   MARLOWS   CHARLES   GENEVIEVE ARTHUR   MARILYN   ALBINA   NANCY   ANTHONY
   KOSKE   KOHLER   SCHRAMM   COVICH   BARKOTT SHUCK   DOLGACUS   GUTTENGRATH DiVARAIA

4

PADDY LEVOY

Oh, Paddy dear! And did ye hear the news that's goin' round?

Dion Boucicault, "The Wearin' o' the Green"

The fiddler ended the reel and was reaching for his beer to take a swig, and a break! It was well into the second hour of the party, and he had been playing awhile. The crowded basement was warming now to the drink, the music, and the blarney.

"Sing us a little song now, Paddy," I heard Uncle Jim say to my father, with his brogue, as he puffed on his cigar. I could see my Dad brighten up at the request, although he didn't need to be lit up, with the beer flowin' and the gab goin'.

"Let's hear a bit o' 'The Rose of Tralee,' Paddy me b'y," McDonough spoke out in a thicker brogue, lilting the "b'y" and letting the sound float around the room as though it took wings.

Daddy looked over at my Mother who was sitting with the ladies in the main part of the basement. She had heard her brother Jim's request that Daddy sing, and knew he loved to show off his Irish tenor voice. She smiled and gave him the approval my father needed.

"The pale moon was shining above the green mountain," sang Daddy slowly. The crowd started to soften their voices as I stood watching my father begin. He opened his hands and arms to include everyone in the lyrics, especially the women in his audience.

"The sun was declining beneath the blue sea." They first met at Uncle Johnny and Aunt Verna's wedding in 1927. Mommy worked with Verna

at Presbyterian-St.Luke's Hospital, and Daddy was real close to his older brother Johnny, or "Whitey" as everyone called him.

"When I strayed with my love to the pure crystal fountain." By now the crowd in Flanagan's basement was quiet. The smoke from the cigarettes was hovering around the ceiling, moving in slow swirls to my father's melody.

"That stands in the beautiful vale of Tralee." My father had an Irish tenor voice, groomed by his mother, Annabelle—as he loved to call her when she played the piano. He had ample chances to practice his voice also with the Irish dances in Chicago in the 20's and 30's that he and his brothers attended.

"She was lovely and fair as the rose of the summer." He glanced at my mother as he sang the high notes for *"lovely"* and smiled. She was slightly embarrassed but smiled in return. I could tell that she really liked the attention.

"Yet 'twas not her beauty alone that won me." The story that we received as kids from our parents, especially my mother, was that she went out with him because he sang to her. Her favorite was "The Rose of Tralee". And he was only half-Irish, his mother's folks, the Lehners, coming from Bavaria, Germany in 1872.

"Oh no 'twas the truth in her eye ever dawning." Again my father lilted the high note in *"truth"* and it seemed as though he was singing for the world as he raised his head and voice, and not just for these Chicago Irish in Flanagan's basement.

There was a pause in my father's voice as though the end was coming, and the best part would be last. He raised his voice in a grand, triumphant sound, and delivered, *"That made me love Mar'gret, My Rose of Tralee."*

The clapping and cheers started as he hit the high notes *"of Tralee"* and the noise was loud in my ears in that small basement. My father was all smiles now.

"Attaboy Paddy," shouted an Irishman, as he patted Daddy on the shoulder and handed him another beer.

"Now if that doesn't warm the cockles of yer heart," announced another fan from the group of men standing by my father.

I looked at my mother across the room. She was clapping for him, with a small tear sliding from each eye down her cheeks, as though she remembered his song to her when they were courtin'. Then she blew him a kiss over the heads of the ladies seated near her, and they all laughed and cheered louder.

*

The organist was chanting the "Gloria" in Latin as my father stood in the pew with Mag and Pat and I. We were at our parish church, St. Anthony's, for the 9:00 AM Sunday Mass. We sat in a side aisle that had room for the four of us. My father liked to attend Mass in the center aisle section, but these were filled with school children and their parents. My mother wasn't with us because she was home with Kate, who had just been born in April of 1941.

When the priest went to the end of the altar to read the Epistle, we sat down. Daddy leaned over to the three of us and reminded us to be quiet in church, and to pray. The Mass was a mystery and we had to keep this mystery by sitting up straight, or kneeling on the kneeler when supposed to, or standing quietly, like at the Gospel that was coming. Father Schmidt was moving along in the Mass at his usual record-breaking speed, so my father decided to give each of us a coin for the collection that would follow the sermon.

He handed each of us a nickel, and right away Mag put hers in a little purse with the long straps she had draped on her shoulder. Pat looked at the coin and put it in his right jacket pocket. "Now remember," my father whispered, "when the usher puts the basket in front of you, drop the coin into it." He smiled at us, hoping that we would remember, especially me because I was only three and a half years old. Mag was six and Pat was almost five.

By now it was time for us to stand for the Gospel. I was too short to stand on the floor and see over the back of the pew in front of me. So I stepped onto the kneeler and came eye height with the top of the back. As I went to grab the top of the pew to hold onto, my right hand was still holding the nickel. It hit the hard wood and made a sound, "Clink."

My father turned to me, frowning and wagging his finger at me for making noise in church. By now I had balanced myself, standing on the soft kneeler and holding the top of the pew with my left hand. When my father looked away, I took the nickel with my thumb and right index finger and hit the edge of the nickel against the rounded top of the pew, "Clink Clink Clink," enjoying the sound as it broke the holy silence.

Daddy turned again to me, this time with a look of controlled anger—he didn't want to yell at me and disturb the mystery of the priest reading the Gospel in Latin at the altar. Instead, he motioned for me to come to him since I was the farthest away, with Mag and Pat in between. I turned my head and looked down at the nickel as I fingered it. But, I didn't move to go to him. I kept staring at the nickel.

"Hughie Boy," he whispered rather loudly, "get over here."

I still didn't move. Pat poked me and said, "Daddy wants you next to him."

By now, Father Schmidt had finished the Gospel and was walking across the sanctuary to the large pulpit that thrust itself into the pews on the left side of the main aisle. I could barely see him as I peered over the top of the pew.

Everyone sat down. I looked around. All of the people were settling into their pew seats, waiting for Father Schmidt to give his "quickie" sermon. I was still standing on the kneeler with the nickel in my right hand. There was no one in the pew in front of me, so I could see up front as long as I balanced on the kneeler.

My father had decided to leave me alone rather than force the issue of me sitting next to him, just as long as there were no more "Clinks". He did however motion for me to sit down because I was somewhat of an attraction to the people behind us. Just as I was ready to let go of the top of the pew I was holding with my left hand, Father Schmidt raised his voice on the pulpit and pointed to the people. He looked right in my direction. I got scared and sat down in a flash, still clutching the nickel.

The sermon lasted seven minutes. Father Schmidt returned to the altar and everyone stood again, including me on the kneeler. Pretty soon a man was walking down the aisle with a basket on a long pole, sticking it in front of each person. People were dropping envelopes or bills or coins into the basket. I watched him as he moved down the aisle to us, wondering what the inside of the basket looked like. When he came to our pew, my father put a green envelope into the basket, and whispered to us, "Put the nickel into the basket."

Mag had her nickel ready and dropped it in. Pat was digging in his jacket pocket, found his nickel, and dropped it into the basket with a smile. The basket came in front of me as I was still balancing on the kneeler. I looked into it and saw lots of money and envelopes.

My father was now motioning for me to put my nickel in, but after I glanced at him, I looked back into the basket at all that money. By this time, the usher gave up and pulled the basket back from in front of me and went to the pew behind us. Daddy gave me such a disgusted look as he shook his head and blew out air from his lips. "For the Love of Jesus" he choked on the angry words while raising his head to the church ceiling.

When Mass was over, I followed Pat out to the aisle, with a sense of guilt and fear of what my father would do. As soon as Daddy got next to me, he gave me a cuff on the back of the head, and called me a "mope" in a subdued voice. I started to cry, as we walked to the side exit on 28th Place. When we got outside, he finally raised his voice and hollered at me all the way home, in between cuffs on the back of my head. "You won't be going to Church again," he said, "until you learn how to act." I didn't say anything, just cried as I walked with them, clenching my hands together.

We finally made it to our house after the block and a half walk, and my father's anger had subsided. It was a cool day in October and the fresh air and walk had helped to calm him. Mag ran up the front stairs right away to our second floor flat, so she could tell Mommy how bad I was in church. Pat was taking the steps one at a time on his own, like a grown-up kid. And I was straggling behind, not wanting to face my mother's stern looks.

I put my right foot on the first step and reached for the banister with my right hand. Suddenly, I felt something drop from my hand and "Clink" on the wooden stair and roll to the edge. I looked behind me but Daddy didn't hear it because he was stamping out his Camel cigarette on the sidewalk that he had lit after church. Smiling to myself, I reached down and picked up "my" nickel.

This was the first time I remember disobeying my father, and there were more occasions to come. I would usually be playing in the back yard, either marbles on the dirt, or swinging on the home-made swing Daddy had rigged under the porch of the two-story alley building that was behind our yard and up against the alley.

My father would call down from the kitchen window for Patrick and I to come upstairs for supper. Pat would go quickly because he was hungry, but I was more interested in swinging and singing, "You Are My Sunshine" and "Mairzy Doats," and seeing how high I could swing before my backswing would bring my back up to the porch floorjoists.

I surely did test his patience on those evenings when I was slow in coming to dinner. But I would eventually suffer, not so much from the verbal punishment from him and my mother, but more because part of my food might be gone. There was only so much food cooked by my mother and put on the table, so each child had to get his share or go hungry.

Both my mother and father required that we eat supper as a family. Daddy would often say to us, "This is not a cafeteria. NO special meals. We eat together, AND what's served on the table."

The kitchen table was eight feet long and three feet wide. It was home-made by my father for our long, narrow kitchen, and had linoleum glued on top of a plywood sheet, with stainless steel edging that my father had gotten from Lawrence Kleifges' metal shop at the Santa Fe Railroad. Up against one wall was a home-made bench that was attached to the wall. When the whole family sat down, the three youngest kids, Maureen, Fred and Kate sat on the bench. My brother Pat was at one end of the table, nearest the kitchen window and the heating stove. Then along the other side were myself, Mag, and my mother, near the cooking stove. My father, of course, sat at the other end, at the head of the table.

Once the table was pulled out from the wall, set with dishes, and the food put on it, milk poured and margarine put out, it was a tight squeeze by everyone to sit down and eat. There was no getting up from the table for the washroom or any other excuse because we couldn't get around where Mommy and Daddy were sitting.

My father always said "Grace" out loud after the Sign of the Cross, and we mumbled with him. As kids we had to serve ourselves from the bowls of potatoes, gravy, meat, and vegetables. There were always arguments by us if one took too much ham, or chicken, or "mashers", as we called mashed potatoes. My mother called them "pradies," the Irish word. No one ever took too much pig's feet or turnips or salmon patty or tuna casserole though.

I loved mashed potatoes with gravy. I could eat them for lunch or supper everyday. I would form the potatoes into the shape of a white mountain. Then with my spoon, I'd make a crater in the center for gravy. Slowly, I'd pick at the sides of my potato "volcano", dipping the forkful of potatoes into the hot, "lava" gravy. Soon there would come a point where the sides of the "white" mountain would leak and the brown gravy came running down onto the green "pea" people living in the valley of my plate.

During WW II, my mother could only get hot dogs for meat with the little, red, meat tokens that were the size of a dime. Wieners were part of the War rationing effort. After the War, we moved up to chili, spaghetti with meatballs, and chop suey once a week. There was always a meal of vegetable soup with home-made bread, or potato pancakes and syrup. Once in awhile Mommy made boiled spare ribs with boiled pradies and cabbage—please hold the parsnips and boiled carrots. "Eat that cabbage," she'd admonish us. "It'll clean ye out."

The "poor man's steak," pot roast, was a real treat, especially when she broiled the meat in the new gas stove we finally bought in the late '40s. It sure was a lot easier for her to control the heat than the old, black, coal stove with no knobs at all.

Rarely did we see or taste pork chops, and never shrimp, steak, ribs, or roast beef. But we did get enough, and if we wanted more, or I was late, there was always bread and margarine. Mommy usually made sure that there was a dessert, especially cookies, or a home-made chocolate cake with white frosting, or my all-time favorite, rice pudding. But our ticket for dessert was a clean plate!

My first major fight over food with my mother came one October morning in 1944. I was now in second grade at St. Anthony's, and she insisted that we start off the day with something warm in our bellies. I was dressed for school in dark pants, a dress shirt and tie, my face washed, and hair combed. I came into the kitchen at 7:30 AM, and there on the table by my place was a big bowl of oatmeal, with a glass of milk.

"C'mon now, eat yer stirabout, and don't be late for Church," Mommy ordered. We had to go to the 8:00 Mass every day before school started at 8:35 AM. Patrick and Mag were already eating their oatmeal and drinking their milk. Kate was still sleeping in the middle bedroom, and Fred, the baby, was in Mommy's bedroom off the kitchen. My father was "sitting on the throne" in the bathroom, having his first Camel cigarette of the day before going to work.

"Mom, I can't eat this oatmeal"—the Irish called it "stirabout" because that's how they made it in the pot, stirring the oatmeal about. I protested after I had tried a little from the top of the spoon and made an ugly face to show her how awful it tasted.

"'pon my word, ye'll sit here and eat it," she answered. "It's yer breakfast and that's all yer getting' 'til ye come home fer lunch."

"Can I put some sugar on it? I said, hoping that would sweeten the sickly meal taste that made me gag. Uggh!

"Go ahead," she said, as my father came out of the bathroom with a cloud of smoke following him. He was now ready to go to work. He took his black workjacket and cap out of the kitchen pantry/closet, right next to the bathroom. Then he grabbed his lunchpail, kissed my mother on the cheek, tapped Mag on the head, waved to Patrick at the end of the table, and poked me in the back of the head.

"You need your oatmeal, Hughie Boy."

I got a clean spoon from the silverware drawer in the cabinet under the sink and scooped a heaping spoonful of sugar from the jar on the table and sprinkled it onto every part of the oatmeal surface in the bowl. Again, I tried the oatmeal with the spoon. Uggh! Och! I began to gag again. "Mom, I can't eat this!"

By now Patrick and Mag were finished, and brought their bowls and glasses to the sink. Then they went into the dining room to get their books on the table from last night's homework. I could hear them putting on their jackets, and my mother reminding them to walk together to Church. I was all alone in the kitchen now with my bowl of "sweet" oatmeal sitting in front of me, getting cold and gooey and greyer and uglier than when it was served. I sat and stared at the oatmeal, not understanding at all how this little bowl of food could stop my life. *What was I going to do? I couldn't go to school until I ate it. Mommy wouldn't give in to me. But I hated the look of it, the taste of it, and now even the sound of it! Oatmeal!*

Mommy returned to the kitchen and started to clean the breakfast dishes in the sink. She didn't say anything to me, probably because she didn't know what to do. No one had ever turned down her stirabout before.

In desperation, after what seemed like an hour of sitting silently, I said to her, "Can I pour some milk into the oatmeal?"

She turned around from the kitchen sink and said, "If that'll make ye eat it, go ahead. God knows ye need something to git ye going."

After half a glass of milk was poured onto the cold oatmeal, I dipped my spoon in again for a small serving. It didn't taste awful now that the sugar had soaked into the oatmeal, and the milk with it as it hit my mouth. I got down three spoonfuls, but now the milk was thinning out, so I decided to put a spoonful of oatmeal in my mouth and very quickly drown it with a swig of milk. It worked! Pretty soon I could see the bottom of the bowl.

By the time I finished the oatmeal, found my homework, and put on my hat and jacket, it was 8:40. "Ye have to go right to school now. The kids will be gone from Church," my mother cautioned me. "I'll watch from the front porch to see that yer all right."

I gave her a kiss, and took off as fast as I could out the front door, down the long front steps, and along the sidewalk. She could see me all the way to school because our second floor porch had a perfect view of the convent and school entrance on the next block.

I opened the big door to school and tip toed in slowly, letting the door close behind me. No one was in the first floor hall, but I could hear the 1st Grade teacher, Sister Theodorine, doing the alphabet with her class because her door was open. The typewriters were clicking in the High School Commercial rooms to my right.

Quietly, I went up the front stairs to the second floor hall. Looking ahead I could see the door to the 2nd Grade was closed. Good! The doors to the Library on the right and the 4th Grade on the left were also closed. But, the 3rd Grade door was open and Sister Ponciana was teaching reading.

As I moved across the hall to the 2nd Grade cloakroom, I could see into the 3rd Grade classroom. Sure enough, there was my brother Patrick, staring at me and smiling from his desk. He was whispering something that looked like, "O meal."

Ever so softly, I turned the knob on the cloakroom door and slipped inside. I didn't dare turn on the light to the cloakroom for fear that Sister Henry would hear it and come in. My coat hook was half way down the line. I took my jacket and hat off without a sound.

The inner cloakroom door was open. I could hear Ray Fendler answering a question from Sister. I could tell by the direction of her voice that she was at her desk on the little platform in the front of the room. Her back was to me slightly, so I thought that I could sneak past the upright piano and into my desk which was first in the row by the piano and windows.

I edged into the doorway and took a step into the classroom. But then, all eyes of the students moved from attention to Sister Henry to looking at me sneaking into the room. I took another step, but now she had picked up the new focus of the children and turned to her right to see what they were looking at.

"Well, who do we have here," she announced to the class in a mock, surprised voice.

For just an instant, everyone and everything was silent. Then, as I realized I was caught, I blurted out, "I had to eat my oatmeal," with a flood of tears. Immediately, there was one sound of thirty five laughters echoing throughout the room.

*

Discipline came in different doses from my mother and my father. Mommy's favorite expression to show disapproval was "'pon my word, ye'll get it if ye keep it up." And "get it" meant the stick across the arms or shoulders or back. She wasn't mean, but with six kids, she made it clear that she would lay down the law with the stick when we were fooling around or disturbing her.

My father would cuff the back of our heads when we were out of line, or too rough with each other, or missed a chore. He was always reluctant to get physical with the boys because he was so strong. He could have easily paddled our rear ends with his hand and sent more pain to our brains than Mommy's stick ever would. But he was afraid to use his strength on Patrick and me. He relied more on his voice, "Cut it out now," or "If I come into that bedroom, you'll be crying," as my brother and I would be roughhousing in the front bedroom at night instead of going to sleep.

Mommy would accuse Daddy of being "soft" with the boys, but he would counter that he was a boy once, and he used to fool around with his brothers, but all his father had to do was come in the bedroom and say, "That's enough!" My father told me once that his father had such a commanding voice that Daddy and his brothers clearly knew it was time to stop.

"Boys will be boys," Daddy would tell Mommy.

Sometimes he would sneak up to our bedroom and poke his head into the doorway. "It's Daddy," we'd both say, and scramble to get under the covers and act like we were sleeping. We'd slowly open one eye and look over to the doorway, and there he'd be with a smile on his face.

"Your mother and I are going to bed. That's enough playing for one night," he would say in a soothing, paternal voice. He'd walk away to the kitchen, and we'd both see the reflection of the kitchen light in the living room go dark. We'd barely hear him getting into bed, and then a slight murmur of voices. Silence followed. Patrick and I would look at each other in the dark, knowing that it was time to stop the nonsense. We both sensed that Daddy really would be upset if we continued and misplaced his trust in us. In five minutes we were quietly asleep.

The name-calling from our parents was clear and consistent. The Gaelic word for fool is "*amadon.*" Pat and I were called that quite a few times by my mother. As we got older and too husky for her stick to be painful, she would add the phrase "ye big amadon," as she hit us. This was especially used if we were picking on our sisters, Mag or Kate. The word amadon has such a disparaging sound that I always felt I had no sense when she would let me have it after acting foolishly (which was very often).

My father's favorite name for someone who was goofing off or didn't show good sense was "mope." "What a mope," he would complain to me if I didn't get up to dinner when he called, or was pig-headed, or forgot one of my chores. And then if Pat or I would really mess up, like not getting the coal for the stoves upstairs after school, we would be tagged with a worse moniker, "Mickey the mope."

Chores were a constant source for trouble or problems in the family. Every child who was tall enough to see over the kitchen sink had to wash or dry dishes on a weekly schedule. For a long time that was Mag, Pat, and I. If one of us wasn't washing, we had to either clear the table, sweep the floor, and take out the garbage, or wipe the dishes that were being washed and put them into the kitchen cabinet. The argument would always occur when the three of us "lost" track of who had to do what that week.

"It's your turn, Mag. I washed last week," said Pat.

"No, it's Hughie's turn because he follows you every week," she would answer.

"But I had to bring up the coal from the shed last week," I'd reply.

"No you didn't," Pat would argue with me. "I brought up the coal last week when it was so cold and I had to go twice. You're lying."

"I'm not fibbin'," I countered. "I remember goin' down to that dark coalshed last Thursday, and the lightbulb was out and I had to carry the flashlight and the coalbucket."

There were two coal stoves in our kitchen, a large, black cooking stove with four covers for depositing the coal to burn, and also to cook on. The center section below the coal area was the oven. The other stove was narrow with just two covers, but a deeper basin for coal to burn. This stove heated the kitchen and Mommy's bedroom, and usually had a kettle on it to keep water hot for "tay", as Mommy would say in her Irish brogue.

"God help us, would you stop the arguin'," my mother would finally say. "Read the list on the wall over there to see who's next for washin'. Yer drivin' me batty and I can't read the paper for the food sales at the A & P." All the fun of arguing was gone now once we had to follow the names and dates on the printed sheet by the icebox.

Going for coal during the afternoon was a scary chore for me because it was stored in a shed below the alley house at the back of the yard. This alley house was three floors high with four, old spooky sheds at the yard level, two on each side of a dark, narrow passageway or tunnel which ran down the middle of the building from the yard to the six steps that gave access to the alley. The tunnel was short, only about five feet high, and had no lightbulb anywhere in its twenty feet of length.

During the day, some light came into it from the yard, and I could always see a crack of light coming from the alley door at the other end. But what also made it frightening is that Andrew Kocet, the renter in the first floor flat, would sometimes be in his shed getting a tool, or working. He was a quiet, old man with white hair and a mustache who spent his days fishing in Lake Michigan, and his nights reading by the kerosene lamp that he used for light in his kitchen. Although he was gentle, he spoke with an accent in a gravelly voice. It made me nervous to meet him in the dark tunnel as I was going for coal, and he'd grunt a sound to me.

Or if I met Sam Guistolese in the tunnel, I'd really get scared. He lived on the second floor flat with his wife Sophie. He was tall, with bronze skin. He looked and talked like an Indian on the warpath. His cheekbones were very high and his eyes were cold. I never saw him smile, and he rarely said "Hello" to us kids when we were playing in the yard. Since he was close to six feet, he had to stoop to get thru the tunnel, and he would take up the whole path because of his size. If I saw him in there when I was going for coal, I'd wait until he got out, or went to his shed.

Pat and I always made sure the tunnel was clear before we went in to get coal. And, we made darn sure that we got the coal in the afternoon when there was light. Our coalshed got light from a trap door that opened to the alley and was the same as a coal chute door. There was a single lightbulb in the center of the shed. We had a shovel for filling the buckets with coal chunks that were the size of golfballs or bigger.

We dreaded having to get coal at night. But if the temperature outside went down, or Mommy was baking, there was a need for more coal. Even with the flashlight, I was scared when I had to go. I needed to put on my warm coat and stocking cap and gloves—and boots if there was snow.

It was cold and mysterious as I would descend the two flights of stairs to the backyard. When I came to the alley house, I would shine the light around the tunnel before I entered from the yard. No rats, no cats, no man waiting to grab me. Then I would walk quickly to our coalshed at the far right side of the tunnel, and open the wooden shed door. Creaks from the old, iron hinges would bother me, but I'd bring the flashlight up again to check the shed. Nobody's in there, only cobwebs hanging in the corners. The shed looked clear.

One night it was my turn to get more coal. I walked into the shed slowly, scanning the room for the slightest movement with the flashlight, for anything! Finally, I pulled the chain on the lightbulb. Nothing happened, except the clicking from the switch. No light. I became more nervous because now I'd have to fill the two buckets with only the flashlight shining.

Quickly I grabbed the shovel and filled the first bucket as best I could because I could only guess where it was on the floor. I could barely see it with the flashlight pointing toward the coal pile. As I was filling the second bucket and feeling less tense, I heard a loud "Bang" followed by an even louder "Clang" just outside the shed in the alley above me.

I panicked, threw down the shovel, grabbed the two buckets and the flashlight, and ran out of that shed as fast as I could. On the way down the tunnel to the backyard, I banged into the wooden walls of Andrew's shed because the flashlight was down in my right hand which was also carrying the half-filled coal bucket.

I could still hear the "Clang" from the alley. I made it to the yard and down the walk, up the stairs to the first floor porch. The wind had picked up since I had come to get coal. I could feel it coming right across the backyards on the block.

Then up the steep stairs I labored to the second floor porch. *Safe! I'm safe now, by my back door.* I was panting now from both fear and lugging the two buckets and flashlight down the tunnel, across the yard, and up the stairs.

I paused and looked toward the alley and listened, but could only hear the slight banging and clanging of the garbage can lids as the wind blew them around the alley.

*

We were in the middle of World War II, but Pat and I only knew about the Germans and Japs in planes and boats. My father wasn't drafted in 1941 or '42 because he worked for the Wabash Railroad, and had four children. Railroad employees were exempt from the draft because they were a vital part of the war effort, moving freight around the country. He'd always say when asked about Army service, "I was too young for World War I and too old for World War II."

My Uncle Zeke, however, was the right age for service. Born in 1920, he was in the Army on leave in Chicago when he met my Aunt Catherine, my mother's sister. They had a whirlwind romance and were married on December 27th, 1942. Zeke's real name was Isaac Washington Cooper, and he was from Oklahoma. Within two weeks of their honeymoon, Zeke was sent to England for training for the invasion of France, and Aunt Catherine became the war bride waiting at home in Chicago.

Earlier that year of '42, on a hot, dry August afternoon, my father came home from work with the news that there would be a "blackout" practice at 9:00 that night in Chicago. At our supper table he told us that this was for civil defense of our city, in case the enemy tried to bomb Chicago. We all stared at him when he said the City would be dark.

Pat looked at me and said, "We can wear our gas masks and helmets." I smiled and started imagining what it would be like with all the street lights out, and no lights in the house. I also tried to remember where I put the toy pop gun I got for my 4th birthday. Mag wanted to know if we had to go to bed early, because she liked to play outside with her friends on the block until it got dark. Daddy told her that she would have some time to play as long as the supper dishes were done first.

We did finish the dishes that night in record time, without a protest as to which kid had to do the washing or drying or cleaning the table. The radio was on afterwards and we heard about three reminders of the blackout, in between our favorite programs.

As soon as the dishes were done, Pat and I started looking for the gasmask and helmets and guns for the battle. Mag was playing hopscotch in front of the house. Mommy was taking care of the babies, Kate and Fred, getting them ready for bed. And Daddy was enjoying a Camel cigarette and a cup of coffee at the kitchen table while he worked the crossword puzzle in the Herald-American.

After an hour or so he'd finish it, except for some foreign word he didn't know. Then he'd balance the pencil down on the newspaper with the point, place the eraser against his forehead, and snooze for half an hour with the weight of his head pressing down on the eraser which was pushing the point into the paper on the table. What a way to nap!

AT 8:45, Mommy called Mag in from the front. Pat and I had put our gear by the front windows. We woke up Daddy at the kitchen table and told him the Germans were coming. He paused for a second, and then started to laugh. "Yawohl," he snorted to us. He told Pat to check the basement to see if any lights had been left on. My job was to go downstairs to Grandma Bosak and remind her of the blackout.

When we returned, it was 8:55, so Pat and I went to the two living room windows and took our "battle stations." As Pat was kneeling down in front of his window near the front door, he bragged, "I know what the Germans look like." The shade had already been pulled down with just an inch of glass showing over the sill. "They wear these square helmets," he said, tapping his Army helmet. "And there's double Zs on their uniforms. I saw a German in the paper the other day. His name was Adol."

To show him how much I knew, I blurted out, "They speak German too." I knelt down by my window, next to the old console radio between the two windows. Slowly I peered thru the opening between the shade and the sill. But I couldn't see much because the living room lamp behind me was still on. It was now time to put on my helmet. I tried the gasmask with the helmet already on and both fit, but I decided to swing the mask around to the side of my face until the "fighting started." I checked my gun and the cork bullet with the string attached to see that the bullet was pressed into the barrel, ready for firing. "Good. I'll get a few Germans from where I'm kneeling," I thought to myself.

All of a sudden, a loud siren went off outside, and continued to wail. The lamp in the living room was turned off and the house was dark. Mag screamed. I glanced outside again and the street light in front of Johnny Stephan's house across the street went out. Now everything was dark, except for a faint bit of light from the moon. The siren kept wailing. I felt a chill down the middle of my back, and my throat started to get tight. "This is it!"

Mag started to cry. Mommy told her to be quiet. "It's only a practice," she said. They both were behind me on the sofa with Kate. Fred had already been put to bed. I could barely see my father in the front hall, peering out the small windows in the front door to the street below. I couldn't see Pat at the next window because the radio was in the way.

The siren finally stopped, but the shrill sound kept going thru my ears.

Now everyone and everything was quiet except for our breathing.

"Did you see that German," Pat whispered to me.

"Where," I blurted out more than a whisper.

"Over there by Schmitt's victory garden, right by the flagpole. He's carrying a gun."

I couldn't see any German soldier, just a slight shadow of the lightpole moving because of the moon and the wind. I slowly raised the shade a little more to get a better look.

Daddy grunted, "Leave that shade where it was."

Looking down at the sidewalk in front of our house, I saw something move and make a sound. "It's a Jap," I whispered to Pat.

"Where?"

"Right below on the sidewalk. I can see it move. It's on our porch steps." I checked my gun again, straightened my helmet, and cleared my throat.

"Where? I can't see him," he protested.

I started to raise the window to get an aim at the figure that was moving on our porch steps. The old window wouldn't go up easily even though my father kept the windows in good condition, always making sure they would open or close. I lifted with one hand and pushed with the other and managed to get it up an inch. Daddy didn't hear me raise the window, but I could hear him breathe from the hall.

I pushed the barrel of my pop gun through the opening of the window and looked through the glass at the porch steps. Nothing was moving. I really concentrated to see because the moon had gone behind a cloud. "Wait. There he is on the third step," I said excitedly to Pat.

Just as I took aim and put my finger on the trigger, the street lights came back on. I was startled and momentarily looked at the light. The sirens started wailing again. Out of the corner of my eye I saw something jump down the steps and run across our sidewalk. Then it ran between Daddy's car and Sam's old jalopy. I stared silently as the neighbor's cat bounded across the street to "her front porch."

After the sirens stopped, Daddy came into the living room from "his station" at the front door, and turned on the lamp. Kate was now sleeping in Mommy's arms. Mag asked if she could go to bed. Pat and I were still at "our stations", taking off our helmets and the gas mask. Daddy looked at the two of us kneeling by the windows and said in a very manly voice, "Good job, men." Then he patted us on our backs. "Time for your bunks."

Almost two years later, on July 13ᵗʰ, 1944, Aunt Catherine called my mother in tears and told her that her husband, Uncle Zeke, had been killed in the invasion of France at St.Lo, Normandy. He would be buried in an American cemetery near there. The War Department had come to her apartment on the Northside with the news earlier that day, and said that Isaac had served his country and gave the ultimate sacrifice, his life.

I had no sense of Uncle Zeke's death and Aunt Catherine's grief. I learned later that the gold star in the front window of the house across the street meant that a member of that family had been killed in action like Uncle Zeke.

After the war ended, I would see a lot of men returning from service. Some had been wounded and some seemed nervous, as though something bad had happened overseas. As kids, we used to hear the expression, "shellshock" whenever the adults would talk about a soldier who was nervous or a little crazy. And then there was the man who walked around our neighborhood with a slight limp and a massive scar and indentation on his forehead. We would stare at him as he came down the sidewalk, talking to himself. I never knew whether to be scared of him, or feel sorry. What kind of blast had hit him in the head?

But, my cousin Jimmy Flanagan was all smiles now that he was back from the Navy. We went to Aunt Annie & Uncle Jim's house in 1946 to see their returning son and congratulate him for his service to our country. When I walked up the hall steps from the side entrance to the house, Jimmy was standing in the hall by the living room entrance. I couldn't believe how tall he was, and how handsome.

He looked at both Pat and I and hugged us. "I brought something back from Okinawa for the two of you. Just wait here," he said. Then he bounded up the stairs to the bedrooms, taking them two at a time. After a minute, he came down, and in his hand was a huge bow that was at least five feet tall.

"Wow," we gushed as he gave it to us and told us he had gotten it on the island after the big battle had ended. Apparently the Japanese used it with arrows to fight the Americans because they were out of ammunition. The string on the bow was so tightly strung that even Pat and I together could not pull it back more than an inch. But, it was ours to keep even though it stood eight inches taller than us.

We thanked Jimmy by shaking his hand like men do. Throughout the afternoon as the families were sitting and talking and later at dinner, I would look at Jimmy with admiration, *and say silently to myself that someday I would be tall and good-looking and I'd be a hero in the war, just like him.*

*

By 1947, Aunt Catherine was living with Aunt Mary in an apartment on the Northside of Chicago. She had remarried after losing Uncle Zeke in the war. Her new husband was Jack Blotz, an ex-serviceman from "WW II." Aunt Mary was still single and working as a waitress in the expensive restaurants and night clubs downtown. She was very attractive with Maureen O'Hara flaming red-hair and a great figure. These paid off at the fancy spots in the Loop. There were stories she would tell us about the $5 and $10 tips she would get at the Latin Quarter from service men and business people. How these same tippers would order and think nothing of eating an 18 ounce steak and washing it down with expensive wine. Aunt Mary would remark to my parents that there was a lotta money in Chicago after the war. She'd follow that with a bit of her investment strategy, "I'm putting all of my tips into the stock market."

Once a year, on New Years Day, Aunt Mary would take all of the LeVoy Family to Chinatown for a big meal. We would always go to Guey Sams at 22nd & Wentworth. In our group of 12 were Aunt Mary, Aunt Catherine, Uncle Jack, and Simo Galve, a Filipino chef who shared a large apartment with them. Then came Mommy & Daddy and the six kids, Maureen, the youngest up to Mag the oldest, with Fred, Kate, myself, and Pat in between.

This was a big event for the kids because we rarely had authentic Chinese food, just Mommy's chop suey, with starchy rice and thin gravy. Definitely not Cantonese! We had no idea what eggrolls or fried rice or egg foo yung tasted like, and especially how to hold the chopsticks. And the only tea we ever drank was Lipton's.

For New Years Day 1949, instead of Chinese food, Aunt Mary decided to invite us to the new apartment that the four of them were sharing on Dakin St. She wanted to serve a real feast for us with h'ordoeuvres, standing rib, and baked ham, as well as drinks and wine, with herring for Good Luck in the New Year. She had Simo help with the cooking and Uncle Jack to serve the drinks. Uncle Jack liked that because he actually worked as a bartender in a Northside tavern, and proved to be his own best customer.

The eight LeVoys arrived around 2 PM after a morning of Mass at St.Anthony's followed by Daddy's homemade breakfast. He insisted on cooking the bacon and eggs himself and serving my mother. She was the "Queen for a Day". After preparing three meals a day for 364 days in the year, Mommy really enjoyed being waited upon on her day.

The night before, New Years Eve, Daddy did his usual "blast" at midnight with the 12 gauge shotgun. It was the custom in our neighborhood of Bridgeport for the man of the house to shoot his gun in the air when the clock struck midnight, ushering in the New Year.

Daddy would load both barrels of his gun with shells, and then go out to our little front porch about one minute to midnight. We'd be inside listening to the countdown on the radio from State & Randolph Streets. We'd pick up the unison count "10,9,8,7,6,5,4,3,2,1."

"Boom Boom", we'd hear from the porch—he always got off the first shot of the New Year. Then there would be a "Pow Pow Pow" from a handgun down the street, followed by some more "Booms" and "Pows" farther away. All the kids would hug each other, make lotsa noise, and Mommy and Daddy would kiss. "Happy New Year Everyone"

As soon as we got settled into Aunt Mary's living room, she and "Suz"—our affectionate name for Aunt Catherine because she was the nanny that we never obeyed when Mommy would go to the hospital with her deliveries—began putting the hors d'oeuvres onto the coffee table. "Wow", we all said as we looked at stuffed celery, three kinds of cheeses, fancy crackers, liver pate with pumpernickel bread, Italian and Greek olives, herring in cream sauce and in wine & vinegar, potato salad, and even assorted nuts. I looked at all of these delicacies that we never saw at home. Could I really get one of each on my little hors d'oeuvres plate, as I was eyeing the cashews.

Aunt Mary, in a very commanding voice like a drill sergeant, would tell us to have a lot because dinner would not be served until 6 PM. "So eat up. I don't want anything left on the coffee table," she'd admonish us. "If ye don't eat it, we'll throw it out," we'd hear as she walked down the long hall to the kitchen at the rear of the apartment.

When I finished gorging myself, especially on the fancy crackers and French cheese, I went back to the kitchen and asked Aunt Mary where her radio was, because I didn't see one in the living room. She was really busy now getting the rib roast seasoned for the oven, so she didn't answer me.

Simo told me there was a small radio on the buffet in the dining room in the far corner. I checked and sure enough it was there. I turned it on and dialed 720 WGN. The announcer was talking about last night's New Years Eve celebration. He reminded the WGN listeners that the 1949 Rose Bowl game would be broadcast today at 4:30 PM from Pasadena, California. It would be the Wildcats from Northwestern University versus the Golden Bears from the University of California.

I was excited because this would be the first Rose Bowl I had ever heard, and the game involved Northwestern from Evanston, the northern Chicago suburb. I looked at the clock in the kitchen. It was 3:15. Aunt Mary said that the dinner would not be until 6, so I could listen to at least the first half of the game.

When I went back to the living room, everyone was feeling fine. Uncle Jack was keeping my father's glass full of Schenleys whiskey—we found out much later in the 50's that Aunt Mary always bought Schenleys because it was made by National Distillers, one of her stocks. Mommy was enjoying her day off, and kept raving about the hors d'oeuvres, especially the celery stuffed with blue cheese.

I didn't want to sit in the apartment any more, so I asked my Dad if I could go outside for a little while until the Rose Bowl started. The weather that day was cold, in the middle 20's, but there wasn't snow. He said it was OK as long as Pat went too. I looked at my brother and he answered, "Yeah, as soon as I finish the nuts and soda."

The apartment was on Dakin St. near Broadway. As soon as we got outside, we heard this loud, rattling sound from down the street. We both looked around and saw an El train on tracks crossing Dakin about thirty feet above the street. We decided to go down the block to take a closer look and see if another train would come the opposite way. The racket from the iron wheels on the rails, and the rattling and swaying of the El cars was so inviting.

Nothing came for a few minutes, and we were getting cold standing around, so we continued to the corner. I looked up at the street signs to see where we were. One sign said Dakin St. and the other said Sheffield Ave. That sounded familiar but I couldn't connect with anything.

We noticed there weren't too many people walking on New Year's afternoon. Everyone was inside probably, having a feast. It looked like Sheffield ended near the corner of Dakin, so we looked in the other direction. At the same time, we both noticed a huge neon sign with red letters about three blocks away, south on Sheffield. The first letter was a big C. There were others that followed but we couldn't see them. We could also see a large wall under the letters, going along the street.

"Look at that sign and wall," I told Pat.

He stared at it with me, but only said, "Yeah, I wonder what it is."

"Let's go down the block to the next corner. We can see it better from there," I answered, with a little excitement in my voice.

As we walked together, I kept my eyes fixed on the sign and the wall. Now I could see what looked like huge ramps and seats above the wall, and farther down the street. The street sign at the corner said Sheridan Road. We stared at the neon sign and now could see other letters, C-h-i-c.

There wasn't anyone walking on our side of the street who we could ask about the sign and building. We were both anxious to find out what the sign said and what the huge structure is.

"Let's go one more block," I said. "I'm sure we can read the sign from there."

As we crossed Sheridan we heard a loud clatter. We looked left to see an El train overhead, going in the other direction from the first one. Standing in the middle of the street, hypnotized by the noise, we never heard the "Beep,

Beep" from a cab trying to get us out of the middle of the street so he could turn. "Crazy kids," the driver yelled after he rolled down his window.

The next block seemed short to walk because before we knew it, we were at the corner. The street sign read Grace Ave. Now we could see the word Chicago in large, red letters up on a wall that curved a little. The other wall that ran along Sheffield seemed lower, but beyond this wall were huge ramps and seats. I got the feeling again that I was looking at something I knew. We both stared at the sign and the building.

"Wow. What is it, Pat?" I said.

He didn't answer and instead looked back down Sheffield to where we had come from. He seemed to be hesitant to go any farther. But we still didn't find out what the sign said.

"Why not keep going. It's only another block." I finally said to him. Hesitantly, we crossed Grace and continued toward the next street, and hopefully the answer. As we walked closer and closer, the feeling became stronger and stronger that I knew this place. Seats, ramps, wall, sign that says Chicago!

All of a sudden Pat yelled out, "Chicago Cubs, I see it now. Look."

And there on the curved wall were mounted the words in red neon, Chicago Cubs. I stared at the letters and the curved center field wall, and then at the right field wall on Sheffield, and the big ramps and upper deck with the seats on the first base side, and finally remembered Wrigley Field.

The street sign read Waveland Ave. just as I heard it on the radio for the 1945 World Series. I began hearing the imaginary crowd roaring as Stan Hack drove in the winning run in the game I had listened to on our old radio. Wow! Wrigley Field! Hank Greenberg. Hank Borowy. They were all here in front of me!

We walked all the way to Addison St. to get a better view of the Field. No one was out in front today because it was January, *but again I started "seeing" the crowds outside the gates, waiting to get in for the World Series. I could hear a "buzz" from the crowd, an excitement for something big that was coming. It was Game 7, Tigers vs. Cubs.*

When we made it back to Aunt Mary's apartment, Pat let everyone know that we had been to Wrigley Field. I asked Daddy if he had ever been inside for a game, and he said, "Yes, in the late 20's when the Cubs had Hack Wilson, the bantam slugger."

We told Aunt Mary about our discovery. She looked frazzled from all the cooking and food preparation. "Oh yes, we hear the crowds from Cubs Park all the time," she said in a hurried voice. I wondered if she had ever been inside for a Cubs game.

It was now time for the Rose Bowl. I grabbed a new plate of "goodies" and positioned myself in the dining room on a chair in front of the radio. I didn't want to turn up the volume real high, so I leaned over more on the buffet to hear. I had read in the paper that California was favored to beat Northwestern because they were undefeated. Northwestern's big star was their halfback, Frank Aschenbrenner. He was shifty and quick, going for long gains once he passed the line of scrimmage. California's star runner was Jackie Jensen, the All American tailback.

The game started slowly with both teams showing strong defense and exchanging punts. All of a sudden the radio announcer raised his voice as Aschenbrenner went around right end and broke into the clear. I leaned even closer to the radio. "50, 40, 30, 20, 10, He's going all the way," the radio announcer was screaming. "It's a touchdown."

I ran into the living room to tell my father that Northwestern scored. He and my mother were laughing with Suz over something that happened when she was the nanny for Maureen's birth. And Uncle Jack was still pouring the Schenleys.

On the next series of downs for California after the kickoff, Jackie Jensen came right back with an awesome run of his own for 43 yards and a touchdown. The extra point was made and the Rose Bowl game was tied 7-7. But now, Aunt Mary was starting to set the dining room table for dinner. I moved around twice to get out of her way, but she kept making faces as I continued to listen to the game. Northwestern was moving the ball again toward the Cal goal line.

Then Mommy and Mag came in to help with the table. I reluctantly turned off the radio so they could continue. I knew I'd get the score and game summary in the *Herald* tomorrow.

By 8:30 PM, the scrumptious dinner was finished; everyone was feeling stuffed. Aunt Mary had finally relaxed from her hectic day of cooking and entertaining. She kept pushing the drinks, asking my father and mother if they wanted a little Drambuie or Crème de Menthe to settle their stomachs. I looked at my father and he was eager; he already had enough whiskey before dinner to last a month.

My mother frowned as she said a firm "NO" to her sister. Mommy looked a little concerned at my father, who started to sing an Irish song, without a request. She didn't want any "Pale moon was shining," now because the kids were tired; she was full; and he had to drive them all home to the Southside; somehow!

As soon as we got into the car, the old '43 Plymouth sedan, Daddy started playing, tapping on the steering wheel and humming a song. My mother was in the front seat with Maureen, and the other five of us were in the back. As we entered the Outer Drive at Belmont Ave., he was till tapping on the steering wheel, and humming louder.

Then, accidentally, he hit the horn; we all cheered in the back seat! Mommy was getting nervous because Daddy was moving the steering wheel slightly right and left in a playful weave, as we drove down the three-lane Drive. She finally pleaded with him, "Patrick, cut it out or ye'll get us in an accident."

But he was feeling good from the drink and the food.

I shouted from the back, "Dad, hit the horn again."

Kate chimed in, "Play the Lone Ranger."

He laughed and started the familiar tune, amid the cheers from his audience in the back seat. His horn sounded just like the radio program we would listen to after dinner at home. I looked out the side window to see if the Lone Ranger and Tonto were riding alongside of us on their horses. HI HO SILVER!

We finally made it to 28th Place in one piece; ending that fun-filled ride along Chicago's lakefront. All of the kids were laughing as we got out of the car and headed for the front steps. Maureen had slept through it all on my mother's lap. Mommy was a nervous wreck; worrying about an accident, or being stopped by the police.

Daddy told her to go ahead with the kids because he wanted to stay outside for a while. As we joyously climbed the stairs to the second floor flat, my father had both his hands on the front yard railing, leaning over it moaning. Then we heard his loud, guttural sounds as he began to throw up.

My mother looked around from the top of the stairs, and sternly said to us all, "And that is what too much drink will get ye,"

*

In the spring of 1949, my brother Pat came down with St. Vitus Dance. He was finishing 7th Grade at St. Anthony's and I was finishing 6th. The illness caused him to have involuntary movements in his arms and legs. The doctor said that he needed complete bed rest over the summer, and large doses of vitamins.

We were told by Mommy that she had the same illness in Ireland; thus Pat inherited it. She had been cured partly by rest on the Flanagan Farm, and by the care of her brothers in 1916, but also by many prayers and petitions to God at the shrine at Knock Monastery, County Mayo.

I shared the front bedroom with Pat. It was difficult at night to sleep with all the movement he kept doing as he jostled around in the bed. In the morning he'd be awake before me, and when I got up, I'd see him being fed at the kitchen table by Mag. I felt sorry for him because his mouth drooled; his arms had very little control. I felt guilty that I was healthy and could go out to play ball in the street; deliver papers; and eat at the table. But he was so helpless.

The complete rest worked: by the end of the summer the St. Vitus Dance had left Pat. He grew taller and heavier by the beginning of school in September. Before his illness, he was always three or four inches taller than me, with the top of my head coming to his eyes. And he was always a little heavier and stronger. (One summer day at Cedar Lake, he decided to drown me. We were in three feet of water when he grabbed my head and pushed me underwater. He held me down for what seemed like forever. I really thought-panicked-I was going to drown because I was not strong enough to break away from his grip on my head and come up for air.)

But now, he had a full head on me when we stood next to each other. His shoulders and arms were much bigger than mine. He was truly "my big brother." I was happy though because, with his St. Vitus Dance gone, I could sleep at night.

Pat and I had done much together from early on. Back yard playing; sports on the street; serving Mass; delivering papers; even smoking. We started puffin' around 1950 because all the guys were old enough to try it. We somehow had a way to get cigarettes and we'd "light up" in the little cave that was dug out under the sidewalk at 29th & Canal. This was our clubhouse. It was always scary to be in the clubhouse when the streetcars came down Canal St. The pressure from the heavy street cars on the tracks would cause the concrete sidewalk above us to vibrate. I always had the fear that the sidewalk was going to cave in on us as we puffed away. We'd do anything for a smoke!

One of Daddy's friends, Lawrence Kleifges, told him one day that he saw Pat smoking as he came out of the alley on Canal. So, at dinner that night, my father told us, "I hear that you were smoking in the alley. Now tell me where you're hiding the cigarettes."

Pat and I looked at each other, shook our heads and denied that we were smoking. And we certainly didn't have any cigarettes. Daddy smiled, and said no more.

After the meal, Daddy headed straight for the kitchen pantry/closet to search our Navy coats for the contraband. He came back in a few minutes without any cigarettes or matches. We could tell that he was flustered because he was sure he would find them in our coats. Again Pat and I exchanged glances. Phew! Daddy had *not* looked in our little brother Fred's coat because he was only seven at the time. The pack of Lucky Strikes and matches were hidden in Fred's right hand pocket!

Our Father was reluctant to come down hard on Pat and I for smoking. He had started when he was twelve and had been smoking Camels for thirty years. It was common in our neighborhood for boys to start smoking sometime early. Yet, it was still hard for him to accept that Pat and I were growing up;

becoming influenced by the gang and the neighborhood, the same Bridgeport neighborhood he got his start with tobacco.

My mother, however, told us we were too young to be smoking. "Ye'er burnin' up hard-earned money with those fags," she'd criticize us. Then she'd turn to my father, "Jest think of how much money ye'd save if ye didn't smoke that pack of Camels each day. We'd all be rich." In the end, five of the six children in our family became smokers.

My father really got angry when he was driving home one June afternoon and saw me shootin' dice around the corner from our house. There was a big game with more than fifteen guys on the street next to Schweih's garage in the middle of the block. Some of the guys were as old as eighteen or nineteen.

I was on the edge of the crowd, making side bets that the shooter would make his point. There were all kinds of coins; nickels, dimes, quarters and half-dollars on the street as players were betting for or against the shooter. I could hear guys layin'odds that the shooter would roll a seven, or make his point in two rolls of the dice. I liked the crap game because the shooter always "spoke" to the dice when he began his roll. "C'mon baby, Daddy needs a new pair of shoes," or "Here it is, Seven come Eleven."

After the shooter "talked" to the dice, he'd blow on them softly in his right hand and then send them rolling along the asphalt street. Everybody in the game had their eyes glued to the rolling, tumbling dice; hoping they'd turn up a seven or eleven if they bet with the shooter, or a two (snakeeyes) or three (craps) or twelve (boxcars) if the better was against the shooter. We'd hear a loud "Yeah" from the group who got the roll of the dice, whereas there'd be silence from all the others if the points four to ten rolled up.

I never saw my father drive by because I was too intent on the shooter making his point of six. Twenty cents of my money was on the street; betting the guy next to me. All of a sudden while the dice were tumbling toward me from the shooter's roll, I felt a strong hand on my shoulder, and a loud, "What in the hell are you doin' here?" Daddy pulled me around to face him. I was so shocked to see him after being jerked around, that I was speechless. "You're goin' home with me right now," he yelled again.

The game stopped as everyone looked at me and my father. Then one of the older wiseguys said, "Hey, let the kid play. It's his money."

My father's head jerked up in the direction of the wiseguy who was across the circle of players. Daddy started to move, like a raging bull, toward this tall, thin smartaleck who was known by everyone as a troublemaker.

I thought to myself, "My father will kill this guy with one punch." But as soon as he saw my father coming, he backed away from the game, pleading, "Hey, if you want to take your kid home, no sweat. I'm sorry I butted in."

Daddy slowed down. By now he was in the middle of the dice game, with coins and guys all around, the dice lying at his feet. He knew the wiseguy from the neighborhood and didn't like him. Some of the guys felt the same way, and were hoping to see this punk get a crack in the face. *I was still in shock!*

The hesitation helped because my father turned slowly, grabbed me by the shoulder again and pushed me to his car. It was still running on the other side of the street.

When we got inside the car, he turned to me with a quiet, angry look. "God help you if I ever see you shootin' dice on the street again! Half of those guys are bums that won't amount to anything. They'll probably end up with the Mob. Don't ever let me see you gamblin' with the likes of them."

By now, though, I was a teenager in seventh grade. Pat was in eighth. We hung around with a gang called Chi-Annies. They were guys mostly ages thirteen to sixteen, who frequented a candy store named Annie's; right across the street from St.Anthony School. The little store was in the basement of a two-flat frame building. Annie let us hang there because she knew practically all of us. We bought lots of soda, candy, chips and played the jukebox. We also brought the girls there. Pretty soon she had a thriving business with three booths filled all the time with teenagers.

My brother Pat was now known as "Jake" after Jake LaMotta, the middleweight boxing champion. All of his friends and half the neighborhood knew of his fistfight with Little Red and called him "Jake."

Jake started giving me a hard time about hanging with the Chi-Annies, his gang. Nobody from my class was in the gang. And besides, I was more than a year younger and smaller than all of the guys. He'd complain to our father that I shouldn't be allowed to hang with the gang. But, my father would say to both of us, "Your mother and I know where both of you are, so let it be."

Jake didn't like Daddy's decision at all, having his little brother around when he was with the guys, especially now that the girls were around a lot.

I knew what Jake was talking about, and feeling, but I also was attracted by the gang; hanging out, smoking, playing ball on the street in front of school and meeting older guys and girls. There seemed to be nothing happening as a gang with my own age group. I had always played ball and hung with the older kids on the block, so I was used to being the youngest kid in the gang.

Annie's was the place to hang for a couple of years. But, like all great places, the luster wore off. The new paint began to fade. Annie got tired of the teenagers, the noise, and cigarette butts scattered on the sidewalk and stoop outside.

Replacing Annie's came The Doll House. In 1951, Karl and Ella, an older Italian couple from the neighborhood, opened an ice cream shop right on the corner of 28th Place and Normal, on our block across from the Convent. Almost overnight, the place became popular, with everyone hanging in the store or on the corner under the street light

And now, guys would pull up in cars with the top down, and girls inside. There were crap games right under the street light as it got dark. I stayed away from the game; just watched at a safe distance. One of the guys was assigned by the players to be the 'lookout". He kinda hung at the edge of the game; always looking for the cops

More than once, however, the cops would glide up to the game without their lights on, then make a big, protracted effort to get out of the squad car to grab somebody. By the time they did get out of the car, all the players had run. So, the two cops only nabbed the coins that were still on the street from the betting. Coffee money for the night patrol!

On the really hot nights of the summer, around 9 PM, one of the guys would say, "Let's turn the pump on to cool off." Pretty soon we had the fire hydrant cover off and a board tied to the spout so that the water would spray when we turned on the hydrant. Wide open, the spray would arch from the spout at one curb all the way to the curb across the street.

Everyone would get wet; guys without shirts or shoes or socks, girls just missing their shoes. Pretty soon the neighbors on the block would get their lawn chairs and come to sit on the sidewalk by the corner. The little kids would perch on the curb; dangling their feet in the cold water running in the gutter. The cool mist from the spray was just the relief everyone needed on the hot, muggy night.

The cops avoided the corner now, even though it was a crime to turn on the hydrant in Chicago. There were too many people enjoying this cooling misdemeanor.

*

Another problem with Jake had been surfacing for some time, but didn't come to a head yet. For many years my father was doing part-time carpentry work on his days off, to get extra money for family support. He was very good at remodeling basements, building porches and stairs, or even putting up a whole addition to the back of a two-story house.

Up to 1947, Jake and I were too young to help him with these jobs. But as we moved into the upper grades in school, Daddy started tapping us to help him after we finished our paper routes. Mostly, he needed a "gofer" to get tools from his car, or hold the end of a long board he was sawing, or get him the Phillips screwdriver from his tool pouch when he was on the ladder. The gofer also had to haul lumber, find the finishing nails, mix plaster, you name it!

I found out later that Jake never took to being a gofer or helper on these jobs. His mind was elsewhere, especially when the Chi-Annies started to hang together. He was much more interested in the teenage life in Bridgeport than knowing the difference between a wood chisel and a wood plane.

So, my father turned to me for help. And I became a very willing gofer, helper, and eventually apprentice carpenter. He showed me all of his tools and how to use them. He'd demonstrate how to line up the teeth of the handsaw with the edge of my thumb as I held the piece of wood to be sawed. "And then, let the saw slowly down to start the cutting groove. Don't push the saw down! Let the weight of the saw and the teeth do the cutting," he would say as he guided my cut on a 2 by 4 piece of lumber.

A trust began to develop in him that I could be counted on to not only get the tool he wanted, or even use it, but also to make cuts on my own while he was on the ladder or scaffold. By now, I was even using the electric table saw, the grinder, and the electric drill on the jobs.

We were working together. There was a quiet harmony as we did remodeling, porches, and stairs. Daddy was a quiet worker who'd occasionally whistle if everything was going smoothly on the job. Once in a while, however, I'd hear a "Dammit" if the last cut of wood didn't fit quite right.

One sunny afternoon, he and I were putting in a new, first-floor porch for Grandma Bosak. We were both standing in the yard; lining up a 2 by 6 by 12 feet piece of planking to nail to the porch joists. Along came Pat Regan, a neighbor on our side of the block. Pat was coming home from work in a bank downtown. He looked quite business-like in his dark suit, white shirt and tie. Just as he came up to where we were working, my father was driving a nail into a plank to fasten it to the joist. But the nail missed the joist: I could tell by the sound it made that it hadn't hit the joist.

"Dammit," shouted my father as he pounded the nail deep into the plank out of anger.

Then Regan, standing above us on the sidewalk, said to my father in a mocking voice, "Well now, did you miss the board, Patrick?" And he smiled.

I saw immediately my father begin to erupt. "Why you little pipsqueak, what in the hell are you talking about me for. You never had a hammer in your hand your whole life. Get the hell outta here before I take this hammer to your head." And then Daddy started to go for the steps leading to the sidewalk.

Pat Regan took off like a flash, scurrying down the sidewalk to his house, sensing full well that my father meant business with the hammer.

"I'll be damned if I'll take anything from a dandy the likes of him who doesn't get his hands dirty with a little work. He won't lift a finger over at his house. Mary Regan has to call me to come and fix the place while he sits and reads the paper," my father continued with his tirade.

It was becoming clear to me that Daddy liked working with his hands, and respected men who wouldn't hesitate to get dirty. His father, Grandpa Hugh, had been a laborer on the buildings in the early 1900's, and later an amateur carpenter. He had taught my father a lot of what Daddy knew about construction and home repairs. No matter how many difficulties my grandfather had with the bottle, my father respected him very much because Grandpa worked with his hands: gotten them dirty many a day.

There were many a night that my father would sit on the stoop of our front porch with me and reminisce about growing up in Chicago. He would talk about "Annabelle", his mother: how she loved to play the piano and have a good time at family parties. But, she had much suffering with diabetes later on in life, limiting her music.

Daddy told me how he was raised on 28th and Wallace, just a block from where we were living. He attended Mark Sheridan School because the family couldn't afford St.Anthony's tuition with five boys and two girls in the family. Then for high school, he attended only two years, because at the age of sixteen he had to get a job as a helper on the buildings to help the family income. His one claim to fame on the buildings was work on the Drake Hotel on the Magnificent Mile, north Michigan Avenue, haulin' mortar for the bricklayers in the 1920's.

Daddy would always go back to his father as if he continually had to explain to himself why his father was a drinker; a binge drinker in fact. There had been problems in Grandpa's family with an invalid mother who made him feel guilty because she was partially paralyzed after his birth. Grandpa was given two years of college by his father, John, but somehow never followed thru with a career in business.

And there was the animosity in his own family when he married a German girl, Anna Lerner, from across the alley on Emerald Ave., instead of an Irish girl like his mother. To compound Grandpa's problems, he was hit in the head while working in the Stock Yards: this affected him emotionally as well as physically.

The two of us, father and son, would settle into that stoop for two hours or more on warm, summer nights. Daddy would go on and on about his older brother "Whitey": how he practically raised my father and taught him how to play baseball. Whitey was big, powerful with a bat. He was known as the "Babe Ruth" of Bridgeport because of his tremendous homeruns in the Mark Sheridan playground. Many a Whitey blast ended up on the third floor back porches of the tenements beyond the left field fence.

I heard from my father all about the Depression: how difficult it was for him not only to get a job and make money for himself and the family, but also to grow up as an adolescent. He'd tell me of the many trials and errors as a young man tryin' to court women. One night, after he had been talking about his youth in Chicago, he looked at me very seriously and said, "If I could throw away the years from when I was fourteen to nineteen, I certainly would. I was miserable during that time of my life."

It was so easy for me to sit on the stoop and ask questions; then listen to his gentle but firm voice. One calm evening I felt heady with the conversation, so I asked him what he wanted to be in life. He laughed, mostly because he was already forty-four years old, married with six kids. "I always wanted"—and he paused—"to work with my hands. I really like being a carpenter, even if it's only part-time." After another pause, he started slower this time, as though he wanted to share something very personal. "You know, Hughie Boy, I could have been a full-time carpenter seven years ago after the War. One of the carpenters in the neighborhood, Bertucci, heard that I could handle a hammer 'n rule 'n saw. Bertucci came to see me. He said there'd be a lot of new housing built on the southside now that the War was over. He needed a whole crew of carpenters. I'd have all kinds of work."

Daddy then touched me on the arm: looked straight into my eyes. "I was afraid to take that job with Bertucci. When I was young, I'd work two months on a job on the buildings and then get laid off for six. I couldn't do that in '46, what with six kids." Again he paused, even longer. "I don't know. The Railroad was a steady job. It wasn't much money but I went to work every day." He looked away from me to the street below.

I sensed a certain longing in his voice, and unspoken thoughts. "I made the wrong decision. I should have taken the chance. I'd be happy now. We'd have more money. I'd be doing the work I love," I interpreted his mind. As I continued to look at my father, I wondered what our lives would have been like if he said Yes to Bertucci. *More income each week, or ups and downs? Rags or riches? A better home and neighborhood? New car? Were things better for carpenters after the War?*

Daddy would then slide into politics and talk for hours about FDR, Roosevelt, as he called him. "Roosevelt saved this country," he would proclaim. "He put men back to work and gave them dignity and just wages, the forty-hour week, with time-and-a-half for overtime." Pretty soon I was listening to his diatribe about the Democrats for the working man and the lousy Republicans for the rich. He'd end his speech with "And don't you forget that," admonishing me to vote Democratic when I was old enough.

There were periodic, lengthy arguments between Daddy Democrat and Republican Aunt Mary, (she of the stock portfolio) especially about Harry Truman. "Was he or wasn't he a good President?" The two of them would dominate the family visit: Daddy staunchly defending Harry's years as President against Aunt Mary's attacks and enthusiastic support of Ike. She knew just how to set him off with a negative comment about the latest Union strike. It seemed as though us kids in the audience learned early on that people should *never* argue politics.

One afternoon, Daddy's political views almost got him arrested. It was a warm, sunny, just delightful afternoon in July of 1952. We were working together, widening the arch between the living room and dining room in a second-floor apartment on 29th and Parnell. The preliminary work to tear out the old arch and extend the opening had been done. We had already installed the drywall on the new spaces; nailed in the corner beading, and were ready to plaster in the nails, joints, and corners.

Daddy sent me down to the car for the bucket and five-pound box of ready-mix plaster.

I returned in no time at all with the bucket, but there was no ready-mix. He then remembered that he hadn't bought it yet for this job because he didn't think we'd be this far along.

Instinctively, Daddy took out his round pocketwatch from his coveralls, flipped the gold cover and read 4:45. "We just have enough time to go to the lumber yard on Halsted and get some mix."

We hustled down to the car and took off, Parnell Ave. to 29th. Then a left turn to Wallace, the stop sign, and on to Lowe and Union, the next stop sign. When we pulled up to Union Ave., a squad car was blocking our side of the street. "Now what the hell is this?" Daddy said in a nervous, irritated voice. Then we heard sirens coming from 26th and Union, heading toward our intersection. The policeman got out of his squad car in front of us and took a position in the middle of 29th.

"Is there an accident?" my father asked, as he craned his neck and head to see more. But all we could see were people coming out of their houses, and cars stopped on the other side of the intersection.

I had an uncomfortable feeling as to what was causing the traffic stop, but I didn't know if I should tell my father. I had read in the *Herald-American* that afternoon that Eisenhower had been nominated last night by the Republicans to run for President. The Convention was being held at the Amphitheatre on 41st and Halsted, just two miles directly south of where we were sitting in our car.

The sirens turned out to be coming from six police motorcycles who were preceding the limousine line of cars carrying the bigwigs and Ike to the Amphitheatre for his Acceptance speech. We were trapped until the whole line of cars passed our intersection.

As the motorcycles passed us, I shouted to my father, "It's Eisenhower. He's going to the Amphitheatre for his Acceptance speech."

My father looked incredulous. "We're sitting here like mopes, waiting for that Republican so 'n so to drive by with a big hullabaloo. He doesn't believe 'n puttin' people to work, and now he's holding me up from making a livin'." At this, he started to turn the car around the police car to move into the intersection.

"I'll stop this motorcade right now," he shouted to me.

I was shocked! He wasn't serious? "No, don't do it, Dad! You'll cause an accident! You'll get arrested! Leave Ike be." I found myself yelling at him and trying to grab the wheel to turn the car back behind the squad car.

Daddy stopped the car; frustrated, pounding the steering wheel, looking at his pocket watch and muttering, "Five minutes to five. For the love of Jesus, can you believe this. Held up by a lousy Republican! No wonder the workin' men don't like 'im."

We could now see the limousines moving thru the intersection; big, long cars with shiny, black paint and dazzling chrome. We couldn't see Ike or anyone else for that matter because the limo windows were tinted. Not that Ike would want to show himself to the people of Bridgeport: who were solid Democrats like Daddy.

Finally, or so it seemed to my steaming father, the last limousine passed, followed by two squad cars: roof lights flashing. The officer in front of us went back to his squad car and turned on his light too. We could see his car slowly creep across Union, heading towards Emerald.

We followed the squad car to Emerald where it turned left and we carried on to Halsted. By the time we pulled into the Carr-Moody Lumber yard a block away, the big gate was closing. But Daddy was waved on in because he was a good customer, what with all the neighborhood jobs he had that needed lumber, nails, etc.

Even with the "presidential interruption" we got back to the plastering job and finished the first coat by 6:15 PM. Dinner was good that night; hamburgers with grilled onions, fried potatoes, and corn-on-the-cob. A fitting meal for two hard-working Democrats!

Daddy had to tell all the kids how he was ready to stop the motorcade on 29th and Union. Mommy shook her head, but all the kids (me too!) laughed when he said he was going to stop Ike from making a speech.

I noticed it was 7:20 PM, so I asked him, with a grin, if we were going to watch Eisenhower's speech on TV tonight.

*

Sister Elizabeth was tired of our class in 4th Grade at St.Anthony's and it was only January. The boys in the back of the room were always distracting her with pokes to each other. The girls were chatty, even though Sister was strict about talking—she liked to bang the pointer on her desk when a "buzz" arose. There were constant arguments about sharing books for reading, or correcting your neighbor's spelling test.

"This is not a 't'. You wrote an 'e' here and it's wrong."

"That is a 't'. That's how I make my 't's."

"But you didn't cross your 't'. Wrong!"

And the little boys in the front desks—like myself—spent more time giggling than reading silently, or answering all of Sister's questions, the reason we were put in the front of the classroom.

So, on January 16th, 1946, after much thought and prayer, Sister announced shortly after lunch that, "Today we are going to change seats."

A loud cheer erupted from all 34 of us! It was so loud that Sister had to quiet us down before the principal came to see what was happening. She looked shocked at our overwhelming support of her decision, but probably saw that we felt the same way about our present desk location, and neighbors.

"Now we'll do this in an orderly way," she said firmly. "Take all of your books and paper and pencils out and put them on top of your desk. And no talking! I mean it!"

There was an instant bustle of activity with books sliding out and being dropped (more like plopped) on desk tops. A slight murmur of voices started cascading into a room full of talkers.

"I said 'Quietly'," yelled Sister, above the growing din.

Pretty soon the floor started accumulating wadded paper and old assignments, even a few personal notes. "Eugene—I think yer kewt. Signed," and the name had been scratched out with pencil so it couldn't be read. I threw the note to Eugene Heinis who was two desks away. He read it and said to me, "That's not me!" throwing the note back.

Finally, we had our desks cleaned and were ready to move. The tension was mounting as everyone wondered who they'd end up with in their row and next to them. I could see girls pointing to each other with their fingers, making like they wanted to be seated next to each other, following the pointing with little smiles. Big George Schramm and Arthur (Bucky) Barrett didn't have to get excited. They knew that they would be assigned to the last seats in a row because of their height. Since I was so small and liked to answer questions, I had been sitting in the third row, first seat, right in front of Sister's desk. I was dying to get a desk further back in the middle, so I could talk and fool around.

"Mr. Adamo! First row, first seat." Sister began the assignments.

Joey looked at Sister with a shocked face. "Me! First row, first seat?" as he picked up his books and supplies to move there. Ray Fendler, who had been in the first row, first seat, smiled and took his things off the desk so that Joey could "move in".

All the other kids in the room moaned in sympathy with Joey. "Awwh. First row, first seat?" even though Joey would now get to answer knocks on the classroom door.

"Now shush," blurted out Sister. "Mr. Amato! Third row, second seat."

Joe laughed out loud and started to pick up his books from the last desk in the fourth row—there were four rows of seven desks and the first row by the chalkboard had six students.

Very quickly we figured that Sister was assigning new desks by alphabetical order. So the kids with last names beginning with M thru W—we had no X, Y, or Z students—relaxed and started chatting or picked up their books and supplies, moving to the windows if someone was assigned to their old desk.

"Mis-ter Barrett," she dragged out the Mister. "Last seat, second row."

"Hey, hey." Bucky said as he moved from the last seat of the sixth row.

"Eleanor Bitten. First row, third seat." Sister kept going.

I looked around as this pretty girl with curly hair and glasses moved from the sixth row. She looked shy. I couldn't remember ever talking to her, even though I didn't talk to many girls. "Boy, would I like to sit next to her," I thought.

"Carol Bowman. Last seat, first row." Sister was now moving faster, realizing that the more time she used, the more talking would erupt. Before Carol could gather all of her books and supplies, we heard "Nancy Butterworth. Fifth row, last seat"

Nancy frowned, "Back there?"

I quickly calculated that Norene Kieneggar and Nancy Koehler and Charles Kundrot were the three K's before me in alphabetical order. I kept watching the third desk in the second row. Still empty. I looked at Eleanor, but she was too busy putting away her books, supplies and papers to catch my eyes. She did these tasks so quietly: *I was impressed! "Do you think it could happen? Me sitting next to her?" I wondered silently.*

"Norene Kieneggar. Second row, first seat"

Norene frowned too, but started to move her things.

"Nancy Koehler. Fifth row, fourth seat."

"Mr. Kundrot. I want you in the second row, fifth seat."

"My" seat was still open. My assignment was next. *I closed my eyes, squeezed my hands, said a quick prayer, and listened to what Sister would say.*

There was a knock on the classroom door. I opened my eyes to see Joey Adamo running to open the door, like he was supposed to. He had a smile on his face.

An eighth grader came in with a message for Sister. She read it and took out her record book to make a note of some sort. In the meantime, the eighth grader was looking around the room to see whom he knew; smiling when he saw a friend.

Finally, Sister said "OK", and told the messenger to leave. "Now where were we?" she questioned the class.

I timidly raised my hand, sitting right in front of her in the first seat, third row.

"Oh yes", she said. "Mr.LeVoy." She read her seating chart, but paused as though she had second thoughts about my new assignment. "I don't know if you'll be able to see from there, but I'm going to put you in the second row, third seat. You let me know if you have trouble seeing from there, Hugh."

I couldn't believe it. I was sitting next to Eleanor Bitten. My face was all smiles as I gathered books and supplies, and waltzed over to the second row, third seat—or should I say, Third Desk, Second Row. It didn't matter that Sister was questioning my ability to see because I was so short, the only desk for me being the first in a row!

Eleanor briefly glanced at me as I got to my new location. I said "HI" to her. She smiled and then got busy with something inside her desk. So I busied myself, putting books away and straightening my supplies. I couldn't remember ever talking to her except to say "Excuse me", once in a crowded cloakroom when I was trying to go to the room and she was in the way.

The rest of the moves went smoothly for Sister even though there were more groans and complaints. "I have to sit next to him?" and "I sat next to her in third grade: I hated it!"

We finally started our afternoon subjects. I could hardly wait for Spelling when Eleanor and I would have to share the book, because we only had 24 Spellers. We'd have to push our desks together like real partners, with the Speller either on her desk or mine. I'd turn the pages for her!

That magical afternoon went by really fast. When we stood for the final prayer before lining up along the chalkboard wall, I was tempted to ask Eleanor if I could walk with her to the corner of 28th Place and Wallace. But, shyness kicked in after the Amen. I hesitated, smiled sheepishly, and said "Goodbye", as we lined up in boys and girls lines.

Mommy was wondering why I was smiling when I came home at 3 PM. I told her about my new seat and Eleanor. Mag was listening intently while munching on a piece of bread with peanut butter and jelly. She always had a snack after school to help her thru the paper deliveries.

As soon as Mag heard Eleanor's name, she blurted, "I know that girl. She lives on Pat's paper route!" Just then, Pat came into the kitchen. Mag announced to him, "Hughie's got a girl friend."

"Who," he questioned her.

"Eleanor Bitten. She lives on 28th and Union," Mag answered.

"Oh yeah! I see her once in a while on my route. She wears glasses." Pat replied.

That evening at supper, after Grace, my Dad asked us how things were at school.

Mag started singing, "Hughie's got a girlfriend!"

Then little Kate picked up the chorus line and repeated, "Hughie got a girlfriend."

Pat poked me in my right arm because he always sat at my end of the table. "Boys don't make passes at girls who wear glasses." Then he started to laugh.

Fred, my four-year old brother was smiling, then giggling as he looked at me.

Even Maureen, the baby, got into the act by pounding her spoon on the highchair tray.

I didn't know what to do. I was embarrassed at their kidding; not really able to handle all this attention because I liked a girl in fourth grade. With my head down toward the table, I started drinking the vegetable soup in my bowl, hoping the hoopla would end. As I lifted my head to look for the butter, I glanced toward my father. He was smiling and looking at me. Then he said, "Aw, don't worry about them, Hughie Boy. You'll have plenty of girlfriends for them to talk about before you're a man. Now the rest of you leave 'im alone, and drink yer soup!"

There *were* plenty of girlfriends talked about, especially by my parents' friends and relatives. It seemed that everywhere we went to visit, the host family had a daughter my age. As soon as we arrived at the house, there would be the familiar "Well Hughie Boy, maybe you should talk to Mary about school. You're both in the same grade and you both like to read."

This always made me uncomfortable because I was shy and small and really wanted to sit in the living room, listening to the adults talk about sports 'n politics and the families. It bothered me to have a girl—usually a redhead—imposed on me for the afternoon. I found myself getting obstinate. Even though I was friendly with Mary or Patsy, I'd vow to myself that I wouldn't get involved, instead running out to the backyard where my brother Pat was playing Catch with the older boy in the family.

But my cousin Betty Jean was different. *What a cute girl with a quick mind!* I liked her right away and had no trouble talking to her and spending time with her when we visited the Flanagans. We both would hear a lot of kidding about Hughie and Betty Jean from Aunt Annie, her mother, and Mommy. I would usually act shy when the conversation turned to the two of us at the dining room table, but it didn't seem to bother me. In fact, I asked Sister Ponciana in third grade at St.Anthony's if cousins could get married. She looked surprised at my question during Religion class. Her answer was something to the effect that first cousins couldn't get married, only relatives to the third kindred—whatever that meant.

Sitting next to Eleanor day by day in class was great. She was easy going, quiet, and didn't complain. We got along well; sharing books, correcting papers and occasionally talking. The glasses didn't bother me because she was so cute. I even walked her to the corner one afternoon. Everyone who went that way home was wondering why I was walking to Wallace, until they caught on that I was with Eleanor. Soon the stares, whispers and giggles started. The next day, some of the boys razzed me at recess about walking with her.

But then Eleanor broke my heart! In June, on the last day of school of fourth grade, Sister announced that Eleanor would not return in September because she was moving to a new home out south. The class went, "Oooh" as a sign of appreciation that Eleanor was going to a nice neighborhood. Everyone turned to look at her and smile. I could only bury my head in my hands. Darnit! I was smitten by Bitten!

As our class continued to move up the grades, my height seemed to be stuck. I continued to be one of the "shrimps". By eighth grade, I had finally, *finally* gotten tall enough to look at the shortest girl in the eyes. But there were no more romances, glasses or not.

Through high school I would occasionally take a girl from the neighborhood to see a movie downtown at the State-Lake Theatre or the Oriental. Afterwards, we would head for the Kopper Kettle Restaurant on Randolph and State Streets for ice cream or a sandwich 'n coke. The girls were all bigger than me. Eventually we just didn't click. Either I was too conscious of my height or she was just too mature for Hughie Boy.

There was still some kidding from my brothers and sisters, but they began to sense that I really didn't like the attention: wouldn't talk about the girls anyway. Mommy never said much about my dates, but would keep urging me to take out a nice Irish girl. She'd remind me of Mary, the daughter of her friend from Ireland. "Mary likes ye, Hughie Boy. Her mother has told me so. Wouldn't it be grand to ask her out, now!"

I felt like telling her that I'd get my own dates, and they wouldn't be redheads. But I didn't want to hurt her feelings about the friend's daughter. Ironically, I really liked girls with brunette hair, just like my mother's.

During the summer between sophomore and junior year in high school, I started to see a girl around the corner named Darlene. She was shorter than me, and really pretty. The word got home to my folks, probably through my brother Jake. One afternoon, while helping Daddy in the basement with some painting, he asked me about Darlene. I told him where she lived and who her father was. Daddy looked at me somewhat quizzical. "You mean that alley house behind 29th and Normal. That skinny guy with the drawl?

I said "Yeah." My father didn't say anymore, but I somehow got the message that he didn't approve of my girlfriend Darlene. The tone of his questions, the look on his face told me he disapproved: she wasn't good enough for me!

As Mag and Jake and I moved thru our teen years, our dates, friends and acquaintances were silently scrutinized by our folks. I began to feel that I shouldn't say anything about a girl I was interested in because they wouldn't approve of her. There were different ethnic groups in Bridgeport; predominantly Italian, some Croation and German, and a lesser amount of Irish families. Not far away, were a couple of buildings with Mexicans, and some hillbillies were scattered around the neighborhood. Maybe I should think twice before I get interested in a girl from around here.

The teen club at All Saints Parish at 25th and Wallace was very active under the leadership of Father Cziedlo, the associate pastor. Some of their big events were the teen dances they would hold on Friday nights, once a month in the Spring and Fall. Everyone from the neighborhood would go because the band was real and lively; playing all the current love songs and rock 'n roll. We saw guys and girls from as far away as St. David's on 32nd and Emerald, three parishes south of All Saints.

These dances were safe. Father Cziedlo and the parent chaperones absolutely forbad drinking or fights. The Boys washroom was checked regularly. Any violators or wise-guys were sent home early. The price was cheap, too! Only a buck to get in! We couldn't beat that for a night out.

One misty night in April of '55, I went to the Friday night teen dance with a couple of friends from my senior class at DeLaSalle Institute. I was wearing my favorite, powder blue jacket—one button roll—with dark pants and black leather shoes for dancing. These dances were held in the basement of the grammar school. The floor was oak that had been waxed, then sprinkled with dancing powder.

The place was crowded when we got there. We walked around the hall looking for a place to stand and some guys to talk to. The band was busy with "Shake, Rattle and Roll" by Bill Haley and His Comets. The dance floor was packed, mostly with girls dancing together. There were some couples, with the better dancers like Ronnie Renaud and Sammy Demma showing all of their swingin' moves with their partners.

It was exciting just to be there, watching these kids having fun, and listening to the rock 'n roll music. We'd hear a great cheer from the dancers as the band blasted the last notes of a tune and the swingers made their final twirl with intertwining hands lightly pulling at each other and movin' in a circle.

It didn't take long before I noticed a short, thin girl with long, dark hair and a cute face. She was just finishing a dance with her girlfriend, and then moving to the side of the floor. My eyes focused on her as she stood talking to a group of girls.

I asked my friend Bill if he knew her because she was not from All Saints or my parish, St. Anthony's. Bill lived around 31st and Lowe, and knew a lot of girls from there.

"Who?" he said, looking in the direction I was pointing.

"That girl," I said. "The one with the light-blue suit and flat shoes. She's wiping her forehead with a hankie."

"Oh yeah, that's Lucy," Bill answered. "She's from 32nd and Union. She went to St. David's. You like her?"

"I don't know. I just saw her dance and she's good. She swings," I said. I didn't tell him that she looked cute.

"Ask her to dance," he shouted above the crowd talk and music as the band began a slow tune.

"What'ya think? Will she say 'No'. Does she have a boyfriend?" I yelled into his ear. Couples began filling the floor now, moving slowly in the familiar two-step to the soft, romantic music. A few couples were cheek to cheek, hardly moving at all.

Bill looked at me, smiled and raised his voice. "Go ahead. I can tell you like her. I don't think she has a boyfriend."

The band was now halfway thru "Blue Moon". I could see that she was still standing on the edge of the dance floor with her friends. No one had asked her to dance, I noted, so I had a chance. I had to move now or the slow one would be over.

I walked around the dancers, past the tables at the end of the hall, past the stage where the band was brightly lit, and toward the group of girls. She saw me coming, and turned slightly away, then back in my direction as I continued to her. I was getting nervous, but determined to ask her to dance.

"Hi," I said to her, as her brown eyes fixed on mine, and a smile came to her face. I noticed her lips had a light pink shade of lipstick, very faint in the subdued light.

"Hi," she answered, slightly bumping into her friend, who now turned around and saw me.

I had to keep going even though I was still nervous. "Would you like to dance?" I said much too loudly, I thought.

She hesitated, so her girlfriend bumped her in the hip, answering for her. "Go ahead, Lucy. He's cute!"

The rest of the evening we were together; dancing, talking, cooling off after the fast ones, having cokes, joking and laughing with her friends and mine. Lucy had no trouble following my jerky, jitterbug moves or stiff-legged, two-step waltz. In fact, when the band decided to play "Rock Around the Clock" for the finale, I was twirlin' her and we were movin' around the floor like Fred Astaire and Ginger Rogers. We were really in rhythm with each other. As the notes of music from the band bounced around that low-ceilinged basement, and we stood at arms length, connected by the fingers of her right hand and my left, we breathed a sigh of exhaustion and joy.

The walk home with Lucy at 10:00 to her house was over a mile. Her friends and mine walked with us part of the way down Wallace, but dropped off as we reached 31st. Lucy and I went down 31st to Union and headed towards 32nd. There had been a slight April shower while we were in the dance. The trees on the parkway were dripping just enough to notice as we walked under them. I could feel the moisture in the air and smell the flowering trees from some of the front yards on Union.

Lucy was talkative. I could tell that she liked me. Our slow stroll came to a stop halfway down the block. We leaned against the iron railing of a three-story house: the tree above us shielding the light from the street lamp. She was a second-year student at St.Anthony's Commercial, and I was a senior at "D". She was the fourth child in her family, and I the third in mine. She liked to dance and so did I. We continued getting acquainted while a soft breeze rustled the tree: tiny raindrops fell on us.

Her instincts said that it was getting late, so we had to leave this sidewalk spot. She had to be home by 10:30. We walked slowly to 32nd and turned the corner. The streetlight cast our shadows in front of us onto the sidewalk, moving hand in hand, leading the way to her house.

"Thanks," I said. "It was a great night. You're quite a dancer."

She blushed, and replied, "Thanks! I really had a good time."

There was just the slightest pause as though we didn't want to part. We made plans to meet at the Wallace Show the next night.

As I walked home, down Lowe Ave. to 29th and over to Normal, *I felt wonderful. Finally I had met a girl I really liked and enjoyed talking to and being with. And I didn't have to look "up" to see her pretty face.* When I reached the front steps of our house, I remembered the kidding, "Hughie's got a girlfriend." I decided as I went slowly up the front steps that I wouldn't tell my family about Lucy. There'd be no "Paddy dear and did ye hear the news that's goin' round" from me.

The Rose of Tralee and her Paddy.
Mommy and Daddy going steady, 1930's.

Mary & Pat

Grandma Bosek with 5 LeVoy kids and her
baby grandchild — on the back porch — 1946

Grandma Anna LeVoy — 1950

Aunt Catherine Blotz and Patrick
In the back yard — 1945

Aunt Mary Flanagan — on the back
yard swing - 1945

Uncle Zeke's grave — Normandy American
Cemetery, Colleville-sur-Mer, France

5

MIKE JUDGE

"Whatsoever you do to the least of my people,
that you do unto me."

Willard F. Jabusch, 1967, "Whatsoever You Do"

The huge, cavernous lobby of Union Station in Chicago on Adams & Canal Sts. was the meeting place each morning for the guys and gals who rode the Canal St. bus to St.Patrick Academy and St. Patrick Girls High School. My first venture to the Station was in early September, 1951 as I began freshman high school year at SPA—as the words of the St.Pat's fight song ended—"keep your eyes on the SPA."

My sister Mag was now a junior at the Girls School, on Adams St., just west of DesPlaines Ave. My brother Pat (now known as Jake to his buddies after his first fist fight) was a sophomore at SPA, which was on DesPlaines, just around the corner. Old St. Patrick's Church was on the corner, in-between the two schools, with its two towers standing guard on Chicago's near west side.

There were other guys and girls who hung with us in the Station who were from Bridgeport, the neighborhood on the near south side where we lived. There were probably 20 of us each morning, hanging around instead of going directly from the bus to St. Pats. We'd sit in the huge lobby and talk, have coffee or a coke, and smoke cigarettes. (We couldn't smoke on the way to school because Brother Patrick was always on tobacco patrol in the morning and after school.)

There were always newspapers to read on the hard, wooden benches, left by the "true" passengers who went off to catch their trains, leaving the news behind. There would also be the latest school gossip, or talk about the "sock hop" that was held on Friday after school. I had learned during 8th Grade how to ask a girl to dance, and how to dance, especially the jitterbug. And we would always have something to say about SPA's basketball teams—the Shamrock hoopsters were doing well in '51-'52.

It was always a special feeling for me as a boy of 13 to enter Union Station on the Canal St. side, and walk down the grand, marble steps that were just inside the doors to the lower waiting area. There was a continuous bustle to the room as commuters hurried from the trains to ascend the same stairs that I just came down, and go to their offices in the western Loop. I loved to hear the announcements. "The Burlington Zephyr, train #34, bound for Aurora, Cedar Rapids, DesMoines, and beyond is now boarding on Track 4. ALL UHH BORD!"

Then there were the bums who had just woken up from sleeping in the Station all night, and were panhandling passengers—and us students—for a dime to buy their morning coffee (or wine). In fact, these derelicts were scattered throughout the area. We'd see them sleeping in doorways of vacant buildings or scrounging thru garbage cans and always begging for money as we walked the 3 blocks from the Station to school. "Hey kid, can ya spare uh dime," I'd hear as the old fella came limping up to me while I was hustling to make it to SPA on time after spending too much time with someone else's sports pages at the Station.

I found these men both intriguing, and disheartening as I would reach into my pocket for a nickel to drop into his outstretched, shaking hand. I'd look at his dirty and unshaven face with beet red cheeks and nose from too much whiskey, and I'd wonder what had happened in his life. *What had gone wrong to bring him to this sorry state? Was there some tragedy in his youth, or a rejection from the girl he loved? Maybe he was a victim of injuries or trauma from World War II. Perhaps it was the "big" job pressures that led him to drink.*

I'd imagine his wife and kids ekeing out an existence somewhere in Chicago, giving up hope of ever seeing him again, even though he was "livin" just west of downtown on Skid Row, a bus ride away.

It truly made me pause to look into that bum's eyes. And one day, after he got my nickel and limped away, I was reminded of my Uncle Domnick and his sporadic visits to our house on 28th Place. I must have been six or seven years old when he first came.

"Now Marg'ret, can ye spare me a cuple uh dollars 'til me nex' pay. I'd not be both'rin' ye, but I'm a wee bit low."

There was Uncle Domnick, one of my mother's older brothers, standing at the back door to our 2nd floor flat, begging my mother for some money to "tide him over." He was dirty, with a week's beard on his ruddy face, and had old clothes on that looked like the suit he wore when he came over from the old country in the 20's. His Irish cap was in his hands as he stood on the outside of the screen door, with my mother and us kids on the inside.

"Well, look at what the cat dragged in. What a sight ye are in front of the chil'ren," my mother said to him, looking disgusted.

Uncle Domnick lowered his bald head in shame, and muttered something about "these being hard times," apologizing for his appearance, and "wouldn't she be so kind as to help him this once."

"I've got a mind to send ye off with nothin'," she spoke sternly to him. "God knows if I give ye anythin', will I git it back. And what will ye do with the two dollers?"

"Ah Marg'ret, I'm goin' now to the Mission to git a shower, a clean bed, and a bit o' food. I'll not be spending the money on the drink. I take me pledge in front of ye an' the chil'ren," Uncle Domnick pleaded with her as he raised his right hand.

There was a pause in the conversation as my mother decided whether to give him any money. I was standing next to her on her right and I could sense the indecision she was feeling. Patrick and Mag were on her left, next to the kitchen sink. Mommy really didn't have two dollars for Uncle Domnick because of the low wages my father was earning at the Wabash Railroad, and five kids to support. Besides, she would send money regularly to Uncle Mick and Aunt Sis and Uncle Tom in Ireland to help them make ends meet in the Old Country. They were living on the Flanagan Farm and barely making do.

But something inside me knew-even though I was so young-that Mommy would give in and help her brother Domnick. I found myself hoping she wouldn't turn him down. I kept staring at him through the screen door as he was shifting his weight between one foot and the other, peering through his side of the screen at my mother, acting nervous and ashamed at the same time.

My wish must have turned to deed because I bumped her accidentally. Then, she glanced at me, sighing slightly. She turned around and walked to her bedroom off the kitchen. The three of us kids were left standing, looking through the screen at our Uncle. He smiled sheepishly at us, and his ruddy, tan face showed many lines and creases from working in the weather for the Wabash, the same railroad as Daddy. Uncle Domnick was a gandy dancer, one of the men who repaired the rails and ties and track bed on the miles of track in the railroad system. These men lived in cabooses while on the rails, generally having a bachelor's life made up of drink and gambling, but no permanence or family life.

"Hi Uncle Domnick," I said softly to him after he smiled at us. Patrick and Mag chimed in with "Hi's" of their own. He smiled again and this time

I noticed that he was completely bald, not a hair on his head. I kept looking at his pink dome as he bent down somewhat to respond to our friendliness, movin' his right index finger up 'n down, sayin' "Hi" back to us.

"Now don' ye be talkin' to the likes of him," Mommy scolded us as she returned from her "bank" in the bedroom. "He'll be askin' fer yer piggy bank next," she warned us. In her left hand was the two dollars. She opened the creaky screen door slightly and put the money through reluctantly.

As Uncle Domnick reached for the two dollars, he became serious in tone. "Marg'ret, bless ye. I'll not be lettin' ye down. Thank ye fer the money. I'll be sayin' prayers and lightin' a candle at Old St.Paddy's Church fer ye an' the chil'ren and yer Paddy. God bless."

And then he smiled, flipped his finger to say "Goodbye" to us kids, put on his cap and turned to head down the steep back stairs.

"Go out the alley, will ye. I don' want the neighbors to see the likes of ye comin' from this house," my mother commanded him.

We followed him onto the small back porch. "That I'll do, Marg'ret. That I'll do," said Uncle Domnick as he grabbed the wooden banister and let himself down the long string of steps leading to the first floor landing. I glanced at my mother. She was watching her brother intently, fearing that he'd fall down the stairs and kill himself. There were tears in her eyes, as Uncle Domnick finally made it to the landing.

We watched while he quickly made the five steps to the back yard. He turned ever so slightly, looked up at us with another smile, and lifted his right hand in a sort of wave goodby. Soon he was across the back yard and into the gangway under the alley flats.

I ran down the back stairs to look out from Grandma Bosak's back porch to see him in the alley, but Miller's fence was too high. *Uncle Domnick was gone!*

Two months later, on a sunny day in June, Patrick and I were playing Bounce or Fly against the front steps of our house. We were using a new, pink rubber ball that really flew if you hit the corner of the step just right. Pat was "at bat" and I was the fielder. He "hit" a squibber that rolled down the sidewalk toward Schmitt's corner. I ran for the ball and grabbed it before it got to the parkway down the street. I looked up and there coming down the sidewalk toward me, with two bags of groceries in his arms, was this older man in a new blue suit. And he had the shiniest bald head I had ever seen.

I stared in disbelief! "Could it be? Was that him?" I ran back to our steps and grabbed Pat's arm excitedly. "Look," I almost shouted, pointing to the well-dressed man who was now getting closer. "Is it him?" I blurted out to Pat.

By now, the man was ten feet from us, peering up at our house to check and see the address. Then, he turned to Pat and I, and I just knew it was him.

"Uncle Domnick," both Pat and I yelled at the same time, as we ran the last five feet to him. We grabbed him around the leg and waist, but he couldn't hug us back because of the two grocery bags in his arms.

"Well now, look at these two laddies. Ye'er great to greet me here in front of the house. Is yer mither home, now?" Uncle Domnick asked us with a broad grin on his clean and shaven face.

"I'll get her, Uncle Domnick," said Pat. Quickly he turned around and bounded up the front stairs. "Mommy,Mommy, its Uncle Domnick," I could hear him yelling as he pulled open the front screen door and burst into the front room.

I held onto Uncle Domnick's coat and walked with him to the front stairs. All of the Miller kids from next door who were playing outside, were staring at the two of us, wondering who the important man was that Pat and I were so excited to see.

My mother was now at the top of the stairs, with Mag and Pat and little Kate. "Would ye look at this. It's Himself," she said with a broad smile to Domnick as she looked down at the two of us coming up the stairs. "Now what have ye in the bags?" she added as Uncle Domnick made it to the landing. Mommy gave him a kiss on his clean face and invited him into the house.

When we got to the kitchen, Uncle Domnick unloaded the groceries onto our table. He pulled out boiled ham, Swiss and cheddar cheeses, olives with pimentos, RYE BREAD, real mayonnaise, fancy mustard, and dill pickles. Following each treat that he uncovered, there came an "OOH" or "AH" from us—all the delicacies we would see in the grocery store, but could never afford to buy.

We had a great time for lunch that summer day. We'd pester him about his work on the railroad and he'd tell us stories about the places he'd been to in Southern Illinois and Indiana, and the work the gandy dancers had to do in the heat and cold and rain. I kept staring at him as he talked with his thick brogue. There were scars above his right eye that scared me, but I was simply captivated by his shiny head. The pink glow of his dome seemed to be drawing every ray of light from the kitchen window behind him. I finally got up enough courage to ask him if I could touch his head. Uncle Domnick laughed loudly and almost had a coughing fit. "Sure, Hughie me B'y. C'mon over here and pat me head. Maybe it'll bring me some luck." All of us kids and Mommy laughed while I went over to him and ran my hand slowly across his smooth, glistening scalp. I could see the sparkle in his eyes, the genuine delight of my touch. And then I got a hug from him that almost took my breath away.

Before he left us that afternoon, he gave Mommy the two dollars. She smiled and tucked them into her apron, beaming as though she had just won the Irish Sweepstakes. And, Oh! Yes. She led him out the front door, with a kiss goodby.

Uncle Domnick's visits went on for seven or eight years. He'd come up the back stairs if he was "down 'n out" with the drink, looking for a handout from Mommy with cap in hand. And then, a couple of months later, just like that sunny day in June, we'd hear the front doorbell ring, and there he'd be standing, "Himself" in his blue suit, clean shaven face, glistening head, holding a bag or two of groceries.

One cold day in November of 1953, my Uncle Jim called Mommy to tell her that Uncle Domnick had died of a heart attack. There were tears in her eyes again. I was stunned to hear her tell me, and to realize that he wouldn't be making anymore visits, front door or rear. Somehow, even though I didn't see him much, I really cared for him. Something inside of me latched on to him. He wasn't just an Uncle. My "pat" on his bald head had somehow bonded me to him. He was such a character to me, so sad and shameful, apologetic at the back door, but bright and cheerful, full of life (and goodies) at the front. He seemed to me larger than life, bigger than the other men I had seen in my young life, with his weakness and contrition mixed in with much generosity and love. But finally, there was redemption. God rest his soul!

*

In the 1950-51 school year at St. Patrick Academy there were about 350 students. Many of these boys came from the western city parishes like Blessed Sacrament, Blessed Agnes, and St. Malachy. A sizable group came from the near west side parishes of Santa Maria, Notre Dame, and from the Mercy Home for Boys on Jackson Blvd. near Racine. There were students from as far north as Rogers Park, northwest from St. Isaac Jogues, and a large group from our neighborhood in Bridgeport.

It was easy to get to know a lot of these students because the enrollment was small, and at lunch and intramurals we had chances to meet students from other neighborhoods. Every morning at Union Station was like a social hour where we could mix with a lot of students, boys and girls.

While there were many contacts for me, as well as my brother and others from Bridgeport, I was generally uneasy at St. Pat's. I felt like a little kid somehow, in a situation where I didn't belong. I was nervous, even though I attended all the basketball games at SPA, the sock hops, and even tried out and made the freshman midget basketball team. I even asked the heavyweight basketball coach, Jim Weaver, if he needed another trainer to help with equipment and uniforms. He said, "Yes". So now I was traveling with the big guys (5'8" and taller) as they visited other city high schools for practice and league games.

There was always a question in my mind as to whether I would get St. Vitus Dance like my brother Jake. At least, I was afraid I would get it. In October,

I developed a hacking cough that seemed to have no source from a cold or upper respiratory infection. The cough didn't seem to bother me during the day at school, but was really a problem at night, in bed! For some strange reason, I would cough and Cough and COUGH, not only failing to go to sleep, but also keeping the whole family awake.

I thought for sure that I had the cough from St.Vitus Dance, that this was another form of it. But when I was checked by the family doctor, he couldn't find anything wrong. My lungs were clear; heart was excellent. Maybe my head wasn't screwed on right, as my father would say.

Everyone at home was frustrated with me. And I was too! I went to bed each night with fears of coughing. And no matter how hard I tried to stop, when the apartment went silent and darkness settled in, the coughing continued.

Finally, in November, out of complete frustration, my folks put me into the hospital to see if any tests could point to the reason for my coughing. Nothing showed! But strangely, after resting in a bed and eating hospital food for four days, I *stopped* coughing. Was it a respite from the daily nervousness that was always present in grammar school because I was younger and smaller than my classmates. Or, was I now getting all kinds of attention from nurses and doctors. Perhaps this coughing was just the sign of immaturity!

Like my schoolwork at St.Anthony's, I was doing well in the freshman subjects at St.Pat's. I had enrolled in the regular course of study, and was getting B's in Religion, Algebra, World History, Latin, and an A in English. I even earned a B in Physical Education. My problem didn't seem to be with the books, but with the growing pressures and expectations both from me and others as I entered adolescence—the teenage years. I always had this feeling I was "in over my head", that I really didn't belong emotionally in high school.

I could do all the things necessary for a freshman in high school—ride the bus, hang out in Union Station, walk thru the west Loop streets, attend classes, answer questions, study, do homework and pass tests. *But everyone seemed bigger, older and smarter: I was just a kid, a shrimp, a Hughie Boy.* It was the same when I would hang with my brother Jake's gang, the Chi-Annies, on the block in Bridgeport. I could talk the street language, smoke the cigarettes, and gossip about girls but I couldn't feel confident or respected as a member of the gang. Maybe I was tolerated because I was Jake's brother!

Throughout this freshman year, the Christian Brothers at St.Pat's kept informing us about the strong possibility that the Academy would move to the northwest side, to Belmont and Austin Avenues. The imminent construction of the Northwest Expressway would take some property and buildings from the existing school, thus the reason to move. Both Jake and I and the other guys from Bridgeport were not happy with the news because we really liked old SPA. There was excellent camaraderie between the students, even though there were some heated intramural football and basketball games at lunch between the Irish kids from the far west side and the Italians/Mercy Home boys from the near west side.

Jake and I even figured out how we could get to the new St.Pat's using the CTA. But it would take over an hour one-way. Mommy and Daddy said we couldn't do it and still work downtown, earning our tuition and carfare and expenses. Those came first!

Finally, the decision was made to transfer at the end of the '51-'52 school year instead of waiting 'til the end of next year, since St. Patrick Academy would be open at Adams & DesPlaines for one more year: then move to the northwest side.

I would miss the hangout at Union Station, the social hour, "recess" at the start of the school day, and watching the hustle and bustle of Chicago's train station. No more "smoking walks" down Adams St., keeping an eye out for tough Brother Patrick who patrolled after school. There wouldn't be the sight anymore of a pathetic man limping to me with outstretched hand, begging for a dime, stirring my thoughts as to Why. I'd miss those tense intramural games at noon, the exciting lights and heavyweight games at night. But what I'd miss the most was the awesome racket we would make in the Gym with our hands and feet as the St.Pat's team came on the floor from the locker room to do battle with the "bigger and better" schools like Fenwick or St.George or St.Mel's.

The Gym was very small, so small that heavy pads were mounted on the walls at both basket ends to cushion the players who drove in for a layup. There was only four feet of space beyond the backboard to the wall on one end, and to the short wall of the stage on the other end. Nine to ten feet above the floor, on three walls, were the precarious wooden balconies for spectators. The ceiling was low and when 300 students started clapping and stomping, the whole balcony vibrated. The noise, the racket kept bouncing around the walls and ceiling of that old Gym, bombarding the ears of the opposing team and their coach, but charging our Shamrocks to play inspired ball. Talk about home court advantage!

*

The curriculum at DeLaSalle Institute in 1952 offered five courses of study for students. First was the Scientific, which required four years of Math and English, Biology, Physics, and Chemistry, two years of History, two years of Latin or Spanish, and of course, four years of Religion. This Course definitely was for students with above-average ability to go to college.

The next Course was Technical—with Wood and Metal Shop, Mechanical Drawing, but only three years of Math, and just Biology for the Science requirement. The other Courses were called Secretarial Commercial, Clerical Commercial, and the General Course.

Since I had experience helping my father with his carpentry jobs, and also had no thoughts about going to college but instead figured I'd be working with my hands, like my father, I leaned toward the Technical Course. I could have taken the Scientific Course because my freshman average from St. Patrick Academy was "B", and my I.Q. results from both 8th Grade testing and the entrance exam at DeLaSalle in the summer of 1952 were at 112. There would be more challenges for me with the Scientific Course, and I would be well-prepared for college if I was successful. It would mean more homework, studying, note-taking, and harder tests.

But the Bridgeport neighborhood mentality swayed me to the Technical Course. None of the guys that I hung around with were thinking—even remotely—about college. High School was four years to suffer through so that I could graduate, get a job, buy a car, date girls, get married, and have kids. Later on in life, I learned that the final catastrophe of all these life-decisions was to buy a house, and lastly—get a dog.

College was for the guys in better neighborhoods or the suburbs. Many of us from the Chi-Annies saw ourselves as truck drivers, or factory workers, or maybe working in a trade, like brick-laying. So, I might as well take the easier Course at "D" instead of facing a tough curriculum each day. Besides, I had to work after school and didn't have a whole lot of time for homework at night. And, I liked the prospect of making things like furniture in shop, and learning how to draw houses in Mechanical Drawing.

My parents didn't add much input to my decision. Daddy liked the idea that I would be in a technical area and would learn things that would help me with my assistance to him on the part-time carpentry jobs. He had attended a technical high school, Tilden Tech, at 46th and Union for two years. He was not allowed to stay there because he had to go to work full-time at the age of 16. Mommy got as far as sixth grade in the town school in Loughglynn, County Roscommon, Ireland.

Daddy even joked to Mommy that if I became a carpenter after high school, I could help him build the house he always had dreamed about.

Both Mommy and Daddy made it clear to all us kids that we *had* to graduate from high school. We *had* to attend a Catholic school. There never was any talk at home about after high school. It was assumed we would get a job, perhaps be an apprentice in a trade, or work in a retail store in sales. They both had the minimum in formal education. Their goals for their children were simple: a high school diploma, a good steady job, and marriage. The effects of the Great Depression on both of them-Daddy didn't have a job in August of '34 when they were married-made them emphasize jobs, instead of careers.

*

Biology class at "D" was on the second floor of the Main Building, in a lab room just at the middle staircase. Sophomores had to take this Science class. There were six students assigned to each lab table, with five tables in all. I was at the far table the day in September of '52 when we began dissecting a frog. I had the short end of the table to work with and Rich was on my left and Tom on my right. As soon as we got our Biology trays, knives, and dead frogs, the three of us started making light jokes about the dissection. Our experiment was to cut the frog, observe the inner parts, and draw them into our Biology notebook.

We had heard that Brother Jarlath John, the Biology teacher, was strict with student behavior, and had been in the Marines before he entered the Christian Brothers at Glencoe, Missouri. He was a short man with blond hair and a baby face. You could tell that he had a muscular build, even though he was wearing the black cassock and white collar of the Christian Brothers. Also, he was the Frosh-Soph football coach. He didn't look mean, and his voice was soft, but I sensed that he could be hard when it came to discipline.

Pretty soon, Rich and Tom and I began to fool around both with our comments and with the procedures for the frog dissection. We even laughed a few times. Apparently, Brother Jarlath heard us while he was helping students at another table. One of the Biology Lab rules was—No fooling around or laughing or unnecessary conversation.

Brother Jarlath came to our table and caught Rich and Tom making jokes about the frogs. Then he looked at me and said, "Are you part of this nonsense, LeVoy?"

Something inside of me told me to say "No". Maybe it was the intense look that Brother was giving me. Or perhaps I was intimidated with the knowledge that he was an ex-Marine, a football coach, and could dish out the punishment. *My pause seemed interminable.* I looked at Rich, and then up to Brother who was now standing right next to me. "No, Brother," I heard myself meekly say.

"Now you two are going to see what happens in my Biology class when you fool around instead of work," said Brother Jarlath to Rich and Tom. He went over to the window behind our table, pulled down one of the large window shades and took out the thin, steel rod that provided the weight at the bottom for the large shade. He came back to our table carrying the four foot long rod.

"You students move away from this table," Brother barked, motioning to the other four at the table, including me. "Rich and Tom, come over here and bend over the table with your rear end up," he directed.

"WHACK" was the sound we all heard so clearly as Brother swung that steel rod like a baseball bat into Rich's extended rear end. There was a shocking cry of pain as Rich's legs and whole upper body jumped up from the floor.

"WHACK" again we heard as he hit Tom. Once more a terrible cry, with Tom's even louder as his body convulsed upward off of the table.

For the next two minutes, we saw and heard the "WHACKS" and miserable cries of pain as Brother Jarlath disciplined the two students. Each swing of the steel rod was the same, but cries were louder and the jumps higher. *The rest of the class was in shock.* Everyone had stopped dissecting their frogs, instead were witnessing the cold, painful punishment meted out by the Christian Brother.

I didn't know what to feel. Relieved because I hadn't been caught, having lied to avoid this terrible punishment. Or cowardly because I had not told the truth and taken my pain like my fellow classmates. Their painful cries kept ringing in my ears, numbing me. I did know, very clearly however, that I would never fool around in Biology again! I would be very wary in any encounter with Brother Jarlath John.

My grades continued to average "B" in my Sophomore and Junior years at "D". I was busy with the part-time job downtown at Chemists Supply, so the studying, homework, and test-taking were manageable. The basketball games at "D" were a lot of fun and excitement, just not as loud as SPA because the "D" Gym was huge. DeLaSalle's heavyweight & lightweight basketball teams were perennial winners in the Catholic League, primarily due to the excellent recruiting and coaching by Eddie Riska. I had a chance one afternoon to see part of his training. As I was walking thru the Gym on my way out, here were all the members of the heavyweight team running up and down the Gym steps, sweating those vertical laps.

It was great to have Frank Mannott, the varsity football coach, for my teacher in Sociology. I didn't like this subject, had a lot of trouble understanding what it was all about. Most of the class felt the same way. Sociology was too theoretical for us "D" boys.

Anyway, we could avoid "Soc" instruction on Mondays and Fridays during the football season. On Monday, a designated student would ask Coach Mannott about a play that the "D" quarterback called in the fourth quarter of last Saturday's game. Pretty soon the Coach was not only telling us that *he* called the play, but also diagramming it on the chalkboard for us. Forgotten was the principle of human group behavior he had written on the board to start the class!

Then on Fridays, we would get a scouting report on St.Rita's football team, or the annual champion, Mt.Carmel, or whomever "D" had on the schedule for the weekend game. It really was great to have the Coach as our teacher. We muddled thru Sociology, but became experts in football strategy.

During each Springtime, I would feel sad though when I heard the announcement of tryouts for the baseball team. I wanted so much to get my glove, crank up my arm, and go out for the team. I'd always glance at the practice field, imagining myself playing there in April and May. But, I knew that I couldn't put on the spikes because of my job downtown each afternoon, earning tuition for a Catholic education. The dream I had to play second base for the White Sox was fading. *Would I ever be a ballplayer?*

The first time I went to Wood Shop class in my Junior year at "D", I was surprised how far it was from the Main Building on 35th St. The Wood and Metal Shops were in a small, single-story building near 34th St., in the middle of an intramural field and the practice football field. The walk over was almost a block long. Students were allowed a little longer time between classes to get there.

Each student had a work area in the Wood Shop on a large work table that also included a large, sturdy vise. Four students could work at one table. The rest of the Shop contained an office for the teacher, Brother Justin, a large table saw—only to be used with Brother's direct assistance—band saw, wood lathes, planer, sanders, and a drill press. By far, the most interesting other space was the paint room. In here, students could shellac or varnish or paint their projects, then set the projects on racks for drying. The interest that we had as students was *not* in using this room to put finishes on our work, but to grab a puff of a cigarette during class, when Brother wasn't looking.

Brother Justin's office was at the near end of the shop, and the paint room was at the far end. Even though there were glass windows on the door of the paint room, students would sneak into there. It was relatively easy to get rid of the smoke from the cigarette because the paint room had a vent fan with a large hose attached. All we had to do was blow the smoke into the hose, turn on the vent fan, and pretend to shellac or varnish our projects.

The Shops Building also provided cover for the boys who *had* to smoke a cigarette after lunch. The Brothers couldn't see the far side of the building from the Main Building on 35th, so quite a few students would innocently wander out there after lunch, and light up. My friend Gerry, leaning against the back wall of the Shops Building each day, used to take his first drag from the cigarette, inhale, blow out, and smile. "There's nothing tastes better than a cigarette after a hot lunch."

One day in Wood Shop, a bunch of us were standing around one of the work tables, sanding our projects. There were DeVallo, Roger, Gerry, Bob and myself. Unlike Biology, conversation was permitted by Brother Justin as we worked on our projects. Brother was newly assigned to "D" when we were Juniors, and he hadn't developed a hard-nosed approach to discipline, or decided that "no nonsense" was what he wanted in the Wood Shop. Besides, there was a lot of noise in the Shop as machines were running, students were pounding nails, or sanding wood, using handsaws, coping saws, or electric drills.

DeVallo was the target of much kidding by our class because he was a meek sort of guy with a very soft voice. Many of the "soon to be men" in our Junior Class used to razz DeVallo about getting his hands dirty, or hitting his finger with the hammer, or making other mistakes with the tools. He just didn't look like a Shop student. His personality and demeanor seemed more suited for hair dressing instead of wood working. He would shrug off our jibes or wave the back of his hand to us, or just be silent as we had a few laughs at his expense.

On this particular day in November, however, all of us, except Bob, were leaving DeVallo alone as we concentrated on the sanding of our projects. I was putting the finishing touches on the shadow box I had planned to give Mommy for our kitchen. A couple more swipes with the Fine sandpaper and it'd be ready for bright yellow paint in the Paint Room, and a Lucky Strike cigarette!

As usual, Bob was really being nasty toward DeVallo, casting questions about DeVallo's gender. I felt the sting in Bob's lousy remarks and told him at one point to leave DeVallo alone. I could hear a couple of "Yahs" of agreement from the guys at the table who felt that Bob had crossed the line between kidding and cruelty. But, Bob persisted with his insults as though our complaints only stirred him on.

The rest of us sensed, however, that the barbs were bothering DeVallo. As mild-mannered as he was, we could see him start to stiffen from the anger building inside him.

Finally, I had enough! I stopped sanding the shadow box and yelled across the worktable to Bob. "Why don't you leave DeVallo alone. He's heard enough from you today."

Everyone stopped working at the table, and looked at me. I stood there with the sandpaper in my right hand, staring at Bob.

He yelled back, "Don't tell me to stop talking about that sissy. If I wanna make fun of him, I will," as he gestured with his hand and sandpaper to me.

I don't know if it was the unspoken challenge from Bob that I couldn't stop him, or the fact that he was one of those guys I just didn't like because he was a loudmouth, or maybe it was his big nose and the fact that he was only two inches taller than me. *I felt brave.* Slowly, I put the sandpaper down on the table, walked around to where Bob was standing, and before he could move back, I cracked him in the face with a quick swing of my right hand.

The "CRACK" was loud and traveled thru the Shop, even with the noise from the students. Brother Justin looked up from his office area to see Bob holding his left cheek, redder than a tomato, and me standing in front of him. The other two guys at the table and DeVallo were staring at me in complete surprise. DeVallo was mutterin' something about, "You didn't have to do that."

Brother Justin came rushing over to our table. "What's going on here?"

Bob was too mad, and embarrassed, to say anything, so I answered Brother. "We had a disagreement and I hit him in the face."

Brother then took me into his office. I explained the reason for the disagreement with Bob, involving DeVallo. Brother understood all that but started to counsel me about fighting. He also told me that I would have to sit in "Jug" for a week, for fighting in school. Jug was detention after school. Brother H. Francis, the Assistant Principal and Disciplinarian took care of Jug students in the Library. Students who were tardy, or absent frequently, caught smoking, or worse (like me) ended the day under the watchful eyes of Brother H. Francis.

As I sat in the silent Library in one of the wooden chairs that afternoon, I was amazed at what I had done. Cracked a kid in the face for botherin' someone else. A kid that was bigger than me! Why did I do it? Did I feel sorry for DeVallo because he was being ridiculed by Bob? Was I identifying with the underdog, the one being picked on? Did Bob go way too far? Or was I just waiting for a chance to slap a guy that I had no respect for? *And since when did I become my brother's keeper?*

Perhaps what I did could not be understood or explained. *But I had an inner sense that it was right. Sitting in that silent room, a quiet satisfaction settled in me.* I had responded to a situation that was patently unjust. Bob's treatment of DeVallo was unfair, and had to be stopped.

*

Grandma Bosak, our own make-believe Grandma, and our landlord, got sick around Christmas, 1953. And, after a long illness, she passed away in the Spring of '54. Her daughters, Carrie and Bertha, came into Chicago for the wake and funeral. They also had to tend to Grandma's business affairs, one of which was the sale of the 2-story houses, front and rear on 28th Place.

My parents were very sad that Grandma was gone because she had been such a wonderful neighbor and landlord—she only knocked on the pipes occasionally when the kids above her were too loud.

Grandma recognized in 1940, when my mother and father moved into the second floor apartment that there would be noise with all the kids above her head—three already here, Mag, Patrick and I, and one on the way, Kate. She figured that it would be too hard to yell up to Mommy if the kids were noisy upstairs, especially in rainy weather or winter time, or call on the telephone, because we didn't have one! So she said that if she rapped on the kitchen sink pipes in her apartment, we would hear the rapping from our kitchen sink pipes, and that would be the warning signal that we were too noisy for her.

It is ironic that this communication system worked because in 1938, Mommy and Daddy moved into a first floor apartment at 3006 S. Normal Ave. They had Mag and Pat, and me on the way. Little did they know that the couple upstairs would have loud arguments regularly. The wife threw so many tantrums up above, that my parents referred to her as "the old battleax."

One evening in the spring of 1940, Mommy and Daddy and we three kids were sitting in the living room of the first floor apartment, when we started to hear the battleax ranting and raving at her husband, even jumping on the living room floor above. Suddenly, half the plaster in the ceiling of our parlor started to crack and fall down on us kids and Mommy and Daddy. That's when they started to look for another flat, definitely on the second floor.

Besides the grief of losing Grandma Bosak in 1954, we all wondered what would happen next. Would her daughters, Carrie & Bertha, keep the house and continue renting to us? This seemed unlikely because they were both married, with children, and lived in Arizona and Nevada, respectively. They wouldn't be interested in absentee ownership, even though my father was handy and had been maintaining the two buildings, front and back, for Grandma.

The more likely event would be that Grandma's daughters would sell the place. This caused more concern for Mommy and Daddy because they couldn't afford to buy it. Even though Jake and I were working part-time, and Mag was now finished with high school and working full-time at Woolworth's downtown, there didn't seem to be enough money to now pay a mortgage. So, the prospect of another family buying the place and asking us to move loomed large. Where could our family of six children get a place to rent at an affordable amount? We were happy here even though the six kids had to double up since there were only three bedrooms and one hide-a-bed in the living room.

But God heard our prayers, especially Mommy's as she read her holy cards each afternoon after the younger ones, Kate, Fred and Maureen had lunch and walked back to school. Carrie and Bertha met with Mommy and Daddy after Grandma's funeral and offered the two buildings to them for $4800. The daughters were very appreciative of all that the LeVoys had done to include Grandma in our family christenings, graduations, and holiday parties. We knew Grandma so well, we could imitate her Hungarian accent, "Yah, vy nah shure," when she needed only to say, "Yes." And the daughters were confident that the buildings were kept up by my father, and that Grandma was looked after by us since both of them lived quite a distance from Chicago.

"Where will we get $4800?" my mother asked my father as we sat around the kitchen table.

"I don't know," Daddy answered. "Maybe we can borrow it from your sister, Mary. She's got the big stock account. I really don't know if the bank will give us a loan because we don't have any credit."

Again, God answered. Aunt Mary came thru with a personal loan for the sale price of the buildings. And she only charged 4.5% interest for the loan. It was to be paid back over four years, with a monthly payment of $125. She never hesitated to help us with the loan, because the three sisters, my mother, Aunt Mary and Aunt Catherine had been close, since they had come to the States from Ireland in the '20s. Mary's stock account and savings could easily handle this loan to my parents.

But now, we had to meet to determine not only how to raise the mortgage payment each month, but also to get enough money to buy the materials needed to repair the foundation and remodel the front building in which we lived. There would be the rent from the new tenants on the first floor where Grandma had lived, as well as the rent from the tenants in the rear building, Andrew Kocet, Sophie and Sam Guistolise.

When it was all put on paper, we were still short of monthly income. So, Mommy said that the three of us, Mag, Jake and I would get a raise in our weekly Room & Board. Also, Kate would be working soon because she was just turning fourteen.

The raise in Room & Board didn't bother us because we were so happy to be able to keep "our home": didn't have to move somewhere else. Even if the space in the apartment was limited, and now we're getting into the teen years, needing more space for clothes and personal items, we still wanted so much to stay put on 28th Place.

The remodeling of our front building began in late April. We had to dig out the west wall of the basement first, because Albert Bosak, Grandma's late husband, had never finished the concrete foundation that he started in the early 1920's. Next we hired a company to come and straighten out the building because the western side was sinking due to the missing foundation. Then we formed up the western wall portion to be poured, called for the concrete truck, and wheeled the wet concrete down Miller's gangway next to our building, pouring it into the forms.

I enjoyed the challenge of wheelin' a full wheelbarrow of concrete from the truck, over the sidewalk, down the ramp, into the gangway, and then the satisfaction of dumping the load where my father showed me into the foundation forms. I'd get a feeling of accomplishment after every "run" of controlling the wheelbarrow, using the strength in my arms and legs to master the load and not spill any concrete. I'd be heady after every dump of concrete into those forms, turn right around and go back for another load. I was sixteen but handlin' the job like a man of twenty-six.

When the concrete in the foundation was set, and the forms removed, my father took the old cedar posts that had been "holding up" the west side of the building with only bricks below them, sawed off the rotten end and set them upright in between the new foundation and the end beam that ran the length of the house. Now the west side of the house was supported by a solid foundation. We could rest assured that the house wouldn't lean to the west anymore, or eventually collapse into Miller's house next door.

The jacks used to straighten the house were removed. We followed that with a complete dig-out of the basement dirt floor, then set up the forms for pouring a new concrete floor. After the floor drains were laid and tied into the main drain to the street, we were set for wheelin' concrete. Once more, I looked forward to the physical challenge of handlin' a wheelbarrow full of wet concrete. Daddy persuaded four of the Chi-Annies gang to help Jake and I wheel, because concrete on floors sets quickly. We had to get it off the truck fast so that the driver could move on to his next delivery. (And not charge overtime)

This time the route for wheelin' was more difficult. We had to fill the wheelbarrow at the truck, wheel across the eight ft. sidewalk, down the front stairs ramp to our little front yard, across ten feet of yard, thru a four and a half foot high opening in the front wall of our house, down another ramp to the basement floor, and finally across the dirt floor to the dump site. Daddy was busy "floating" the poured concrete with a long 2" x 4" homemade trowel.

Each trip was a challenge to see how close we could come to hitting our heads as we wheeled thru that short opening in the house. We'd get a cheer from Mommy and Mag when we made it safely to the basement. There was banter among us wheelers about "that near miss" and "Look at that sissy. He can't even wheel concrete without spilling it." The challenge turned to friendly competition. Who could keep all that wet concrete in his wheelbarrow?

Jake, however, didn't seem to get caught up in these macho movements as the rest of us. Instead he acted like a supervisor, just standing there as each guy would return to the truck to get another load.

The whole project of remodeling the front house involved not only a new foundation and basement floor, but also new windows, new siding, and a new roof. This was just the outside of the house. Once the building had been leveled off by the blocks and jacks, most of the old plaster in the second floor cracked. The upstairs living room and dining room would have to be gutted, and new plasterboard installed. And my father planned to take out the old-fashioned archway that was between the two rooms.

As it turned out, the exterior work was finished by August. Then my father told Jake and I that we would have to help "gut" the living room and dining room, and give him a hand with the archway, plasterboard, plastering, new trim, and painting. I looked forward to this work because I found it challenging both physically and mentally to move thru the remodeling: from design thru dust to development.

But Jake was of a completely opposite frame of mind. For the four years of high school, he had worked as an apprentice pharmacist at Goldman Pharmacy downtown, in the Stevens Bldg. at 31 N. State St. Ira and Libby Goldman owned the Pharmacy. They developed an affection for Jake, almost like the son they never had. Jake was tall, good-looking, out-going, and had the tight, curly orange-red hair the Goldmans really liked. They joked with my parents when they came for Jake's high school graduation in May of '54 that Jake definitely looked Jewish. "Our son the pharmacist."

The Goldmans were very instrumental in persuading Jake to apply for the Illinois School of Pharmacy program for the Fall of '54. Although he had done fairly well at "D" in his last two years, he had not taken the Chemistry and Physics and Math that would have given him a solid background for the Science courses he would have to take for a Pharmacy degree.

The Illinois School of Pharmacy was located at Navy Pier on Chicago's lakefront, next to downtown. Since it was a State of Illinois school, students with a high school diploma and an interest in pharmacy could enroll for one semester. That first semester was the determining factor as to whether a student could continue his studies, or be dropped because of poor grades. There was no second chance, or probation.

For Jake it was ideal to attend pharmacy classes in the morning and early afternoon and then hop a bus to Goldman Pharmacy to work the late afternoons and Saturdays. What wasn't ideal was at home in the evening as he tried to study for three or four hours, the time needed each night to prepare for the next day's classes, and for tests.

My father had begun the inside remodeling of our flat in September, working early evenings and his days off on Wednesdays and Thursdays. I had the time to devote each evening to help him with breaking the old, cracked plaster in our living and dining rooms, tearing out the wood lathe underneath that was nailed to the old, wall studs and carting the refuse to the backyard. My high school senior course work was not demanding.

For Jake it was the opposite! He didn't have the time each evening for remodeling when waiting on his desk was Chemistry. And, the only place available for him to study was at a small desk just inside Mommy and Daddy's bedroom, just off the kitchen. Since Daddy and I were tearing up the two front rooms, there was a bedsheet fastened to the doorway between the kitchen and dining room to keep the dust out of the kitchen. All of the other kids, Mag, Kate, Fred, Maureen and Mommy were stuck in the kitchen to do homework also, and listen to the radio.

Daddy insisted that Jake help him and I with the remodeling, even though he was in college and needed the time for study. Jake had to do his share of "eatin' dust" as the rehabbers call it. But eatin' dust was not Jake's problem. It was finding the quiet and time to do the course work for a tough, scientific curriculum at the School of Pharmacy.

The remodeling reached a critical stage when Daddy was ready to take out the old, archway frame between the dining and living rooms. He told Mommy that he wasn't sure if the whole ceiling would come crashing down on us when he cut the last stud for the partition wall. He advised her to get her Rosary, stand back, and start praying that nothing happened when he cut that last, vertical 2" x 4" stud that supported the partition.

I noticed a sly smile on his face, remembering what he had taught me about supporting walls in a house. If the wall ran parallel to the ceiling joists above it, it was *not* supporting those joists. But if the wall ran perpendicular, it certainly was a supporting wall. I kind of knew ahead of time what to expect from his final cut—nothing! The partition wall ran in the same direction as the ceiling joists.

But Mommy didn't know. She trusted him again, forgetting about his $50 bill story, but remembering the ceiling that came down on their heads when the old battleax was stomping above their flat on Normal Ave.

"Now Skeezix, as I cut this last stud at the bottom, if it binds in the wood, we're in trouble," Daddy said to Mommy as he started the cut. (He liked to call her Skeezix once in a while—a famous and lovable female comic strip character from the 20's and 30's.)

Jake and I were standing there in the torn-up rooms that now would become one big room, except for that solitary stud. Mommy was moving away from the area of his cut, still working the Rosary beads. Mag and Kate came in from the kitchen to announce that the dishes were done—Jake and I did get out of these every night now that we were doing the manly work of remodeling.

Half-way thru the cut, the hand saw started to bind, and even though my father put more pressure onto the saw strokes, it was becoming hopelessly bound in the stud. Daddy looked a little perplexed as he stood to survey the cut, the stud and the ceiling. So far, nothing had come down from that ceiling, and only the slightest creak from above had been heard.

I looked at Mommy and she seemed worried because Daddy was not smiling. He told Jake and I to get a couple of the old studs that had been cut from the wall and were lying in the living room. He laid one stud next to the half-cut stud and jammed the second stud up to the ceiling area next to the top of the half-cut stud. Slowly he hammered the bottom of the second stud into the stud lying on the floor, creating a brace for the area where the half-cut stud still stood. Pretty soon we could see the handsaw loosen in the half-cut stud.

Daddy finished the cut, and nothing happened! He loosened the brace he had just made, and nothing happened! The ceiling didn't collapse, nor did any plaster fall. Mommy and I were relieved. Daddy smiled. He then explained that the binding occurred because there was a little pressure on the last stud from above as the ceiling joist it was under had settled just enough. Our faith in father was restored.

The remodeling was finished just in time for Christmas. New windows, new walls, new door, window and baseboard trim, and one, big, open room for living and dining. The latest in home design! New carpeting was installed along with drapes. We were all so relieved that the big, dusty job had been completed. We had been living in dust since April when Mommy and Daddy—with Aunt Mary's money—had bought the two buildings at 469 West 28th Place. Happy Holidays were just ahead.

But Jake wasn't smiling or laughing "HO HO HO" at Christmas. The constant demands for his work time with Daddy and I, coupled with his poor study area with kitchen noise and limited time, were resulting in poor grades at the School of Pharmacy. He looked confused and resentful. This career in pharmacy meant so much to him—and to the Goldmans—that it seemed to be slipping away.

In January of '55 the bad news came. Jake could no longer continue at the School of Pharmacy for the second semester because his grades were not passing for the first semester. I felt bad for him, not only because I was beginning to think of college now that I was in my last semester of senior year, but more importantly because Jake really had a dream of working as a pharmacist. Now that dream had burst, not only for him, but also for the Goldmans.

*

The only information at "D" for Seniors interested in college was in a file drawer in the Library. The file contained catalogues from various Midwest Catholic colleges like St. Joseph's in Renssalear, Indiana—where the Chicago Bears trained every summer—College of St. Thomas in St.Paul, Minnesota as well as DePaul and Loyola in Chicago.

I had no idea what I wanted to study, although Accounting caught my eye in the St.Joseph's catalogue, and Pre-Engineering at St.Thomas. I had heard that Civil Engineering was an exciting field, with lots of travel and big projects. What I did have a good idea about was going away from home to study. After the experience Jake had at home with study place and time, I knew that I would be better off at a college dorm. Plus, I could feel like a real college student if I lived on campus; write letters home, go to Saturday football games, and drink beer. No one in my father's or mother's family, as far as I knew, had gone away to college, except my cousin, Father Joe LeVoy, who was in the seminary at Mundelein, Illinois until his ordination in May of '54. I definitely wanted to be "Joe College."

Brother H. Conrad, my religion teacher in Senior year at "D", tried to interest me in Christian Brothers College in Memphis, Tennessee. This was a new college that the Christian Brothers had built to go along with their high schools. Since I was doing well in his Religion class, and I was on the quiet side, Brother Conrad had approached me about becoming a Christian Brother. He said that I could finish at DeLaSalle, spend some time in the seminary at Glencoe, Missouri, and even study at Christian Brothers College for my degree. He confided to me that the Brothers were always recruiting young men who seemed to have the right orientation to God, wanting to serve others by teaching.

I listened and thought about Brother Conrad's inquiry. I tried to imagine myself as a Christian Brother, living a religious life in a community of men, and teaching at a Brother's high school, like DeLaSalle or St.Pat's. He told me that I wouldn't have to worry about money anymore because I would be part of a religious order of Brothers.

But the road to religious life was still not in my view or thoughts. I really didn't have a picture of where I was going, or what my career would be. I liked a whole lot of areas—Accounting, Mathematics, Construction, Engineering—and of course, baseball. I still had the deep desire to play ball, even though the reality of a career was fading because I couldn't play ball in high school due to the part-time job to pay tuition. Maybe I could play in college!

And then there was Lucy. I thought about her quite a bit after all that dancing and walk home from All Saints Teen Dance in April, that Saturday night. I called to talk to her on Sunday, and we agreed to meet at the Wallace Show that night at seven. The movie that was showing was not important, but seeing her was. And, I kept it quiet from my parents, Mag and Jake included.

We began to date regularly, and soon I was meeting her parents and older sisters and brother. I got a good feeling from meeting her mother and older, married sister, and in fact knew her other sister Theresa, because one of the guys in the neighborhood was dating her at the time.

I wasn't quite sure though how Lucy's father received me. He seemed brusque when I went to pick her up for a date. One time in their kitchen, before Lucy and I left for the evening, he asked me what would happen to Lucy when I went away to college. "What about her? What's she going to do if you're away at college?" he blurted out to me. The tone of his questions and the way he seemed to demand an answer for these ridiculous questions flustered me. I didn't know how to answer questions that seemed foolish or unanswerable, especially since I liked her so much.

In the past, whenever I had encountered someone who badgered me with a stupid question, I would most likely give a stupid answer instead of being diplomatic. Because of my immaturity, I couldn't imagine that the best way to handle an awkward situation is to be pleasant and try, somehow, to give a reasonable answer.

But no, I didn't have any finesse with Lucy's father. My answer was just as ridiculous as his questions and only angered him further. I was embarrassed with the negative attention I was getting in her kitchen because even Lucy and her mother responded poorly to my awful answer.

Lucy and I did have moments to ourselves on the next door neighbor's front porch. There was a concrete wall about three feet high that we used to sit on and talk about neighborhood gossip, our future plans for school, and romance. It was great to hold her and smell the freshness of her hair in my face, having my arms around her as she snuggled closely to me. Fortunately, her father worked as a bartender and was away from home in the evenings. So he couldn't yell at me for holding her.

In early May, the All Saints Teen Club held another dance. Lucy and I were excited to go because we really liked to dance, especially the jitterbug. I picked her up at 7 PM. Again, her mother reminded us of her 10:30 curfew. The Spring weather was still cool so we both wore jackets. She smelled so sweet as I caught the scent of her perfume while we walked hand-in-hand down 32nd to Lowe Ave. *And I just loved the light, pink lipstick she wore. Just enough on her small, soft lips!*

The music was great, with another band from the neighborhood playing. We saw friends, danced fast, had soda, danced cheek-to-cheek and enjoyed the evening. By now, most of the guys and girls who knew Lucy and I were aware that we were dating. This included my brother Jake. He didn't say anything to my folks, however, as far as I knew.

The walk home after the dance was another Spring stroll. The trees were now in full bloom, the air was dry, and there was a slight breeze as we walked down the 3100 block of Union Ave. to our favorite spot: the three-story building that was shaded from the street light by a huge, maple tree. What an ideal night to lean against the railing, hold each other, and kiss!

After a few minutes of intimacy, Lucy broke the silence. She asked me about the girl at the dance that I was talking to for a few minutes. I told her the girl was a friend I had met in my Junior year when I started to go to the dances at All Saints. Lucy asked more about the girl, slowly becoming testy with me as my answers didn't seem to satisfy her. I assured her there was nothing between this girl and me, but pretty soon Lucy was pouting, telling me that I didn't care for her, and liked the other girl more. One cold remark led to a harsher one. Soon she was breaking away from me, announcing "I'm walking home by myself."

Lucy stood defiantly on the sidewalk six feet in front of me. I was still leaning against the railing of the three-story building. By this time, I was starting to get a little upset with her performance. Something inside of me said, "Call her bluff."

I found myself responding negatively to her. "Go ahead. Walk home by yourself," I said to her as I kept leaning against that railing, shrugging my shoulders with an "I don't care" attitude. Then I looked away from her for a moment to the street.

Lucy hesitated as though she was not sure what to do. She had challenged me with her "I'm walking home by myself," and I told her "Go ahead," in defiance. We stared at each other like our whole relationship was on the line, and neither one was willing or knew how to back off that imaginary line we had drawn in the sidewalk. Or better yet cross the line to each other.

She turned and started walking slowly down the sidewalk to 32nd. It wasn't a determined walk like someone trying to get somewhere, just a meandering in the semi-darkness.

I followed her with my eyes as I stood up from the railing. "She'll stop and come back," I said to myself, with bravado. "She won't walk home by herself."

But she kept on walking and made it to the corner. I expected her now to stop and turn to look in my direction, although she couldn't see me due to the shade from the maple tree. I could see her under the street light at the corner.

She kept on walking down 32nd in the direction of her house. She was out of sight almost immediately. I stood under that tree, half-gloating because I didn't give in to her pout, and half-scared because I might have made a foolish mistake with the one girl I really cared for.

The walk home to my house was heavy with thought. "Did I do the right thing?" "Did my pride get in the way of walking her home?" I kept remembering the phrase I had recently read in a historical novel. "He had won the battle, but lost the war."

*

"Ev'rybody works tonite. 12:00 Start." The stocky foreman yelled to the freight dock hands below, as he stood on the top stairs leading to the freight office. There was a happy buzz to the throng below as they were ready to punch out from a night's work.

"Well, it looks like an few extra bucks fer ye, kid," John Hennigan said to me in his brogue. He poked me in the ribs and grinned widely.

"Yah! I'm sure to make it to college with all this overtime, John," I answered, patting him on his broad shoulders.

I grabbed my time card and punched out from my job as a "Caller" at the Acme Fast Freight terminal of the Wabash Railroad that was located at 14th and Plymouth Court, near downtown Chicago. My shift was from 1:00 AM to 9:30 AM each night—or was it early morning. The 12:00 Start meant midnight, and one more hour of overtime.

My father worked here as a "Checker". He had used a little influence to get me hired in August after graduating from DeLaSalle and leaving my part-time job at Chemists Supply downtown. He was reluctant to bring me to the freight docks after high school because of the hard, physical work, and the foul language of the men working there, as well as the drinking. But most importantly he was concerned that I might prove to be an embarrassment to him among his colleagues because I was just a kid.

I was 17 ½ years old, 5'9" tall, and weighed only 160lbs. Handling freight was considered men's work because some cartons weighed as much as 80 lbs. Could I pick up that freight and move it, or stack it? And, did I have the stamina to work outside for eight hours or more in freezing cold or 90 degree heat? Get up from sleep at 11:00 PM, and go to work all night while everyone else in the world was in bed?

Mommy didn't like it either, especially because of the kind of men who worked on the Wabash Railroad, and how much they drank. She reminded me of Uncle Domnick and his "visits", and how Uncle Packy—who worked at the docks before my father in the '30's and had gotten my father on the Wabash—had all kinds of trouble with the bottle before he took the Pledge.

I told my folks that my plan was to work for a year, saving enough money to go to college, maybe at College of St. Thomas in St.Paul. I finally settled on Pre-Engineering for a major field of study. I was used to working since fifth grade, used to the Chicago weather from deliverin' papers, and had developed a willingness to handle freight and "get my hands dirty" by helping Daddy with the remodeling of our home, wheelin' concrete and "eatin' dust."

I didn't drink whiskey like my mother was concerned about, only occasionally having some beer, usually with my father on the porch during the hot, summer nights. The foul language from the dock workers would not be embarrassing to me because I already knew every curse word in English, some in Italian, and one in Spanish after growing up in Bridgeport and hanging with the Chi-Annies. No one had to teach me the slang terms for different ethnic groups either because I already had learned the derogatory words for the Irish, German, Jewish, Polish, Negro, and Mexican people—my father himself had unintentionally taught me quite a few nasty names while he watched the Friday night boxing matches on TV, or spoke about public figures that he didn't like.

The bus ride to the freight docks was a short one from 29th and Wallace to State St and Roosevelt Road. I always felt odd being the only one waiting on the corner at 11:30 at night for the bus. Older guys from the neighborhood would drive by in their cars on the way home from a date or from drinking with the boys. Here am I, going to work: they're going to bed. I felt all the more lonely as the weather turned colder in October and November. I'd be stompin' my feet, shiverin', waitin' for that bus, alone on the corner.

The 200 feet walk from Roosevelt Road and State St. to the docks, after I got off the bus, was scary because I had to walk about ½ block under the dark overpass that was really Roosevelt Road. There were no lights under the overpass, just street lights from State St. *I'd always imagine someone waiting behind a concrete support, ready to jump out and demand my money or my life.* And would you believe that the Chicago Police headquarters was only a block away at 11th and State!

I started as a "Trucker" in John Steed's gang. His gang was made up of a Checker (John), a Caller, and three Truckers. Our job was to take the freight off of a boxcar and move it to local trailers that would deliver it to Chicago destinations, or move it to spots on the floor of the freight house, or to another boxcar that was on the tracks next to the dock.

The Checker was the most experienced freight handler. He had all of the freight bills and check-off lists. When the Caller started taking down boxes from the boxcar, he would call out the Acme #, the destination, and the number of cartons he would be putting onto the Trucker's two-wheel truck. The Checker would then tell the Caller the location in the freight house, and the Caller would mark this on the boxes in black crayon, and finally tell the Trucker. Then the Trucker would wheel the two or three or whatever number of boxes he had on his two-wheeler to the spot on the docks.

Very soon, I discovered that "Truckin'" was not for me. I didn't mind the walking, but I kept falling asleep with the early morning work schedule. One time I fell asleep while walking and almost tumbled off the 4 ft. dock as I was pushing my two-wheel truck. And, as the winter started to come, I couldn't seem to keep warm, walking around the cold, damp freight floor, absorbing the icy breezes from the open dock doors. Long underwear, double socks, and good gloves didn't seem to help. My body was freezin'.

So, I asked some of the Checkers if they needed a Caller. The Caller stayed in the boxcar all of the time, unloading freight. He never had trouble with sleep walking, and there was always the heat from the lantern to warm up his hands and face. Besides, the Checkers were always looking for men who could read the labels and Acme #'s on the cartons because some of the truckers couldn't read too well.

"Well now kid, do ye think ye can handle those big cartons and break down the loads?" John Hennigan challenged me after I asked him if he needed a Caller one cold, November night. "Ye'll be handlin' ev'ry bit uv a hunnert tausen pound uv freight. I wouldn't want ye to hurt yerself, bein' a young man, if ye know what I mean," he continued with a sly grin.

"I can handle the load, John. I'm used to hard work," I responded, looking forward to the challenge of my body against the multitude of boxes in the boxcar. I was confident I could move all that freight, and feel good about it. I had watched the other Callers operate as they were loading my two-wheeler, and I made mental notes of how they used leverage and sliding of the heavy cartons to get them onto the lip of a two-wheel truck. They didn't have to lift them! I relished the task of this manual labor.

John Hennigan and I worked together from November thru the Winter. He carried the long extension cord that we used to bring light into the boxcar at night. I had to open the boxcar door and set the heavy, wide metal plate that bridged the gap between the dock and the floor of the boxcar. Sometimes, there would be two or three boxcars in a row that were being unloaded, each having a metal plate for its entrance, bridging the gap between boxcars. We always knew when someone was coming into the boxcars by the "Bang" of the two-wheeler hitting the uneven metal plates.

As I expected, working as a Caller was good for me. I never had to worry about warmth during that winter because the physical effort of handling a hundred thousand pounds was a heater by itself. In fact, sometimes I had to take off the gloves and heavy outer jacket because I was so warm. *I always felt invigorated half-way thru the boxcar load as my body was so warm and alive, sweating thru undershirt and heavy work clothes.*

The only problem I had with the cold was my feet. They would always be cold from the time I left the house to catch the bus until an hour after I started working. Even though I'd wear two pairs of socks, and stamp my feet a lot, they still wouldn't warm up until the rest of my body started sweating. No matter what I did, those feet would get cold and be uncomfortable until my head, chest, arms and trunk was steaming. It was their independent message to me that they had a temperature of their own, and would only warm up after the furnace of my body started the blood boiling and circulating up and down.

It was such a good feeling at the end of a load to send the last piece of freight on its way. John would put his bills together to bring to the office after giving me a pat on the back. I'd stand at the open end of the boxcar, sneak a cigarette, and look at the stars in the western sky as they were fading into the eastern dawn. It was always quiet in Chicago at five in the morning, a kind of silence that's holding on until the sunrise brings the city noise.

Sure enough, my thoughts would slide slowly from the satisfaction of a job well done to the nagging reverie of Lucy. I didn't even have to try to remember her. She was there, right below my work and movements, just waiting for the peaceful moment to surface in my heart.

After the night when she walked home by herself, I called her from the usual phone booth at Warzynski's drugstore on 29ᵗʰ and Wallace. She wasn't home. I tried again the next night, and the same answer. Finally, I did reach her at the end of the week. She was friendly: we talked, but she was not available for a date that weekend.

I continued to call her. Sometimes she was home: sometimes not. When we did talk, she had a lot to say about her family and friends, and other boys she had met. But still no dates with me!

It just didn't enter my thick head that maybe our relationship was over. I insisted on calling her thru the Summer and Fall, consistently trudging to the drugstore, waiting my turn for a phone booth. The response was always the same. She was friendly and informative. I'd tell her about my work on the Wabash, and plans for college. She'd talk about school. *It wasn't going anywhere for me, but I couldn't face that, accept it, move on from her. I liked her too much!*

The male ethic I had learned growing up in the late '40's and early '50's was to be the "strong, silent type." Keep your troubles to yourself, suffer in silence, and do your job. Don't bore people with complaining about this one or that one in your life. See how Joe DiMaggio runs out to center field every day and shags those fly balls and line drives, even though he has a chronic sore heel. And watch how Alan Ladd keeps riding even though his love is back at the farm and he hears her son calling him, "Shane, come back. Come back, Shane."

So I kept it all to myself about Lucy!

The work schedule at the freight dock turned my life upside down. Not only was I waking when most people were going to sleep, but I also had the opportunity to work seven days a week, 2 full nights of overtime. We consistently were told, "Everybody works tonight. 12:00 Start." I needed the overtime so that I could save enough money for college tuition and Room & Board.

There were some paychecks where I actually made more money than my father because of all that overtime. And he was a Checker! On the job for over 20 years! While he was happy that I had made the adjustment to freight handling, and was making good money with all the overtime, it hurt his pride that I brought home a check bigger than his. I could tell by his silence that it bothered him.

My social life however was non-existent. I'd come home from the docks around 9:30 AM, eat a little, shower and go to bed, hardly saying anything to my mother because I was so tired. Even though I met the physical challenge of work nightly, my body felt it. I never could get a full, restful "day's" sleep because my body couldn't adjust to day sleeping. I tried to eat supper with the family and then go out to see the gang, but then I knew at 10:30 PM I would have to come home and dress for work. I'd be out on the street by 11:30PM, waiting for that bus to take me to the docks.

Finally, in early April of '56, after working seven months on the night shift, at one point 28 days in a row without an Off day, I had a chance to work days, like my father. The hours were from 8AM to 4:30PM with Monday and Tuesday off, less overtime, and no early starts. I was so happy that now I could live a somewhat normal life, and work in daylight. I didn't mind the drop in my paycheck. I could even drive to work with my father instead of waiting for that old bus.

There were more characters working days than nights. It always seemed as though the men on nights were like zombies, just going thru the paces, trying to stay awake, and warm. It was like they were leading a half-life, all work but no normality. On the day shift, I soon discovered there was a lot of kidding, some mischief, and a whole bunch of smoking, drinking, ridicule and horseplay. What a difference the day makes!

One Mexican trucker found out that an Irish Trucker had been confined to a mental institution in his young adult days. Every time Pancho would see Lawrence across the dock moving some freight on his two-wheeler, he'd yell to him, "Lemme out. Lemme outta here," acting like he was Lawrence in a straight jacket.

But Lawrence would come right back. "Pancho. The Feds are looking for you, you wetback. You gotta swim that river back to May-he-co. Ad-ee-os Pancho."

There was Muletrain, a hulk of a man, standing 6'2" tall, weighing 263 lbs., wearing the same black clothes he wore when he started on the docks eight years ago. He also "wore" a constant mouthful of Copenhagen that would move around his mouth when he talked, sometimes drooling down the side of his left cheek. At lunch, he would take out a grocery bag full of sandwiches—try ten—and proceed to eat them, with some of the Copenhagen still in his mouth. Ickkk! No wonder no one wanted him to sit at their table for lunch.

A Checker named Ray stopped each morning on the way to work for three bottles of 16 oz. Pepsi. During the day, while he was sitting on a carton in the boxcar taking the Calls from his freight Caller, he would drink some of the Pepsi from a bottle, and then secretly add a little Jim Beam whiskey to the Pepsi. This would go on all day long: drinking some Pepsi, secretly adding the Beam to top off the bottle. But no one was supposed to know. To the guys and foremen—Ray thought—he was only drinking Pepsi.

Smoking was forbidden either on the dock or in a trailer or in the boxcars. Those guys with the "habit" had to walk off the dock during their break or lunchtime to smoke. I was Calling for my father soon after I switched to days. His regular Caller, Sergio Papini, was taking some vacation time. My father needed a cigarette—he really didn't smoke cigarettes, he devoured Camels, the strongest American cigarette on the market. He took deep, prolonged drags from the Camel that made me wince for my lungs and want to cough, and I wasn't the smoker.

As I was moving cartons in the boxcar, Daddy was sitting on another carton by one of the open doors, so that he could get the fresh Spring air, and also blow out the cigarette smoke when he would sneak a smoke. As he lit one of his Camels that day, after pounding one end of it on his metal Zippo lighter to pack down the loose tobacco, he could hear one of the foremen, Reggie, coming closer to the boxcar.

So my father cupped the cigarette with his right hand and let the hand dangle outside the open boxcar door. As soon as Reggie came in, he knew my father was smoking because he could see the faint little curls of smoke outside the door, behind my Dad. He didn't yell at my father though. After we both said "Good Morning" to Reggie, and he returned the greeting, we figured that he would look over the boxcar load, and move on to the next boxcar. That was the usual foreman visit to each load. But since he knew that my father was smoking, Reggie decided to stay and talk a little.

"How are the kids, Pat? Is your bowling average going up? Boy, this weather is nice! Do you think the Sox will go all the way this year?" Reggie kept asking the questions, and getting briefer and briefer answers from my Dad.

By this time, the cigarette was starting to get close to my father's thumb and index finger. It was also heating his right hand as it continued to dangle "out of sight." Daddy started to move uncomfortably on his carton, showing some pain on his face from the hot cigarette burning his hand and fingers. Finally, in desperation, he let the butt drop to the ground outside the boxcar, and brought his right hand slowly around to his lap to rub the burns.

When Reggie saw the right hand without the cigarette, he smiled at my father and me, and said, "Everything looks good here. Good Work!" and walked out of the boxcar.

"Son of a bitch," I could hear my father mutter under his breath. He was massaging his burnt fingers and palm. I couldn't help but smile slightly as I turned back to the freight, not only because Daddy got "burned" by the foreman for smoking, but also that he didn't want to look bad in front of me and hear him swearing because of his pain.

*

"Well now, kiddo. I'll be lookin' for an Announcer t'day. Do ye want to work wit' me gang?" Mike Judge said to me one morning as the day shift was assembling at the time clock. We were waiting for the Checkers to get their loads upstairs in the freight office. He gave me a straight left jab to my right shoulder as he asked me, bobbing slightly with his shoulders and head, and making somewhat of a grunting sound.

I had heard about Mike from my father and the other guys on both the night and day shifts. He was from Ireland and had come over to the States in the 20's like a whole lot of Irish we knew, my Mother included. He got into boxing because he was young and tough and had the perfect build—short, compact body with big shoulders, strong arms, thin waist and a jaw that could take a jolt. But most of all, Mike liked to punch, to hit people.

Part of the legend was that Mike had some fights as a pro, and did fairly well. He even picked up a nickname, "The Babe", as he fought in the middleweight division, 148 to 160 lbs.

But like a lot of fighters, The Babe stayed in the ring too long. Not only was he hard to knock out, so he took a lot of punishment from the better boxers, he also continued fightin' when most guys would hang up the gloves for fear of permanent brain damage. Mike didn't know when to stop. His fists kept comin' even though he was in his late thirties.

As I looked into The Babe's face after he asked me to "Call" for him that morning, and after I was jolted by his firm left jab to my shoulder, I saw a man whose eyes were saying that something was missing, left behind in the ring a long time ago. His head was bobbing slightly again, and the lower false teeth were moving around his mouth with his tongue like a boxer's mouthpiece. Alternately, he'd show the yellow lozenge that he perpetually would suck on. There was the slightly, audible grunting of a person who was uncomfortable with the wait for a response, and besides moving, had to be making sounds.

I felt some pity for Mike that morning, but said, "Sure Mike, I'll do the Calling for you today." I slapped his right arm with my left hand in a sign of affection and agreement. Then all hell broke loose!

Mike backed up from my friendly slap, dropped the clipboard and freight bills on the cement floor, and yelled at me, "C'mon now, put 'em up. Put up yer dukes and we'll see what'cha got." He continued to back up from me with his hands cocked, now moving around in a semicircle like a fighter in the center of the ring.

I was totally flabbergasted at Mike's actions. I could hear some of the other guys yelling, "Go ahead Mike. Git 'em. Show the kid what'cha got." They were making a circle for The Babe to dance and shadow box and grunt on the dock floor.

I just stood there, not catching on right away. But then somebody snuck behind Mike and bumped into him on purpose. The Babe turned quickly on one leg, continued his stance and dance and left hand jabbin' the air toward the new tormentor.

Pretty soon the whole crowd of men were laughing and yelling, "Knock 'im out. Knock 'im out."

The new opponent would dance around, making believe he was going to punch Mike. But Mike was always the aggressor, stalking the guy to get in a shot with his left.

It finally dawned on me as I saw all of this horseplay—and no one getting hit—that this was a big joke. The Babe was both the jokester and the butt of the joke. Bump into him, or make like you're going to punch him, and quickly Mike would be taking a boxing stance, urging you to face up to him like a man, warning you that he had "sudden death" in his left jab. It was true male entertainment, and I, the kiddo, was initiated into the ring. Ding Ding! End of Round One!

I continued to "Announce" for Mike each day after that. Every day was a new adventure with him in the boxcar. He really needed someone who could read well to help him with the checking of freight as I called out each lot of boxes. Occasionally he couldn't find the lot on his set of bills, so I'd stop and find it for him. And then, just to show he was in charge, he'd take the pencil and wet the lead with his tongue, mark the bill with the correct amount of strokes for the number of boxes, and then, grunt some phrase.

After a couple of months, the men and bosses got used to me and The Babe working together. I was known as The Babe's Caller, the Kiddo. We'd get "visitors" all the time to the boxcar we were working in that day. Once, my father came in and asked The Babe how I was doing as a Caller. We were standing together by the door, and The Babe gave me his little jab to the chest as he said, "Ye've a fine lad there, Paddy. I'll not be needin' any help with him doin' the announcing."

I feinted with my left shoulder as though I was goin' to punch Mike. He backed away with his fists up, ready to start dancin'. The three of us started laughing simultaneously, realizing the lightness of the moment, and the good feelings we shared.

All of the visitors came into the boxcar for one reason; to get The Babe to put up his fists, grunt and dance around like a prizefighter. It was live, boxcar theatre! He surely did love to step around with his "dukes" up in the air in front of him. No one ever hit Mike, or if they did, it was a tap. Once in a while, Mike would forget and thrust that left jab like he meant it. And he'd usually connect, like the day he floored the DP trucker from Lithuania with a solid punch to the guy's heart. This guy made the mistake of getting in too close to Mike.

One hot afternoon in the middle of July, Mike and I were working on a load in the third boxcar in a line, with the second car still being unloaded by another gang, and the first car by the dock already unloaded. It was humid too, and everyone was sweating. The day was typical of the hot, steamy summer days in Chicago. Not a breeze in sight!

In walked John, the General Foreman, and Bill, one of the Foremen, to the car we were unloading. John nodded at me as I turned around from breaking out a big carton from the stack midway down one half of the boxcar. He then went to Mike who was standing against the wall on the other half, right by the open door, holding his clipboard and bills.

"How ya doin', Babe," John said slowly to Mike in a voice that was full of foreboding. Then John hit Mike in the right shoulder with a medium, hard right cross punch. I had never seen any of the Foremen "play" with Mike, so this seemed strange. Why is John hitting The Babe, and so hard?

Mike couldn't back up because he was already against the wall. His reactions were hesitant, as though he wasn't sure what to do since this was the General Foreman hittin' him. He just grunted and shifted his weight from one foot to the other.

"Is it too hot for you?" John asked, and again punched Mike in the right arm and shoulder, but this time much harder. Bill winced, looked down at his feet like he didn't want to see this. John's face had a determined look to go with his calculating voice.

I could hear a slightly audible whimper from Mike's mouth as the pain in his shoulder and arm was recorded in his brain. His breathing became deeper, pronounced. His eyes seemed frantic as he was cornered against the wall of the boxcar by the General Foreman. He couldn't move away or strike back. Rage and frustration were beginning to erupt in Mike's body and face. Confusion, however, was in his eyes. He didn't know what to do!

"What's the matter, Babe," John asked in a sarcastic, mocking tone. He sensed the helplessness in Mike as he continued. John started to pull his right hand and arm back to cock them for another punch. His jaw was set, his face intent as he stared at his target, The Babe.

"Leave him alone, John," I heard myself say. I stood up straight from the carton on the floor I had been handling, and looked directly at the General Foreman. He and Bill turned their heads to me instantly, their faces showing surprise. "You're hurting him, John. Leave him alone," I said in a pleading voice.

After a long instant, John regained his composure and still looking at me, said, "This is none of yer biz'niss. Get back to work." Then he turned back to face Mike again.

Something clicked inside of me that hot afternoon when I heard John's "none of yer biz'niz" and saw his cold face. There would be no more pleading or doubt as to what I was prepared to do. Somehow I had crossed the line. There was no hesitation or turning back. I stared at John's profile and told him, "Mike Judge is my biz'niss," and took two steps toward him.

The General Foreman turned again to look at me. There was the ever so faint recognition in his face that I meant it, that I was for real, and that he'd be dealin' with me if he continued to punch Mike. I sensed a mixture of surprise, and then slow resignation in his face. I think he slowly realized what he was doing to The Babe.

Bill was clearly uncomfortable too, moving his head and body to respond to his inner tension, looking up to the ceiling, and out the door.

But The Babe was quiet as though he was holding his breath.

A Trucker hit the metal plate, "BANG", with his two-wheeler, coming thru the first boxcar to the second in the line. The confrontation on our boxcar stage was ending: the drama had been played. All that was needed was a silent exit to stage left. John turned abruptly around and walked out of the boxcar, with Bill at his heels.

The Babe came over to me and gave me his familiar left jab to my arm and shoulder. "Ye shouldn't uh dun it, kiddo. Ye can't be talkin' to the boss like that. Ye'll lose yer job."

I could tell that the left jab to my shoulder was Mike's "Thank You" to me for helping him, but he didn't know how to say it because he was a tough guy. A pat on the back, a tap in the chest, a wink or a smile is supposed to do it for a man. Mike still appeared confused by his own reaction to John's punches.

"Mike," I said, "you don't have to take that crap from him. You're not a punching bag." (I had seen too much of how the bullies of Bridgeport had punched on kids. And I had been punched on by my older brother).

On the drive home that afternoon, my father was all over me for challenging the General Foreman. "How in the hell can you stick up for Judge. John not only gave you a job, he also hired me to remodel his back porch on my days off," he yelled at me.

"John was hurting The Babe, and that's unfair." I stammered to my father. "I can't take that," I said softer but clearly while I was staring out the windshield.

The crudeness of John's punches stirred something in me. How could he do that to a fellow Mick? Had he no remembrance of injustice in Ireland? How the bloody English took it to the Irish for 700 years! *I could feel my blood course, as I saw again the pain and panic in Mike's eyes. I couldn't allow anyone, especially another Irishman to take advantage of his position to harm The Babe. Like my pat on Uncle Domnick's bald head ten years earlier, all the jabs and horseplay between The Babe and I had bonded me to him. No one was gonna hurt The Babe in my presence.*

*

I boarded The Milwaukee Road train at Union Station in the middle of September, 1956, headed for the College of St.Thomas. Daddy drove me to the Station with my luggage after I said good-bye to Mommy and the family at the house. I promised them to write often. It was somewhat strange going back to Union Station, my old hangout when I went to St.Patrick Academy as a Freshman in high school five years earlier. Now, instead of sitting around the old benches, watching the commuters and passengers, I *was* a passenger to a far off place called St.Paul, Minnesota.

Actually, I had already made one trip to the College in the winter of '55 to see what the school looked like. That was my first train trip ever. It didn't cost me much because as a Wabash Railroad employee, I was entitled to a 50% discount to ride another railroad's train.

For the September train ride, I sat in the car that was two car lengths behind the Dining Car. I had a window seat and watched as the train moved slowly thru the western Loop rail yards into the near North neighborhoods, headed to Milwaukee, the first big stop on the way to St.Paul.

There was a feeling of excitement in my mind and body because I was "going away to college." *I had a sense of adventure, a challenge to do something, be somewhere that was beyond Chicago, a far and different life from the freight docks.*

From my winter trip to St.Thomas, I remembered that the campus was very nice, and the scenery along the Mississippi River just west of the school quite dramatic with high bluffs overlooking the river. The surrounding neighborhood looked like a pleasant community with tree-lined parkways in the middle of the main street, Summit Ave. Only the "B" Barracks where I was scheduled to live had a worn, plain look on campus.

There was a sense of satisfaction within me, knowing I had worked on the docks for thirteen months after graduating from "D", sometimes for seven or fourteen or more days in a row. I had adjusted to the midnight shift, then the day shift, earning and saving over $1500 for school. I had overcome the cold weather in winter, the muggy heat in summer, and the strenuous tasks of handling heavy cartons. Just as important, I had fit in with the Wabash cast of characters who were playing out their lives on the dock stage each night and day.

It was hard to say "Goodbye" to the men I had admired while working the freight. But the most difficult farewell was with The Babe. I had grown attached to him while calling the freight in his boxcar loads, not only because he was entertaining and unique, but also because Mike was at the mercy of those who would take advantage of him.

I thought a lot about the incident with the General Foreman, wondering what was this determination in me that challenged John to leave Mike alone. Again it was almost as though there was a bond between Mike and I. And

John was violating it. *Was I the protector for The Babe? Was it the same as with DeVallo and Bob in the woodshop at "D"? Was there some sense of injustice that arose within me?*

I do know that after the confrontation, a couple of guys on the dock came to me and thanked me for sticking up for The Babe. They said that what I had done was right, that The Babe shouldn't be treated that way even though there was a lotta horseplay around him.

As the train reached the Chicago northern suburbs, I could see fields of open space, signs for housing developments, and roads with traffic. My mind went roaming, from farm fields to college campus to walking with Lucy. After a year of not seeing her, I still had thoughts about her. I had stopped calling in the Winter because there would be a conversation on the phone, but no commitments for a date. Lots of pleasant conversation, but no time together. Besides, my nights and days were all confused with the night shift at the Railroad.

That first night we met slipped back so easily to my mind. How we danced, so softly slow, and rockin' fast. I'd rerun the walk home, our conversation, the spring mist in the air and the stop under the maple tree. Seemingly to add to my loneliness, I continued to keep Lucy a secret from my parents. It would be even more awkward for me now to say I was pining for a girl they never met or knew I had dated. *I was confused and went on with this confusion, tucked away into my private world that no one got to see or hear.*

The screeching of iron brakes jolted me back to reality. I now saw the beginning of the southern Milwaukee suburbs. I had never been here before. The views of the neighborhoods and factories—don't they make a lot of beer in Milwaukee—were interesting. The city looked so much like Chicago, the neighborhoods I had just left.

After Milwaukee, the train headed west and north toward northwest Wisconsin and the Mississippi River. Pretty soon we were in dairyland. In the distance were large farms with frame houses, tall silos, and short, squat barns and milkhouses. Once more my mind drifted, first to what was coming with classes, homework, study, beer blasts and football games. And then it came to me that I would be on my own, away from home.

I'd get an edgy feeling again that I wasn't mature enough to go away to college. Maybe I wasn't old enough for this. No one in the family had any experience of leaving Chicago to study. *Would I act foolish, or show a lack of sophistication with coeds? Could I carry on conversation with a bunch of guys in the Barracks? Can a Kiddo from Bridgeport succeed outside the neighborhood?*

I vividly remember riding back to Chicago from St.Thomas after my winter visit to see the College. It was nighttime, just after dinner. Sitting in the window seat, I was watching the snow-covered fields whiz by. Every minute or so there would be a well-lit farmhouse in the distance, nestled alongside a country road. I would imagine the family in that house sitting around a heater or stove, reading or watching television. *As I peered thru my window at that home, I'd start to feel lonesome, wishing that I was there instead of rattling along the rails on this impersonal train. There seemed to be warmth coming from that farmhouse, drawing me to look even more intently and crane my neck as the house started to move out of my field of vision. My imagination continued, and I saw Ma and Pa sitting on the sofa, with a space for me.*

I didn't have a chance to be lonely, or nervous or pining during the first week at St.Thomas. There were tests to take, my "B" Barracks room to organize, meals in the cafeteria in Ireland Hall, class registration, books to buy, and finally classes. In between, and at night, I was occupied with strolls on campus and to the nearby stores in the community, fooling around with the combination of my Post Office box in the Student Union, smokers for Freshmen, a Variety Show, and a genuine college dance. Since St.Thomas was a men's College, the girls came from St.Catherine's College, the women's school a mile south of campus.

Each of us in B Barracks had our own room which measured 12' by 12'. Inside were a bed, desk, dresser, book case, and chair. The clothes closets were on each side of the door. They were open, with no doors. A built-in shelf was at the bottom of each closet about 24" high. The front panel below this shelf was painted plywood. I noticed the first day in the room that one of these closet shelves was loose. When I picked it up, I could see something shiny on the ground three feet below the Barracks floor. I found my new flashlight and shone down the opening. I could see hundreds of aluminum beer cans and vodka bottles strewn on the ground. Now where did all those come from?

The Barracks were built during the Second World War as housing for officer candidates in the Army Air Corp. This single-story building was very simply built with wood siding and double-hung windows. There were three wings of eight to ten rooms per wing, coming out as spokes from a central area of bathrooms and lounge, with a suite of rooms for the Barracks Dean.

One of the tricks we learned for entertainment was to crawl into a student's room thru the unlocked window from the outside yard. Then we'd push his desk against the door, the bed against the desk, the dresser next, and finally jam the chair between the bed and the far window wall. Obviously, we'd exit thru the same window.

When the unsuspecting student would return in the afternoon from classes, tired and ready to take a nap, or just relax, especially if he had an 8 AM lab, he'd put the key into the door lock, turn the key, and push. The lock opened but the door wouldn't move. He'd turn the key again, and push harder, but his door would not budge because the desk and other furniture were jammed against it.

The first student that was victimized was the big, loud-mouth kid from Texas whose father drove him to school on the first day in a shiny, new, baby-blue '56 Caddy convertible, tail fins and all. "Tex" kept pushing on his room door, complaining that "Nothin' works aroun' heah," and finally yelling for help.

Darryl, the Assistant Barracks Dean, came out of his room and immediately knew the cause of Tex's problem. He led Tex outside and around the yard to Tex's window and told him to look inside. "Holy Sheet," yelled Tex. "How'm I gunna git in theah?"

Darryl pointed to the window and said, "You're going to have to crawl in thru the window and undo the furniture to open the door."

You should have seen this big guy trying to squirm into the window from the yard. A classic scene from Winnie the Pooh!

We had plenty of occasions for drinking beer. Since Wisconsin had a drinking age of 18, we would head east of St.Paul every Friday night to the bars on the Wisconsin side of the border to enjoy some brew. We were able to drive these distances because three or four guys chipped in to buy an "old clunker" auto called a Nash. We pulled the back seats out, and put benches on both sides of the expanded rear seating area so more guys could ride. Sometimes on a Friday night trip to Hudson, Wisconsin, there would be ten thirsty students in the Nashmobile.

I wrote home every week and was honest to my folks and brothers and sisters about the school work and study. I took eight courses that first semester of college; English Composition, U.S.History, Elementary Algebra, Air Science, P.E., Introduction to Logic, General Physics, and of course, Catholic Theology. The Algebra and Physics were required because I had not taken them in high school at "D". And the Air Science was part of the Freshman requirement to be enrolled in Air Force R.O.T.C. Altogether, I had eighteen credit hours of classes.

Besides a uniform and cap, I received a pair—no, really two pairs—of black shoes from the Air Force for R.O.T.C. When I was measured by an Air Force personnel for shoes, he found that my left foot was size 11 E, but my right foot was 10 1/2 EE. He said that I had to be comfortable when marching, so he split two pairs of shoes insuring that each foot would be perfectly sized. I felt the difference right away while walking to my next class.

After a month of classes, I knew I would have trouble with Logic. No matter how hard I studied and read, I couldn't understand those syllogisms. Which came first, the Minor Premise or Major Premise?

"Everything that glistens is gold.
Uncle Domnick's head glistens.
Therefore, Uncle Domnick has a golden head."

Now that sounds like a perfect and logical Conclusion. But Uncle Domnick doesn't have a golden head!

"Tommies" was the nickname for the College of St.Thomas' sports teams. During the Fall of '56, the varsity football team developed into a powerhouse, going undefeated in the MIAC, the athletic conference for that area. I chose to get into the action by trying out for the Freshman team. I was still 5'9" and weighed 160lbs. The strength I developed from the docks, and my large hands led me to dream that I could make the team as an End. After all that Touch football on the street in front of my house on 28th Place with the Bears' football, I was sure that I could catch a pass and survive the tackle.

Daily calisthenics and drills left me pretty tired each afternoon on the football field. I thought that I was doing okay, but the coaches thought differently, cutting me after the first week. "You're too small for football," they told me.

For some reason it bothered me that I didn't make the team. I would lie in bed in the late afternoon, trying to take a nap before dinner, but listening to the yells and whistles from the practice field next to the Barracks. *I started to feel sorry for myself that I wasn't big enough to compete. Why wasn't I 6' tall and 180lbs? Then the loneliness would kick in, the thoughts of home, reveries of Lucy and feelings that I didn't belong here. Maybe I was too immature to "go away to college."*

I was also aware of the different upbringing between me and most of the guys at St.Thomas. They came from the suburbs of cities like Chicago, St.Louis or the Twin Cities. Or from smaller towns like Kankakee and Aurora in Illinois and St.Cloud in Minnesota. I sensed that the neighborhood I came from in Chicago couldn't command the same respect that Oak Park or River Forest would. There was the nagging feeling that I just didn't have enough social skills to relate well with the guys—or girls. I didn't know much about living away from home because I had never been away, either to summer camp, or Boy Scouts, or even a Church retreat.

"How come you let your father call you, Hughie Boy?" Pat Breen questioned me the next day when my parents left for Chicago, after visiting me on Parents' Weekend. He and I were standing in the Barracks hall in front of our doors, which were directly across from each other.

"What did you say, Pat?" I queried him

"Your father calls you Hughie Boy. Doesn't that bother you?" Pat added, in a somewhat incredulous voice, and then a smile.

"I guess I never paid attention to what he calls me. Hughie Boy? I never noticed."

What I had noticed all of my young life, from as early as five years old, was that very few people outside my family knew how to pronounce my name—or spell it.

"Hue, Hug, Huge, Huh, Hugo. Everything but my name, HUGH!" I would meet people in school, or neighbors, or fellow students who would look at my name in print and just butcher it, or refuse to even try to pronounce it, resorting to "Whatever". Even my mother—who also called me Hughie Boy—added some differences to the pronunciation because of her brogue. When I'd ask her to spell my name, she'd say; "HAYCH—U—G—HAYCH", instead of AYCH, which requires an aspirated sound. All the kids in the family—and me—would laugh at her Irish HAYCH.

I grew up thinking that I was the only Hugh in the world, and all my life I'll be meeting people who will have trouble pronouncing my name. I thought about using Edward, my middle name. That came from my mother's brother, Edward Flanagan. Early in life he had contracted tuberculosis in Ireland. He lingered with this illness for quite a while, with little hope of recovery. My mother told me that one fine day in 1916, Edward was lying in the "hag", a small bedroom cut into the side of the Irish cottage, next to the turf fireplace in the kitchen. The room is so small that only a bed could fit within its three walls. There is a small window on the outside wall that faces southwest.

The sun was shining so brightly that Edward could see it and feel its warmth. He also noticed the bright, blue sky with hardly a cloud. My mother had propped his head up in the bed so that he could enjoy the beautiful day through the window. He was much too weak to sit up in bed by himself. As he looked out that window with the light coming in, he turned back slightly to my mother and some of her brothers in the kitchen, and whispered, "Och. 'Tis a sight! Lovely! 'Tis a grand day to die!

Hugh is my name, however. I'll have to live with it. Actually, the name has much history in the LeVoy Family. There is my Uncle Hugh, nicknamed "Red" who is one of my father's older brothers. He worked as a marble setter in Chicago, claiming many of the downtown marble buildings as his skillful work. He was named after his father, Hugh James LeVoy, my grandfather. Grandpa Hugh was born in Chicago in 1879, and grew up on the near South Side at 31st and Halsted. Most of his life was spent laboring on new construction. Grandpa Hugh got his name from his mother Margaret's father, Hugh Campbell, in Canada.

One day I looked into the dictionary to see if my name Hugh was there. Sure enough, it was listed. And better yet, the entry said that "Hugh is an old Irish name, meaning 'fire'" Now that's a good reason to keep Hugh, even if I don't have bright, red hair.

Finally, at the age of nine, I found another Hugh in the world. I was following the 1947 World Series between the Yankees and the Dodgers in the *Herald-American* paper. Reading the reporter's account of the third game in Brooklyn, there it was, my name, in black and white on the front of the sports section. "Hugh Casey, Brooklyn's ace relief pitcher, came in to pitch in the top of the seventh inning with the Dodgers leading 9-8. He shut down the Yanks for 2 and 2/3 innings to preserve the victory."

Wow! I was so happy to know that I wasn't alone in the world. There was another Hugh. And he was a ballplayer. Now I could confidently move on, grow up, and be comfortable with my name and myself. I was not alone in the world.

Less than four years later, in July of 1951, my self-image suffered a jolt, however. I read in the newspaper that Hugh Casey took his own life, after leaving the major leagues in 1949. I was sad for him and his family, wondering what had happened to cause his suicide.

*

There were good times at St.Thomas that Fall and Winter of '56. Besides the beer trips to Wisconsin on Friday nights, and the panty raids at Augsburg and Macalester Colleges the night that the Tommies football team won the MIAC championship, there were dances and mixers with St.Catherine's, all night bull sessions in someone's room, and visits to the homes of some students that I got to know well.

Pat Breen invited me to spend a weekend at his home in Brainerd, Minnesota. His father was a John Deere tractor dealer in town, and the Breen Family had a very nice, modern home, with a formal dining room. I remember Pat telling me on the drive from St.Thomas to Brainard that there would be steak for dinner that night, something we never got in the cafeteria at Ireland Hall.

When we sat down at the Breen dining room table on Saturday night, I was a little nervous with the formal setting. Then the steak platter came around to me. I looked at these broiled, slightly charred, round pieces of meat with some surprise.

"Is there something wrong?" asked Mr.Breen who was waiting for the platter.

"I've never had this steak before," I quietly replied, taking one off of the platter and passing it to Mr.Breen.

"These are filet mignons from fine Minnesota cattle," Mr. Breen announced to me. "I hope that you like medium rare."

I surveyed the thick, round piece of meat on my plate, wondering to myself, "What's medium rare?"

One of the enjoyable parts of college life for me was the chance to read novels, strictly for the fun of it. There was so much required reading, note taking and study, that I hungered for the complete leisure of reading fiction with a strong plot just for enjoyment. I found *War and Peace* by Tolstoy in the College bookstore and settled in one night around 10 PM to start it. All I wanted to do is get a sense of the story before going to bed. Tomorrow was another full day of classes.

By midnight I was still up, working my way into the complexities of the plot. I already had the characters down, and the historical setting. I kept glancing at the clock, telling myself I'd stop at the end of the chapter, and go to bed. But I'd rationalize and say to myself that I "needed" this time to keep reading because the book was engrossing.

By 1 AM, it was time for another cup of tea. I turned on the hot plate and listened to the early morning sounds in the Barracks. There were none! I could hear a slight wind outside my window, blowing from the South across the practice field. I wondered if anyone else was up this late—probably Rafael Ortiz, the hombre from San Juan, Puerto Rico. He was constantly complaining that he had to work past midnight to understand Calculus.

I glanced out of my window and could see Rafael's lights were still on. Although, I could see a few other lights on. The word in the lounge was that some guys just had to sleep with a light on.

Anyway, I continued to indulge myself with this classic novel about Russian nobility. I couldn't put it on the shelf for another time. I had to read it through to the end, absorbing, digesting, and finally sitting back in the silence to appreciate this great literature.

My clock said 4:15 AM when I finished the last page. I just sat in my chair, numb, rubbing my eyes, realizing that I had read a major novel in one night. I thought about the characters, the conflict, the tragedy, and had a good but tired feeling from such sustained reading. The reading was a totally personal challenge between me and this book. *I sat in satisfaction of my accomplishment. Finally, I laughed, realizing that if I flunked my courses because I stayed up all night to read this novel, and was kicked out of college, I could always tell my kids, "Well. I didn't graduate, but I did read* War and Peace *in one night."*

After much effort and study and help from the professor, I salvaged a C in Logic for the semester. The other courses were C's except for a B in English Composition—I did enjoy writing—and a B in Physics. I was passing for the semester. No academic probation!

The money I had saved was getting low, but I would have enough to pay tuition and Room & Board for the Spring semester. After that, I couldn't say.

Tuition for the year was $500. Room was $185, and Board came to $440 for both semesters. With fees and book bills, I had about $75 left for expenses until May. The savings would be gone by then. *All of that work on the docks for one year of college!*

The second semester began quietly in the middle of January. I had a full load of classes again, 17 credit hours. No more Logic, but a harder Algebra class. I was tired from the first semester and feeling the strain of the cold, snowy Minnesota winter. Except for an occasional Tommies basketball game, life was pretty much classes, study, and tests, with eating and sleeping in-between. One of the guys mentioned a contagious disease going around called "Cabin Fever."

In the middle of March, a Barracks meeting was called for 7 PM in the lounge. "As of tonight, no one can get a can of Coke from the machine in the lounge after 10 PM. The machine makes too much noise when it delivers a can down the chute and hits the bottom. And there's noise from students walking down to get the Coke and then back to their rooms. All of this noise keeps people up at night." Darryl Merkens, the Assistant to the Barracks Dean, Dr. Ivery, was telling all of us in the Barracks what he and the Dean had decided.

There were moans and groans from the guys, with a few "That's unfair. It's our Coke machine," and "We don't mind the noise. We need our Coke at night." Everyone knew the real culprit in this decision, and he wasn't at the meeting. Dr. Ivery spent very little time in the Barracks, except for sleeping and changing clothes—it was rumored that he had a ladyfriend. Significantly, the Coke machine was on the same wall in the lounge that was the other side of his bedroom wall in his suite. He couldn't sleep, we surmised.

As Darryl walked out of the lounge amid more "Boos" and discontent, I impulsively yelled at him, "If you're worried about sleep, maybe we should wake you up early tomorrow." Darryl looked at me as he digested my foolish threat.

After the meeting, I was still bothered by this unilateral Coke machine decision. I also felt that I should carry through with my threat to wake up Darryl. So I got together with Jim Kennedy, one of my friends, who had a room two doors from Darryl's. We put together a plan to wake up early the next morning—around 5 AM—creep over to Darryl's door, and bang for a few seconds. Then we'd run back to our rooms and crawl into bed like we had been sleeping all night.

The next morning I did get up at 5 AM. I tiptoed down my wing, past the lounge with the Coke machine—running quietly—to Jim's wing, and finally to his room. He wasn't up yet, so I softly knocked. After what seemed to be a minute, I could hear him slowly get out of bed. When he opened the door and saw me, he was surprised. He couldn't believe that I was serious about banging on Darryl's door.

The two of us tiptoed the short distance to Darryl's room. We looked at each other with the light from the Exit sign casting red tints to our intense faces. I nodded to Jim. We both banged on the door, yelled his name "Darryl", and ran.

As I crawled into bed again, panting from the running across the yard from Darryl's exit door to the exit door for my wing, through the door and into my bedroom, I could hear footsteps coming down the hall. I stiffened as soon as I heard the key in my door. It was Darryl. "I know it was you and Kennedy. I'm reporting both of you to Dr. Ivery for disciplinary action." Then I heard the door close quietly and footsteps back down the hall.

Our prank was successful in waking Darryl early in the morning, but his threat of disciplinary action was ominous to me. I began to worry as I lay in bed with my face to the window, instead of the door. *What would happen? Would I be suspended or get kicked out of college? Why did I have to rashly yell at Darryl at that meeting last night? Why didn't I keep my mouth shut and let the Coke machine alone? Was it a sign of immaturity again?*

Jim and I had to wait four days before we were called to see Dr. Ivery for discipline. He lectured us about respect for others: told us that this incident was serious. He'd recommend disciplinary action to Father Vashro, the Dean of Students. Father Vashro would then meet with us individually and decide what action to take. I felt like telling him that the Coke machine conflict was all his fault, but I decided that I was in enough trouble.

It was now the end of March. Besides the tenseness from worrying about the consequences of our pounding on Darryl's door, there was the daily pressure of classes, studying and Mid-term tests. Once again, I was just getting by with C's, even now in English Comp. and Physics. It seemed as though school work was getting harder and I was running out of energy.

Winter was dragging on in the Twin Cities. I couldn't get excited about tryouts for the Tommies' baseball team, set for the first week of April in the Gym. The stress from fear that I would be disciplined began to wear on me. I found it hard to concentrate on classes and studying. I had worked so hard to get to college and, being a pessimist, I imagined the worst. I saw myself packing my clothes and calling my folks to tell them I was kicked out of school for banging on Darryl's door.

Finally, after a week of worry on my part—Jim Kennedy didn't seem to be overly concerned—I was called to Father Vashro's office in Barracks A. I didn't know whether to start apologizing right away as soon as I got into his office, or just keep my mouth shut and listen to my fate. He began by talking about the need for rules and quiet time and proper rest in order to succeed in college. On the other hand, he understood the tendency that college students have to protest authority, break rules and pull pranks on others. Since I had admitted my part, along with Jim Kennedy in banging on Darryl's door, I would have to apologize to Darryl and Dr. Ivery, *and* I would be grounded to the Barracks for one weekend.

That was it! No suspension. No expulsion. No ranting and raving about irresponsibility. I was totally relieved that I could stay in school and not have to call home with bad news.

The next weekend I stayed in the Barracks with Jim Kennedy. We watched a lot of television, read for pleasure, and tried to catch up with homework. I found, however, that the tenseness was returning: that nagging sense of loneliness, and ever present, under the surface thoughts of Lucy. During classes that week, the first week of April, I came to the conclusion that I needed to go home to Chicago for a rest. I had been at St.Thomas since the middle of January without really having a break away from school. I had spent the December Christmas break working ten hours a day at the Main Post Office for the mail rush. Even Mag and Buck's wedding in the middle of January was just a Friday night to Sunday morning rush visit home on the train

When I made it home, Mommy and Daddy were very concerned because I seemed depressed and uncommunicative. I didn't offer any explanation or talk about the door banging incident, or as usual about Lucy. I just told them I was tired. I guess that I didn't look too good to the family doctor, Dr.Coleman, so he suggested I spend a day or two at Mercy Hospital to get some blood tests. Maybe I had mono, the college kids' disease!

As I sat on the edge of the hospital bed in my pajamas, I could see Mommy's concern in her eyes. So far, after some testing, there was nothing physically wrong with me, even again, no indication of St.Vitus Dance. She knew that something was bothering me but she couldn't get it out of me. Finally, Daddy asked her to wait in the hall because he wanted to talk to me alone.

"What's bothering you, Hughie Boy?" he asked, looking directly at me while putting his hand on my left shoulder.

I squirmed a little on the edge of the bed, and glanced around at the other patients in the ward. They were either talking to visitors or lying quietly in their beds. Slowly, I began to talk to him, to unravel, tearfully telling him about the door banging incident, how I was so fearful of getting kicked out of college and being an embarrassment to myself and my family, especially since I was the first one to go away to school.

I told him of the pressures I felt with daily classes, studying for tests, and grades that were just passing. What would I do next year, if I did pass, but had no money to continue at St.Thomas?

And then, after a long pause, as though I was holding it back from him, I blurted out that I kept thinking about this girl named Lucy. I told him how it didn't work out, but I still cared for her! My head was down now, showing the shame of my confession.

I could feel his hands on my arms, squeezing them to tell me of his concern and hoping that the tension I felt would ease with his squeeze. "I know how you feel, Hughie Boy. I was in your shoes when I was eighteen, before I met your mother. It's tough to be down," he said in a calm voice.

After I looked up to his face, he smiled. "We'll have to do something about all of this," he added. Then he cupped my head in his strong, right hand, shaking my head slightly to get rid of the nonsense that had been in it for so long.

"I'm sorry for the troubles I put you and Mommy through," I whispered to him. I tried to force a smile, but the depression and tension in my face and body was still ruling.

Daddy told me to call Lucy as soon as I was home. Ask her directly how she feels about me. Settle it once and for all. Don't let it hang with you for another day. The door banging fiasco was finished. I didn't get kicked out of college. He and Mommy were proud of what I had accomplished. Even though I was getting C's, I was passing. I was doing the best I could, Daddy emphasized. He also made it clear that I had to return to St.Thomas to finish the year. After that, he had no answers, or suggestions.

After leaving the hospital the next day, I called Lucy and asked her if I could meet her after work on Monday in the lobby of the Field Building where she worked. She was surprised on the phone, thinking that I was away at college. But, she did agree to see me in the lobby the next day.

It was five minutes to five when I entered the long, narrow lobby of the Field Building from the LaSalle St. entrance. Still the same busy place from the days of my deliveries in high school when I worked for Chemists Supply. I found a position across from the elevators to wait for her. *I mentally went over what I would say to her. Just ask her if she cares for you like you care for her. That's all! Don't get complicated or wordy. Be direct, like my father said!*

I saw her first, getting out of the elevator and walking toward the LaSalle exit with another girl. She looked good with her raincoat on, long hair, pretty face and light pink lips.

I stepped out from the opposite wall to the elevators and called to her, "Lucy."

She was somewhat surprised as she looked at me, and stopped walking. Her friend must have known that I wanted to talk to Lucy alone, because she quickly said "Goodbye" to Lucy, glanced at me with a polite smile, and kept walking to the doors.

I motioned for Lucy to come over to the wall where I was standing to get out of the traffic from the people who were hurrying home.

"I've thought about you a lot since we stopped seeing each other," I began to tell her. I felt so awkward standing there with all of these people walking past us, instead of sitting in some nice, quiet place with privacy and music. "I really need to know if you care about me, or whether I should forget about it." I finally got it out to her!

"Well, I've been dating a lot of fellows since we were together. I don't know. I like you. But, just as a friend," she said uncomfortably. "I didn't know you felt this way about me," she added in a nervous voice, kinda like she wanted to get this over.

"OK, I understand," I whispered to her, dropping my face somewhat. I took a breath, looked at her and said in a stronger voice, "Thanks for meeting me." Slowly I turned. "Good by," I almost shouted to get over the mass clicking of pedestrian heels on the marble floor. I left her standing there and joined the throng heading for the revolving doors.

As I walked down Adams toward State St. and the bus home, I kept saying to myself, "It's over. It's over. I don't have to think about her anymore. She doesn't care about me." *I smiled: clenched my fist. I was free, free of Lucy!*

But it wasn't over! Six months later, after I had returned from St.Thomas where I had completed one year of college—C average—and out of money needed to return. I was working in Chicago as an apprentice sheet metal worker for the Santa Fe Railroad in the passenger train yards at Archer Ave. & Cermak Road, just two miles from Bridgeport. I had the day shift: free at night except for the two nights a week I went to Loyola University's Lakeshore campus to Chemistry classes. This was another college course I had to make up because I hadn't taken Chemistry in high school at DeLaSalle.

Lucy called me one night. She had heard that I wasn't away to college anymore. She was taking a course in night school and was having trouble with the outline of a term paper. Could I come over to help her?

Sitting in the small chair and table in the dining room of our house where the phone was setting, I couldn't believe what I was hearing. Lucy was calling me? After I had gone through all those phone calls to her, the rejections to get together, the mental anguish of not seeing her, I finally had confronted her about my feelings. *Now she wanted me, me to help her!* I held that phone ever so tightly in my left hand, wanting to lash out to her, "Lucy, it's over for me. Forget it. Get one of those hotshot guys you're dating to do the outline."

But I didn't yell at her. I was silent: thinking. "Why not. If she needs help with an outline, I can do that. I'm pretty good with organization now that I took a year of English Comp at St.Thomas. Besides, maybe she's changed about me. Maybe she's been thinking—about me."

We met the following Friday night in the apartment behind her father's tavern on Archer and Throop. After we sat down at the kitchen table, Lucy was very talkative about her office job downtown and about the course she was taking in night school. She complained to me about the amount of homework in this class, that she didn't have time to go on dates because she was always home; reading and writing. She admitted that she wasn't very good at organizing what she wanted to write. I looked at the topic sheet she handed me, along with her notes and her attempt at an outline.

All through our first minutes together, I kept getting a message in her voice of unhappiness: too much to do at work and school. She continued her monologue as though she realized I was receptive to her sorry state of life.

I looked across that table directly at her a few times. It seemed as though she'd talk on and on, with me sitting there, the quiet listener. There was no interest in her for me. *Why was I here? Did this girl need an audience, and not an advisor? Was I being used?*

Lucy offered refreshments, and eventually we put the outline together. But the feeling kept growing that this wasn't the same girl I walked home from All Saints teen dance over two years ago, on that misty Spring night. The pretty face, the long hair were still in front of me. But I saw no pink lips, or bright eyes. I heard no sweetness or soft laugh in her voice. I felt no stir inside me, no urge to hold her. There were no smiles or looks at me to encourage, or words from her that she cared, even a little.

Sadly I slumped my shoulders and lowered my head. *It wasn't there anymore.*

There was nothing, nothing between us. The Lucy I had cared about for so long was not in front of me. That girl was just a memory. It was over. Now, it was truly over.

Finally, over!

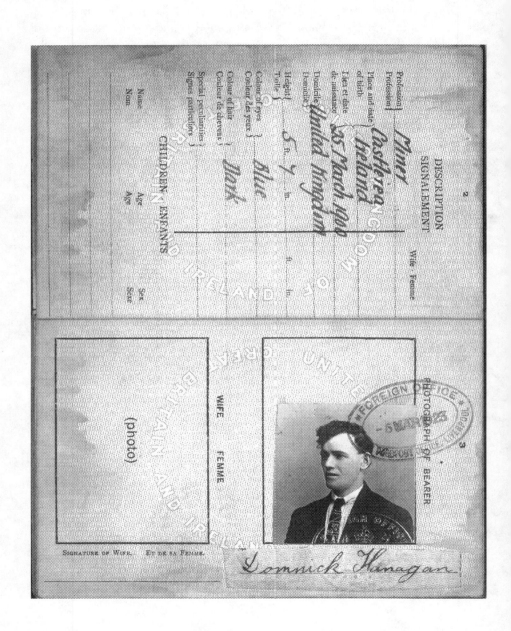

DESCRIPTION
SIGNALEMENT

Wife / Femme

Profession } Profession	Miner
Place and date of birth } Lieu et date de naissance	Castlepolloragh, Ireland, 25 March 1900, United Kingdom
Domicile } Domicile	United Kingdom
Height } Taille	5 ft. 7 in. ___ ft. ___ in.
Colour of eyes } Couleur des yeux	Blue
Colour of hair } Couleur des cheveux	Dark
Special peculiarities } Signes particuliers	

CHILDREN / ENFANTS

Name Nom	Age Age	Sex Sexe

WIFE   FEMME

(photo)

SIGNATURE OF WIFE.   ET DE SA FEMME.

3

PHOTOGRAPH OF BEARER

Domnick Flanagan

FOREIGN OFFICE 6 MAR 1923

St.Patrick High School

De La Salle
Institute
3455 South Wabash Avenue
Chicago, Illinois 60616

The remodeled LeVoy House.

Daddy going to work.

FROSH BASKETBALL
T. Babiarz, A. Alonzo, D. Kesman, A. Ranucci, C. Dohoney, H. LeVoy, D. W

Hughie and Mommy outside the
Barracks at College of St. Thomas.

Hughie's grad photo from DeLaSalle.

UNIVERSITY *of* ST. THOMAS

MINNESOTA

Jan. 19, 1957 The Wedding of Marge LeVoy & Charles Hans

6

JOHN KENNEDY

The hero comes when he is needed.
When our belief gets pale & weak,
there comes a man out of that need
who is shining—and everyone living
reflects a little of that light—and stores
up some against the time when he is gone.

Anonymous

"The time is ripe, the hour has struck and the man is ready. Ladies and gentlemen of this convention, it is my privilege to present to this convention as a candidate for President of the United States the name of a man uniquely qualified to follow in the path of Jefferson, Cleveland, Wilson, Roosevelt, and the man from Independence. Fellow delegates, I give you the man from Libertyville, the next Democratic nominee, and our next President of the United States, Adlai E. Stevenson."

I watched our TV intently as young Senator John Kennedy almost challenged the microphone on the dais at the 1956 Democratic National Convention to send forth the nomination of Governor Stevenson of Illinois to the throngs of delegates who were waiting to cheer, holler, hoist their signs, and parade around the convention floor at the International Amphitheatre in Chicago. I could hear the noise erupting as Kennedy withdrew from the platform. The TV cameras turned to the hundreds of Stevenson supporters who were pumping ALL THE WAY WITH ADLAI signs up and down.

It was August of 1956. I had turned on the TV as soon as I got home from the freight docks to catch the Convention and hear this Irish Catholic

Senator from Massachusetts. I had read in the paper that Senator Kennedy was given the privilege to nominate Governor Stevenson, probably because Kennedy was Catholic, and also a possible Vice-Presidential running mate for Stevenson.

Actually, the first time I saw Kennedy on TV was Monday night of Convention week when he narrated a documentary history of the Democratic Party, and was later introduced from the floor to the delegates, with a lot of applause.

There were slight feelings of pride and interest in me after watching Senator Kennedy twice on TV, noting the publicity he was getting. I had never looked closely at political figures before, having scarcely bothered with the 1952 Republican and Democratic Conventions which were held just south of Bridgeport at the International Amphitheatre. I did know, however, from the newspapers that Eisenhower and Stevenson were nominated by the Republican and Democratic Parties, respectively. After those conventions, I would read a little about the campaigns of '52, and later follow accounts of President Eisenhower and other officials, including the televised Army-McCarthy hearings of 1954. But I never was attracted to any political figures, or identified with them.

John Kennedy was different. He was young, good-looking, with a full head of hair. He seemed to have an air of confidence in his voice and demeanor. Speaking with a New England accent—Ah-frih-ker instead of Ah-frih-kuh (Africa)—my ears perked at his differences from Chicago English. Much was said about his book, *Profiles in Courage*, published in 1955. And, most significantly, he was Irish and Catholic, the Kennedy ancestors coming from Dunganston, County Wexford, Ireland in 1848, during the dreaded potato famine.

When Stevenson threw the nomination for Vice-President open to the Convention delegates on Wednesday evening during his acceptance speech, I got caught up in the ensuing speculation, drama, politicking, and eventual floor fight. Did Kennedy have a shot at the nomination?

The papers and television were full of Kennedy stories. The city of Chicago was abuzz about this fresh, new, political leader, giving him much more publicity than the Democratic Party leaders and Stevenson wanted. Senator Kennedy held his own for the nomination on Thursday night, with at least four other candidates.

Sadly I watched, however, as the third ballot Vice-Presidential nomination votes slowly showed a majority of delegates for Senator Estes Kefauver of Tennessee. He had been the favorite from the beginning of the Convention, with the TV commentators suggesting that he was the person Stevenson really wanted.

I was surprised when I saw Senator Kennedy approach the microphone on the dais after the vote clearly went to Kefauver. Kennedy was hesitant, with his head down. "Ladies and gentleman of this convention," he began, raising his head. He paused and again lowered his head as though he was uncomfortable with what he had to say. "I want to, uh, take this opportunity first to express my appreciation to Democrats from all parts of the country, (I watched intently as he took the gavel in his right hand and slowly turned it in the palm of his left hand) North and South, East and West, who have been both generous and kind to me." (now his eyes made direct contact with the delegates, as though his initial hesitation was gone).

The gavel was put down. Senator Kennedy grabbed the sides of the lectern like a preacher ready to deliver the closing line of the sermon. He looked directly again at the throng of delegates, raised his voice, and firmly stated, "I hope that this Convention will make Estes Kefauver's nomination unanimous." He nodded his head ever so slightly and walked away from the microphone.

Sadness and anger came over me that Kennedy had lost the nomination ballot. But I also admired him for standing in front of all those delegates and thanking them. And finally for making the graceful gesture, asking his delegates and others to make his opponent's nomination unanimous. Again I felt a measure of pride that Kennedy had done the right thing, and a feeling of anticipation that there would be another day.

During all of this, I would talk to my father, showing great interest in Senator Kennedy and national politics. Daddy would remind me of Al Smith, the Catholic politician from New York, who ran for President in 1928. Daddy would tell me how everyone he knew was in favor of Governor Smith because he was a Democrat, knew the problems of the working man because he grew up poor in New York City, with little education, and most importantly, candidate Smith was opposed to Prohibition.

Daddy would describe how Al Smith always wore a derby hat, and had a cigar in his hand. Smith talked simply with a low-key voice, but had a vigorous campaign in '28, even being called "The Happy Warrior." My father felt so good when he turned 21 in March of '28 and voted the following November for Smith. He always said his vote for Smith countered the guy down the street who voted against Smith because he was a Catholic.

I thought about the discrimination Governor Smith had faced, the difficulties I had read in books about the Irish when they first came to the U.S. in large numbers during the 19th Century—NO IRISH NEED APPLY—and the servitude that my mother grew up with in a peasant Irish family in Ireland under English rule at the turn of the century. Combined with my father's experiences in the 1920s looking for work, and then joining the growing

Labor Movement thru the 30s and 40s with Roosevelt in the White House, I found myself becoming politicized, strictly Democratic.

A growing sense of unfairness and anger was feeding my identification with my parents and their roots. Although I had never experienced rejection in my 18 + years as an Irish Catholic boy growing up in Bridgeport, Chicago, I could sense my parents' pain when they talked about whence they came. My father seemed to suffer most, consistently railing against the Republicans and the rich. Mommy was quieter, trying not to answer the questions of her children, especially me, about her young life in Kilroddan, County Roscommon on the nine acre Flanagan farm. She did tell us once about the vicious deeds of the Black & Tans, who were little more than mercenaries hired by the English government to stop the Irish rebellion in 1920. She described how neighbors were burned out of their houses if the Tans thought they were Sinn Fein sympathizers or active militia.

I was affected by Daddy's bombastic remarks about growing up in Chicago, and my mother's reluctance to talk about the harsh scenes of rural Ireland in the early 20s. I found myself internalizing their feelings of injustice. *Silently, perhaps unconsciously, I vowed to do something.* I didn't consciously say to myself that I would follow a career of concern for others, or let the injustices that were part of my inheritance govern my life, but the seeds were planted within me at a time when I was emerging as a person standing on my own. Reflection helped me to understand the role of leadership in changing the conditions of society, especially now that this vigorous Irishman from Massachusetts was emerging both in my eyes as well as the view of many Americans.

*

"Charles, do you take Margaret for your lawful wife, to have and to hold, from this day forward, for better, for worse, for richer, for poorer, in sickness and in health, until death do you part?" Father Ackerman, the pastor of St.Anthony de Padua Parish, asked Buck, using his forceful, liturgical voice.

"I do," Buck responded, looking at Mag, holding her hand, and smiling.

Charles "Buck" Hans met my older sister Mag in 1956 through his sister Evelyn, and her husband's sister, Violet. Mag and Violet worked together at Woolworth's State St. store downtown. Buck was originally from Charleroi, PA, a New World Belgian community south of Pittsburgh on the Monongahela River. In Chicago, he worked as a crane operator for a large scrap metal company on Goose Island.

"Margaret, do you take Charles for your lawful husband, to have and to hold, from this day forward, for better, for worse, for richer, for poorer, in sickness and in health, till death do you part?" Again we heard the rich tones of the pastor's voice as he faced Mag with the marriage question.

"I do," Mag answered with a serious tone to her voice as she squeezed Buck's hand and then smiled at him.

By the time of her wedding to Buck, Mag was 21 years old. In fact, Buck had proposed on her 21st birthday in June at Chicago's Lakefront, in between the submarine races. She had been working at the State St. Woolworth's store since her first year at St. Patrick Girls High School in the western Loop. She was only fourteen when she started working after high school each day to earn the money for tuition and books, carfare and Room 'n Board.

There were smiles from Patsy Hughes, Mag's best friend and maid of honor when she heard Buck and Mag's "I do." Standing opposite to Patsy in the sanctuary and smiling also was Bill Hans, Buck's younger brother and best man. He now moved toward Father Ackerman, reaching into his black tuxedo jacket for the two rings. Bill handed them to Freddie, my younger brother, who was serving the Nuptial Mass with his friend Carl, both of them in eighth grade at St.Anthony's School.

Father Ackerman blessed the rings and then asked Buck to take Mag's ring and repeat after him, as Buck put the ring on her finger. "Margaret, take this ring as a sign of my love and fidelity."

"Charles, take this ring as a sign of my love and fidelity." Mag repeated as it was her turn to slip Buck's ring onto his left hand ring finger.

My younger sister, Kate, was the bridesmaid. She was really smiling now, eagerly awaiting the big moment, the first kiss by the newlyweds. I could see Jake, my 20 year old brother, who was "standing up" as an usher with Kate as his partner, facing the altar and Mag and Buck, wearing a big grin on his red face. Mommy's eyes were tearing, and Daddy was smiling broadly like the Father of the Bride. I poked my little, ten year old sister, Maureen, who was standing next to me in the pew, kinda letting her know that the big moment was coming.

By now, the sun was shining thru the stained glass on the south wall of the sanctuary, transforming the wedding couple with a glow of approval from the heavens, adding to the wedding scene. Time seemed to be momentarily stilled with this holy, marital picture.

Father Ackerman cleared his throat, adding a sense of anticipation to this moment in LeVoy history. "By the powers invested in me, I now pronounce you man and wife," he stated loudly in a majestic voice, the words flying forth to friends and family and neighbors in the pews. As though on wings those words rose above their heads to the choir loft where they bounced against the pipes, rebounded up the arched ceiling and finally found their way back to the sanctuary with a faint echo of "man and wife."

Now, Mag and Buck were embracing with their first marital kiss, evoking "oohs" and "aahs" from all of us present in church. It was a joyful scene as we shared in the most public and sacred display of their love, a kiss.

Then the Nuptial Mass continued.

At the end of the Mass, after a final blessing of the bridegroom and bride, the traditional "Wedding March" by Mendelssohn was played by the organist. Mag and Buck joyfully led the bridal party and our families to the back of church and vestibule for greetings, well wishes, congratulations, and many hugs and kisses.

It was Saturday morning, January 19th, 1957, a rather warm, winter day in Chicago, with no remnants of Friday's snow flurries on the ground. I had come into Chicago by train the night before from the College of St.Thomas. My job for the wedding was to help tend the bar at the wedding reception. This was held in the recently remodeled basement at our house on 28th Place. My father finally found the motivation to finish the basement, namely, Mag's wedding reception. He installed plasterboard on the walls from the concrete floor to chair rail height; then pecky cypress paneling from the chair rail to the ceiling, leaving the floor joists, pipes, and wires in the ceiling exposed.

We had a great party! Over 60 family, friends, and neighbors crowded into that "old" basement for the celebration of Mag and Buck's wedding. There was music from my father's HiFi kit that he had bought and assembled. Two beer barrels were under ice in the stationary tubs of the wash sink. Sitting on Daddy's long workbench was the cold buffet, put together the day before by Mommy and Kate.

None of the guests minded walking down the narrow gangway and across the cold, dark backyard, descending the three steps to the basement door to join the party. No one seemed to notice that the bulky, old oil stove was supplying heat to the basement, or that a cobweb or two were still hanging from the exposed ceiling along with party bunting. And not a person complained when I took their winter coats and hung them on either the water pipes or gas lines in the corner of the basement next to the stove.

There was room for everyone to sit or stand, get a drink, and feast on baked ham, potato salad, rye bread, baked beans, fruit jello, and condiments. It was so easy to get a group together for photos since we were all within thirty feet of each other. I felt cozy, looking around the basement from my bar station, watching groups of relatives or family friends engaged in conversation, erupting occasionally in a chuckle or loud guffaw and pat on the back as one of the group said something funny.

I was amazed how Daddy and Mommy had transformed this basement from a dirt floor, cobweb filled, mice laden, unsavory place that I didn't like to come down to when I was the kid to get heating oil for the stoves, or a tool.

The "lower level" to our home was now a clean, warm gathering place. Our family couldn't afford The Martinique for the wedding party of their oldest daughter, or even the Knights of Columbus Hall on 31st St. The "down home" wedding atmosphere of our "new" basement surely welcomed all who came to share in the love feast of Mag and Buck.

*

Mommy spoke to me after I returned in June of '57 from my year away to college. She said, with a stern voice, that there was only one Commandment in this house. No, it wasn't the one about stealing, nor #9 about coveting thy neighbor's wife. And it certainly wasn't Love thy Neighbor. It wasn't even the 4th Commandment, To Honor thy Father and Mother (That was Daddy's favorite). Her Commandment was *not* one of the Top Ten. Maybe it was #11 or #15 on someone else's list, but for her it was the big one for me to follow now. I think this is how she would phrase it. THOU SHALT NOT SIT AROUND the HOUSE and READ BOOKS. And the second half of the Commandment followed. THOU SHALT GET A JOB.

I had made the mistake of telling my family how much I read in college, and that I stayed up one night to read War and Peace. Mommy knew that I was a voracious reader of newspapers, magazines, and books, especially novels in paperback form. Hard cover books always seemed to be a waste of money. And I never had the money to buy one. *Battle Cry* by Leon Uris cost $4.95 in 1953 when it first came out in hardbound. I waited until the Bantam paperback version hit the racks in '54., and paid 95 cents. Same story, smaller print!

As I was growing up, Mommy would see me regularly camped out in the Lazy Boy chair in the front room by the windows, with total attention in the latest novel, like *The Young Lions* by Irwin Shaw, or *From Here to Eternity* by James Jones. (I read the Jones book first and then saw the film version. After seeing the torrid beach scene with Deborah Kerr and Burt Lancaster, I always thought a better title should be *From Here to Maternity*)

At the age of fifteen I read my first "dirty" book, called *The Hoods*, a tale about New York gangsters and their dolls. I'd become so engrossed in this "literature" that I wouldn't respond to Mommy's mundane request to take out the garbage. I'd just grunt and say, "Yah, just a minute," knowing I would read to the end of the chapter to see what would happen to the main character. (Fifteen minutes later)

Mommy would never question what I was reading, Thank God! But she was afraid that I'd become one of those "bright bums" who sits around all day, reading everything in sight, and then goes out at night to tell the rest of the world how smart he is. So, she told me that there were only two choices in this house. Get a job or go to school! "There'll be no sittin' round actin' like Himself," she let me know in no uncertain terms.

Since I had no money to go back to St.Thomas, or even enroll part-time in a college in Chicago, I really had just one choice, WORK. I did tell Mommy and Daddy that my plan in the summer of '57 was to work in Chicago, and start taking classes at night in September until I had enough money to return to college full-time. Most likely, I would apply to a school like Illinois Institute of Technology. I.I.T. was an engineering college located within two miles of our house at 33rd and State St., just north of DeLaSalle High School, and east of Comiskey Park. I could save a lot of money by living at home and commuting as a day student.

By the summer of '57, the Chi-Annies Club moved from 29th and Lowe Ave. to a bigger space at 28th Place and Wallace St., right next to the Neighborhood Playlot and across from St. Anthony Church. The Chi-Annies were my brother's gang from grammar school, which I tagged onto, although Jake didn't like it. He didn't want his younger brother hangin' with him and his buddies.

The Club rented the first floor front of what was an old store in a 3-story turn-of-the-century brick building. The store had been converted into three rooms that fit our uses. We furnished the front room with two sofas, a couple of easy chairs, and the TV. The middle room had lots of chairs and tables, used for meetings, cards and eating. And the back room had an old bar with mirrors behind, indirect lights and side booths we had purchased from the old Annie's store, the namesake of the Chi-Annies (Chicago Annies).

There had been a tradition of Social Athletic Clubs in the Bridgeport neighborhood, groups of guys who grew up together, hung around, played softball—sometimes tackle football—drank beer, and eventually pooled their monthly dues into rental of an old storefront. The members used their carpentry and painting skills to remodel the place, get a hold of an old bar from a tavern that closed, used tables, booths, sofas and lighting.

As I grew up, I saw quite a few Clubs; the DOBS at the corner of 28th Place and Normal Ave., the Orioles on 26th and Lowe Ave., the Jugheads from 31st and Wells, the Aristocrats at 29th and Normal, and the Hamburgs at 37th and Union. Mayor Richard J. Daley grew up as a member of the Hamburgs.

Each Club had to apply for a license with the City of Chicago. In the case of the Chi-Annies, our sponsor was Johnny Annerino, the local Democratic precinct captain, who worked in the City Clerk's Office in "The Hall"—as politicians called City Hall.

I found that being a Chi-Annie meant having a place to go at night to hang out, talk neighborhood gossip, swap jokes—mostly dirty—smoke, have a few beers, watch the Sox or Bears on TV, and play cutthroat pinochle for money until the wee hours of the morning. It was good for me to talk to the guys regularly, especially about baseball. We all were Sox fans, (Correction—Billy West was the lone Cub fan in the Club). By 1957, the Sox had moved up to second place behind the Yankees, and were still the talk of the summer on the South Side.

Then there were parties in the Club on a Saturday night, with a full bar of whiskey, beer, wine, and soft drinks. Music from the HiFi, dancing, and sometimes a little romance in the front room.

I volunteered to be in charge of cleaning the Club for the first, big party after we had moved in, remodeled and decorated. Three of us, Joe, George, and I spent all day on Saturday washing booths, chairs, tables, and floors. We had to get the liquor, beer, ice, and glasses set up, and put simple decorations in the barroom. I didn't finish the preparations until 7 PM, and the party was set for 8.

I ran the block from the Club to my house, took a shower, dressed, and had just enough time to eat one potato, a left-over from the family dinner. Mommy and Daddy were not too happy that I had spent all day cleaning the Club, and couldn't sit down with them and the kids for dinner. Jake was just finishing dressing for the party, hoping to be on time to pick up his girlfriend, Bobbie Jean.

Sure enough, I made it back to the Club by 8 PM. I wanted to be there to make sure the bartenders were all set and check out the place. The music was on when I entered; the place was warm, heated by our oil stove in the middle room. Everything looked great. The barroom was especially cozy, dimly lit just like a nightclub. Even the bathroom smelled clean. This was gonna be a real good time!

Some of the guys patted me on the back for doing such a great job to get the place ready for our first party. The wives and girlfriends were impressed also, after having fears that the place would be cold, dirty, or unwelcome. (After all, what can you expect from a bunch of guys).

I was feeling so good by 8:30, and the place was almost full, that I pulled up a stool to the bar and shouted, "Gimme a shot un uh beer,"—my first boilermaker. I was going to drink just like my father did in Down's Tavern when Mommy would send me there to get him. Now I could relax and enjoy the fruits of my labor.

Joe Agate, one of the bartenders, said to me, "Can you handle that whiskey?"

I cockily answered, "Aw yah, nuttin' to it." The whiskey was Canadian Club, nuttin' but the best. "The best" tasted sharp as it rolled around my mouth and down my throat. Wuh! I made an ugly face, shook my head, and grabbed the beer to chase down that sharp-tastin' whiskey.

Joe was watching me, laughing, "Nuttin' to it, eh?"

So, I slowed down, wizened by the "shot" I just took to my digestive system, and sipped my beer. There were a lot of guys and gals in the bar now, so it was easy to join a conversation. "Chances Are" by Johnny Mathis was playing on the HiFi. Cigarette smoke was rising to the high ceiling from all the smokers at the bar. And I was beginning to feel warm inside, both from the whiskey and the fact that I had helped put the party together, gaining the appreciation from the guys.

George pulled up a stool next to me, and we started talking about jobs. I ordered another shot of CC. Joe looked at me with raised eyebrows as he poured, but I told him, "Don't worry, Joe, I don't have far to go, and I'm walkin'."

George asked me what it had been like at college in St.Paul. I took a sip of the whiskey before answerin', slowly lettin' it roll over my tongue until I could adjust to the sharpness, and then letttin' it slide down my throat. Not bad! A lot smoother than the first shot. I savored the taste and warmth as it worked its way down to my stomach. Didn't even have to grab the beer to chase the whiskey this time.

The two of us kept talkin' at the bar for the next hour—neither of us had a date for the party. He was interested in goin' back to school to get a GED, having left Tilden Tech High School when he was a Junior, and just turned 17. He said that he could handle night school later on, eventually working into sales or a management position with the company where he was now employed in shipping. I sensed that he respected my goal to get an education in college. He wanted something better than what he had. There was more to life than a steady job that brought home a few bucks, having a car, and drinking beer on the weekends.

In the meantime, I finished the second shot of CC, and my first beer. I was really feelin' warm inside now: quite mellow. Someone put Bill Haley on the HiFi and the decibel level went way up. I started dancin' in place with my upper body to the loud rhythm.

"Joe, I'm gonna have one mo' shot and beer and that will be it," I yelled to him when he came to our end of the bar.

"Are you sure? You're lookin' kinda so-so," Joe shouted as he took his right hand and made it wobble from side-to-side like an airplane shaking its wings.

"I'm OK," I yelled again above the bar noise and music, clapping my barmate George on the shoulder and letting out a big laugh.

"Yeah, you say so, Hugh, but I'm not carryin' you home. Got it," Joe raised his index finger and wagged it at me. He reluctantly poured my whiskey, and then grabbed two beers for George and me.

"I can walk 'ome," I retorted with a slight slur, swallowing the "h" in "home". It's only one 'loc', I slurred again, unable to clearly say "block."

George slapped me on the back with his left hand. "You're feelin' pretty good tonight. You gonna make it for 9:00 Mass tomorrow?

I laughed again, really loud this time, and leaned over to George's ear. "I'm servin' the Mass."

Both he and I erupted in laughter again, slappin' each other on the shoulder. I could see my brother Jake over in one of the booths lookin' at me with wonder.

The third shot of Canadian Club went down real smoothly, although part of it didn't get into my mouth, rolling down the left side of my chin instead. I didn't feel any sharpness or strong taste now. There was just a slight warmth as it traveled thru my throat and esophagus to my stomach.

"Well Georgy, I gotta peepee." I put my right hand on his left shoulder and started to twist to get off the stool I had been sitting on for over an hour.

"Don't fall in," he answered, laughin' softly.

I swung the rest of the way around to get off the stool, putting my right foot down on the floor and then my left. I took one step toward the toilet, and the strangest thing happened. *I could see the floor coming straight at my face! What's this?*

I started laughin' just before the floor hit me in the face. And then the shock! The crash didn't seem to faze me though, as I continued laughin' my drunken head off on that linoleum floor.

I could hear cries from the girls, laughs from the guys, and a loud, "I told you so," from Joe the bartender.

Twenty minutes later, at 10:00 PM, after George and Jake scraped me off the barroom floor, I was neatly tucked in bed at home, a block away, nursing a nasty bump on my forehead, along with a heavily bruised ego. Mommy was upset, telling Daddy that I shouldn't be in that Chi-Annies Club, resurrecting memories of the drinkin' her brothers had done, and fears that I'd turn out the same. But Daddy was quiet, just listening to her, perhaps silently thanking God that my first voyage thru the Sea of Spirits did not result in a shipwreck and drowning.

*

The Chi-Annies, however, were the source for my new job in the summer of 1957 at the Santa Fe Railroad. Nickie Spata, Joe Bova, Bobby Humbert, and Frank Kubiak were all working there as pipe fitters. They told me that the Railroad was looking for apprentices in sheet metal and plumbing. Also, my father's best friend, Larry Kleifges, nicknamed "Foots" because he walked so much in the railyard, was working there as the lead man in the air conditioning shop.

The apprenticeship I was hired for amounted to two years of study and work in plumbing, pipe fitting, sheet metal, and air conditioning on the Santa Fe passenger cars that traveled between Chicago and California. I would work with a journeyman in each of these areas, and go to classes once a week for half a day.

The air conditioning (AC) shop gang turned out to be quite unique and fun to work with daily. Gus Voss, the foreman, was born and raised in Germany. He had the look, build, stride, and accent of a U-boat commander. The sheet metal shop men, Elmer and Pappy, were Kansas-born boys who could bend and twist and solder or weld sheet metal into all sorts of shapes, whether for the passenger cars or for private need. The pipefitters were Hanky Dank Rosset, Philly Dispensa, Nickie, Bobby, Bart Tobar, and little Augie Saccaro. I spent most of my time following them around, being a good gopher, or putting the safety flag on the end knuckler of the last passenger car in line, to make sure that no switch engine would come and hook up to the passenger car while the pipefitter was under the car fixing a broken AC condenser.

Finally, there was the plumbing crew who took care of both the dining cars and passenger cars. We had Joe Bova and "Big Job" Louie, who called everyone "Pal". "Got a big job, today, Pal," he would say to me as I met him in the shop each morning at 7 AM. Felix Kaskie and Eddie Sidabras worked exclusively on dining cars, always trying to please the chefs, and getting some free fruit and coffee in the process.

The Santa Fe Railroad had a certain prestige with its passenger business. At the head of the train, traveling from Chicago thru southwest Illinois to Missouri and then to Atchison and Topeka, Kansas and on westward was a set of red and golden diesel locomotives. The front engine was streamlined, giving it the appearance of power and speed. Following the locomotives were the sleek, shiny stainless steel passenger cars, with either coach or Pullman accommodations. The pride of the line was the Super Chief, a train that took only 39 hours to travel from Chicago to Los Angeles. Many a celebrity who were afraid of flying, would ride the Super Chief, sleeping in the comfort of a bed, eating excellent, chef-prepared meals in the dining car. The non-celebrities rode in the new El Capitan, the double-decker train that gave passengers great views of the Southwest from sixteen feet above the track.

"Watch out fo' the Big Guns from the East," shouted Brooks, the Negro steamman to me as I was walking down the tracks crossing that separated the north end of the trainyard from the south. There were passenger cars on both sides of the crossing for six to eight tracks, waiting for inspection, cleaning, and service before being put together as a train, and then shoved down to Dearborn Station by a switch engine. I was pushing the tool cart back to the AC shop after Hanky Dank and I made a repair on a car on track 6.

"The Braves got some Big Guns of their own," I yelled back to Brooks. "The Yankees ain't gonna stop Mathews and Hammerin' Hank and Big Joe."

Brooks was standing near the steam line that he had just hooked up to a string of cars on Track 3. I could see thin sprays of steam leaking out of the coupling, dissipating into the early October air. "Burdette and Spahn ain't gonna stop the Mick and Yogi and Hank Bauer," he laughed, poking me in the chest with his dirty glove to intimidate me into believing that the Yanks were going to sweep the Milwaukee Braves in the World Series that was starting today in New York.

"Put your money where your mouth is," I said seriously, looking him right in the eyes. "I got a fin says the Braves will take 'em in seven games."

He started laughing again. I could see the superwhiteness of his teeth against the black face and mustache. "Naw, kid, I don' wanna take yo' money. It's bin decided. The Big Guns from the East got the Series all the way."

I walked away toward the shop, chuckling to myself that he didn't want to take my money. Five years before, and about five miles south of the Santa Fe yard, a Negro kid took my money, all 50 cents of it. The Santa Fe was my first experience working with Negroes. There was no trouble that I encountered, unlike the area around DeLaSalle. In fact, there was a lot of jivin' between Brooks and myself over baseball—he hated the White Sox and loved the Yankees, the Big Guns from the East.

Then there was waterman Brown, a chunky, jovial black guy who always carried a waterhose to fill the tank on the side of each passenger car. He usually had a cigarette in his mouth. When I'd see him filling a tank on the track that I was working on, I'd go up to him and say, "Hey Brown, give me a cigarette," knowing what his response would be.

"Hugh-Hugh, uh-uh, my pack i-is-isn't opened," he stuttered, gasped for air, and smiled at me. Then he'd pull out the pack of Tareytons from his shirt pocket and show me that the pack wasn't opened. He would conveniently hide the bottom of the pack with his fingers, because that's where he had opened it to get the cigarette that was in his mouth.

I really didn't want one of his Tareytons because I had my own pack of Winstons. I just wanted to see Brown fake the full-pack story, which he had invented to turn away all the cigarette moochers in the yard.

There always seemed to be tension in Bridgeport between blacks and whites. Part of it was the nearness of neighborhoods, with Negroes living both east and south of Comiskey Park. And I'm sure the bigger part was just plain prejudice from both groups. I remember walking to Sox Park down Canal St. one afternoon with one of the toughguys from our block. I was sixteen at the time, and he was a little older and a lot huskier and rougher.

We could both see ahead, halfway down the 3200 block, that a black teenager was walking toward us. It was such a dead summer day that no one was outside, or on the front porches, and no kids were playing on the sidewalk.

"When the nigger gets in front of us, you take a swing at him. When he ducks your punch, I'll smack him in the head," Andy said to me.

I was already getting' nervous before Andy talked to me, knowing that he'd want to punch the black kid for walking in our neighborhood. I really didn't want to get into this.

As the Negro walked within 30 feet of us, I saw that he was a little bigger and older than Andy. His eyes kept darting between us and the street, as though he was looking for an escape route. He must have known what was comin'

I was hopin' that he'd run now to get away from the trouble he saw with us white boys, and also for me to avoid havin' to punch him. But, he kept on comin' toward us.

As soon as the guy got within five feet of us, he moved out to the grass parkway so that we could pass him on the sidewalk. Andy yelled, "Now."

But I didn't swing. Andy did. He missed though because as soon as the black guy heard, "Now", he ran across the parkway and easily avoided Andy's punch. A second later he was on the street, running as fast as he could down Canal to 32nd. We watched him turn the corner and head for the viaduct under the tracks.

Andy was really pissed off at me, calling me a sissy, yellin' at me that "you can't let those niggers walk thru the neighborhood. Pretty soon they'll be livin' next door." I hung my head in silence as we continued to Sox Park. *I couldn't swing at that guy. I didn't have it in me to just punch a stranger who was walking down the sidewalk. I wasn't the tough guy like Andy.*

But I wasn't reluctant at the age of eight one summer night when the kids on the block decided to "greet" the hillbilly family that had moved into the second floor rear at 456 W. 28th Place, on the other side of the street. The Craig family were from southern Illinois, and had four kids, two of them boys our age.

Five of our gang, including me, waited until dark to sneak down the alley, picking up stones from an empty lot where an alley house had been torn down some time ago. We each had a handful of rocks and plaster chunks. Slowly we moved down the alley to the backyard next to the three-story where the Craigs lived.

Now we could see clearly that the lights were on in the rear apartment kitchen, and someone was moving inside. There wasn't anyone in the backyard, so we had them all to ourselves. One of the guys flung a rock toward the back porch. We could hear it bounce around the wood floor. Yeah! That was the signal for all of us to take aim and fire a rock.

"Wow! I think I hit the window," one of the guys whispered, and laughed.

"Yeh! Watch this one," I boldly stated, letting go with a screamer right at the back door.

"Crash" We heard the window break.

It took about ten seconds to fire the rest of our ammunition, all the while laughing to each other.

Then right at the entrance to their yard from the alley, we saw a man come limpin' strenously toward us, yellin' "You sonsabitches. I'll getcha."

We all ran, with my brother out in front, headin' towards Normal Ave. I got a late start because I was still savoring the sound of the broken window and didn't see Mr. Craig sneak up on us. I was behind the other guys by ten feet. That's all he needed—limp and all—to catch me by the shirt and pull me violently up to him.

"What's yo' name, boy," he yelled into my face after he turned me around, holding me by the back and front of my shirt. He started shakin' me. "Where's yo' daddy, boy," he screamed again before I could answer him. I was cryin' and scared, worryin' about getting' hit by this crazy man. "Yo' take me to yer daddy, or I'll call the cops," he shouted again, pushing me down the alley to Normal Ave., still clutching the back of my shirt.

I was so scared I couldn't talk. I squirmed but couldn't get away from his iron grip on my shirt. Craig finally found someone on the corner of 28th Place and Normal who knew me and told him where to find my father.

Daddy was working at his bench in the basement when Craig pushed me through the open door and told my father what I had done. After Daddy saw my guilty look, I got a whack in the side of my head from him right away, and a lecture not only for throwing rocks and breaking the window, but also because I followed the older guys, my brother Pat included. And I had to apologize and help Daddy replace the window that night.

Just as Craig was leaving the basement, in walked Pat, guilty as can be. He got the same punishment as me, only harder because he was older.

There was always an underlying tension between people of different nationalities, besides races, as I grew up. I learned the derogatory names quickly for each group of people in the neighborhood. Krauthead, Frog, Dago, Polack, Lugan, Limey, Bohunk, Moje, Spic, Shini, Chink, Jap, as well as Turkey for the Irish. For some reason, the Jews were labeled with more than one moniker, as I heard it from my father.

Daddy told me about the tensions in his parents' families. In 1901, his grandmother Margaret, who was Irish, would not accept her son Hugh's bride, Anna Lerner, because she was from a German family. The LeVoys and Lerners were Catholic. They had lived across the alley from each other on 31st and Emerald Ave/Halsted St. for 20 years. But they might as well be living 1000 miles apart—the distance between Ireland and Germany.

This prejudice was reversed in 1937 when Daddy went to St. Anthony's Rectory to register our young family as parishioners. He was told, rather coldly by Mary, the German housekeeper/secretary, to wait on the porch for the pastor.

When Father Leiser, the old German priest came to the door, he took one look at my father and said brusquely, "Vut du vant."

"I'm Pat LeVoy. My wife and I and two kids (and one on the way) live on 30th and Normal. We want to join St.Anthony's Parish," Daddy said to him, with a smile on his face.

"Du Ireesh?" Father Leiser blurted out to my father.

"Yah, well I'm" and that's all Daddy could answer before he was interrupted.

"Den du gost to da Ireesh Church," Father Leiser commanded while he was jerking his thumb north toward All Saints, the Irish parish. Then he closed the door in my father's face.

There were always unspoken feelings between the Italians and other nationalities as though it was taboo to date and, God forbid, actually marry—especially for a girl to marry an Italian guy. "Don't be bringin' home any Dago to this house, let me tell you," more than one Irish or German girl heard from her father.

As an older kid and later as a teenager, I had trouble digesting all of this hatred, disrespect, class consciousness, labeling, whatever it was called. Even within the Irish culture, there was the clear distinction between Lace Curtain and Shanty Irish. "Now what self-respecting, educated American-Irish lad would go out with a girl who had an Irish name all right, but who lived by the tracks, didn't go to a Catholic school, 'n had no roots to the Old Sod? And did ye see the sorry state of the curtains on the windows."

It seemed as though I couldn't get past the person I met or played with or sat next to in school or worked with at the job, and then worry whether he or she was of another nationality, race, color, whatever was our difference. Fortunately, I was able to see the person, and not a problem with his or her background. Instead of rejecting the differences between us, I became interested in the diversity of another culture, a foreign language perhaps, and most certainly food.

"Whatsa matter for you," the old Italian neighbor said one day when I didn't understand what he was handing me over the backyard fence. "Basilico, basilico. No capeesh?" he'd plead, imploring me with the fingers of his left hand pointing upwards, coaxing me with his right to smell the sweet basil leaf from his garden. The same leaf that did wonders for his spaghetti sauce. "Mangia! Mangia!

*

"C'mon Pat, pick us up. We need a strike," Tom Scalia said loudly as my father went up to lane six to get his ball from the rack.

"You can do 'er," yelled Sergio, standing behind the curved booth where most of the bowlers for the two teams were sitting.

I looked down at the score sheet on the small scorer's table. We had been even in marks with the other team, Dalcamo's Funeral Home, going into the 10th frame. But then we lost a mark when Tom, our leadoff man, didn't pick up his spare, and the other guy did. Now it was down to the fourth bowlers on each team. We needed a strike or a double from my father to pull even.

Daddy was set in his stance. I looked at the Tom's Barber Shop lettering on the back of his jersey as he began his approach. Silently I said, "Pocket. Hit the pocket."

His steps were perfect. He laid the bowling ball right on his spot over the foul line, two arrows in from the right gutter.

We all started getting excited as that black ball rolled straight and then broke on a short curve towards the one-three pocket. Yeh! Yeh! He put it right in there. My father was still suspended at the foul line, balancing on his left leg as the ball moved perfectly into the pocket.

One big explosion of sound came back to us from those pins falling and banging into each other. One big cheer from our teammates started, but was quickly swallowed as we watched all the pins go down except for the ten-pin. Our aborted cheer was quickly followed by moans, a "Dammit", "You got tapped", and "You wuz robbed". Each of us, the other team included, couldn't believe the injustice we had just seen.

My father slapped his hands together so hard upon seeing that lonely ten-pin still standing instead of being kicked down by the six-pin, like a normal pocket strike, that the bowler in lane five was distracted and couldn't begin his approach.

And then my father turned to us, his face a mask of rage, his mouth cursing the gods who had provoked him by stealing this strike from him. He viciously kicked the ball rack with his left foot, sending two balls off the rack, one rolling into the still-waiting bowler from Dalcamo's on lane five, and the other rolling all the way to lane four.

The civilized world had not seen such rage from a Patrick, since the 5th century when St. Patrick took his shillelagh to the snakes in Ireland and drove them to the sea.

My father's anger was not new to me. In the past, whether it had been hammerin' a nail and missing the connection to the board underneath, or waitin' in traffic for Ike's motorcade, or other occasions when things didn't go his way, I understood and accepted his behavior. (After all, why was the four-letter word "shit" invented by Old English carpenters, but for just such occasions).

But this outburst, this tirade because he was tapped by a ten-pin, made me embarrassed. Further, as I saw this happen more than once as we bowled together a lot—I was the anchorman for the team, the fifth bowler—I sensed some self-pity in my father. "That ball was a perfect hit, God, and you denied me," is probably what he was saying to himself as he briskly strode back to the bowlers' bench.

I found myself not only embarrassed but also irritated that he would launch these tirades in a fully-packed bowling alley, eventually making his teammates and the other bowlers uneasy with his actions. The more it happened, slowly I realized that their protestations and my admonitions to him weren't working.

So I developed a coolness to all of this, a stoicism that no matter what happened to the pins—or didn't—when I bowled, whether I would miss a spare, or get a railroad, I would remain calm, accepting my fate, even cold to the disappointment that befell me. I was not going to show any emotion when walking back from the foul line after an unjust fall of the pins, except one.

I silently vowed that I wouldn't get excited when I was bowling with my father, serving instead as a counterpoint and silent message to him that I was not accepting or even understanding his anger. I'd hope that he'd notice my calmness and silently say to himself, "See, Hughie Boy doesn't get all worked up when the pins don't fall. Why can't I do the same."

By the age of 19, I was bowling in three leagues each week, and holding a 165 average. There was the Holy Name league with my father and Tom's Barber Shop on Friday nights. The Santa Fe Railroad employees put together a league for Wednesdays, after work. And, my favorite league was on Sunday afternoons. I liked it because the teams were mixed with guys and girls. The resulting atmosphere was calm, social, and full of fun. Gone were the pressures of waiting to see when my father would erupt, and the tenseness of combat that always creeps into male sporting events, whether they be baseball, bowling, chess or checkers.

In the mixed league I could bowl for fun. I could relax between frames and talk to the girls and guys about work, career, and social life instead of constantly scanning the score sheet to see not only how well—or poorly—I was bowling, but also where the team was in competition with the opposing team. In fact, there were times when I didn't even know what my score was, or what frame we were bowling. It didn't matter to me that our team might be losing. The joke was on the serious bowlers in the league. Our team was there for the fun of it, whether we were in first place or last.

One Sunday afternoon in January of '58, I walked into Nap's Bowling Alley, where all the leagues bowled. I checked the posted sheet to see which pair of alleys our team would be using, and went there to put down my coat and put on my bowling shoes. I noticed an attractive blond sitting on the bench at our team's alleys, talking to a fella from our team. *Now this should be an interesting day, I thought, as I pulled my bowling ball out of the bag and brought it to the rack.* I smiled. She smiled! In a matter of a few minutes, I knew that she was Judy, and she lived at 34ᵗʰ and Wallace. *Very, very nice!*

I hadn't been dating too much since high school because the experience with Lucy had its lasting effects. But more importantly, I didn't have a car. My savings from work always went toward college costs so I couldn't invest in a vehicle, even a jalopy. And then there was the exorbitant cost of insurance. My father couldn't afford Jake and I as drivers on his auto insurance, so that proved to be another problem when I asked Daddy if I could use his car for a date. His answer always was, "Wait until you're 21, and then you can buy your own car and get your own insurance. 21 was a year away.

All of that didn't stop me from asking this good-looking girl from the bowling league for a date. During the week, I talked to my brother-in-law, Buck, about using his car. I told him there was this attractive girl named Judy, who I wanted to ask to the hockey game on Sunday night. He and my sister, Mag, were living on the first floor of our house with their little girl, Susan, having moved into the flat in the spring of '57. Buck knew my situation—interested in girls, but no wheels—and readily let me borrow his 4-door DeSoto.

Judy said "Yes" when I asked her at Sunday bowling if she'd like to see the Black Hawks game with me that night. It was a good evening, being out in a big car with a sharp girl. The Hawks won the game, so to celebrate, we went to Nap's Bar to get a drink and dance a little to Johnny Mathis. I took her home, talked a little in the car, and walked her to the door. The weather was getting colder, so we said "Thanks" and "Good Byes".

For some reason, I didn't call the next week to follow up the first date. I thought that I'd see her at bowling anyway on Sunday. To my surprise, when I got to Nap's the following Sunday, Judy was talking to my brother Jake. And they were smiling so nicely! Immediately, I interpreted that I was not going to get much further with Judy after watching those two together. After all, I was no competition for him, being 14 months younger, 4 inches shorter, not as good-lookin' as him, with his curly red hair, ruddy cheeks, broad smile, and wheels.

Yes, Wheels! Jake had bought a red, '53 Mercury when he turned 21 in December. He had the perfect car to impress the girls. Little did I know that Sunday at the bowling alley the gods, led by Venus, had already divined a Judy-Jake romance which would eventually lead to matrimony in 1960.

*

"Oh would I love to vote for Kennedy for President. He's going to run. All the papers are saying. And he'll win, too. I know it. He'll beat that Nixon. Ach! I don't like him. I don't trust him. I sure wish that I was a citizen," Aunt Mary said, in-between sips of her Rob-Roy Manhattan. We were celebrating New Years Day as usual, with her and Aunt Catherine in their small apartment on north Kenmore Ave. We had just finished another Flanagan Feast, and were relaxing, just catching the 10:00 news and sports scores from the Bowl games.

It was January 1st, 1959. John Kennedy had just won a 2nd term in November as U.S. Senator, with the biggest majority ever achieved by a candidate for office in Massachusetts. He was attracting attention all over the country, much more so than the brief bid he made at the 1956 Democratic Convention for the Vice-Presidential nomination. And most importantly, he was being invited by Democratic organizations throughout the land to come and show his handsome face, and speak about the future.

My interest in Senator Kennedy had been growing also. I read his book, *Profiles in Courage* and was amazed at his sense of history. The one college course that caught my imagination and zeal for study at St. Thomas College was the two-semester survey of American history. I was so impressed with the drama of the Colonial and Revolutionary periods, as described by the authors of the textbook, Morrison and Commager, that I connected immediately with the politicians in "Profiles", and devoured the rest of the book. It was easy for me to imagine these men and their conflicts with early American issues of governance. I even began to think that I would rather be an historian, instead of an engineer. Was this the beginning of a "call"?

I felt a sensitivity in Senator Kennedy to the dilemma of elected officials between voting their constituencies versus voting their conscience. There unfolded a depth in his writing of *Profiles* that drew me on to read more and digest the role of elected public service in our country.

Kennedy wrote that elected officials did care for themselves. They needed to respect themselves, which was more important than popularity. Their need to maintain a reputation was stronger than maintaining an office in government. Conscience, ethics, and integrity were the bulwarks of their personal belief. They believed that their course was best and was more important than the negative feelings of the public.

This emphasis on integrity was very attractive to me. I was beginning to see that public officials can be honest and still tackle the thorny issues ofthe day.

At the age of 20, I was maturing to an appreciation of our country's history of over 300 years. And just as the day follows night, and November comes after August, my thoughts shot ahead—after looking behind—to 1960, the next Presidential nominating convention, campaign and election.

"What was it like when you became a citizen?" Aunt Mary asked my mother when the commercial came on the TV.

"Well, 'twas hard fer me," Mommy answered. "I had to read the his'try, study the parts uv the guvermint, and then learn the answers to a flock uh ques'yuns. Would ye believe the judge never asked us a bit 'cept who was Pres'dent," she added. "He made cit'zens out of the lot of us in the room," she laughed, still with the brogue after all these years in America.

How well I remember sitting at the kitchen table in '51 when Mommy had begun the process of Naturalization. She'd push the book in front of me and say, "Now ask me them ques'yuns on the page."

I'd read the first question slowly. "On what date was the Declaration of Independence signed?"

She'd look at me as though she didn't know, fidgeting with the oil cloth border on the kitchen table, then looking out the window at the clothes hangin' on the line.

I didn't know whether to help her or not, so I just smiled and read the question again. This time she picked up on it, something connected, and slowly said, "July 4th."

"Good, Mom. Now what year for July 4th?"

Again I could see the hesitation, the mental searching for that elusive year. She became frustrated, sighing, pushing her hands across the table as though she was distancing herself from the disappointment in front of her, wondering if it was worth it.

"It was 1776," I told her. "Now here's an easy one. Who was the first President of . . . ?"

"George Washington," she blurted out before I could finish the question. She was smiling now, feeling better about her knowledge, confident that she would learn what was required by the Court, and become a citizen.

And she did on January 29th, 1952 with Sadie VanHecke, our next door neighbor as her sponsor. It had been almost 30 years from the time she emigrated from Ireland to Ellis Island, and then Chicago. Mommy was now a United States citizen, just like Daddy and the six of us kids.

Aunt Mary brought me back from my memory of Mommy. "But how will I get started with my own papers when I'm illegal in this country for over 20 years," she complained in a dejected voice. "If I call the government, they'd kick me outta the country."

How well we all knew of Aunt Mary's secret entry into the United States. She had emigrated in 1929 to Canada because the U.S. would not take a foreigner who had TB as a child, even though she had a sponsor in Chicago. But, Canada would take her because her passport was good for all countries in the United Kingdom.

Aunt Mary worked in Montreal as a waitress and was successful, even moving up to waiting in the finer French restaurants. But she longed to be in the States, especially with her sister, Margaret, and her brothers Jim, Packy and Dominic. There were no Flanagan relatives in Canada, so she was lonely.

Mommy and Daddy had heard that the new Ambassador Bridge, which was the border crossing between Canada and the States at Windsor, Ontario and Detroit, Michigan, was very busy, especially with commuters and travelers. Perhaps the border agents on the American side of the bridge wouldn't ask for Aunt Mary's passport if she was riding in an American-licensed car.

So, Mommy and Daddy agreed to pick up Aunt Mary on the Windsor side at her apartment, have her sit in the back seat—like Herself—with Mommy in the front, and Daddy doing the driving.

It worked! They were waved on by the American guards, past the U.S. border, and merrily drove the rest of the way home to Chicago. Within a month, armed with a fierce determination to succeed in her "new" country, a willingness to learn, and a Social Security card, Aunt Mary continued her career as a waitress in Chicago restaurants. There were The Latin Quarter, The Conrad Hilton, and other *haute cuisine* restaurants. She saved her tips, invested in that icon of American capitalism, the Stock Market, and—after 25 years—had a diverse portfolio of investments. These gave her additional income and value with dividends, stock splits, etc. She was paying income taxes on these capital gains, even though she wasn't a citizen, just an illegal alien.

But Aunt Mary didn't make the call to the government to see how she could be naturalized. She procrastinated and let the years pass by, fearing perhaps the worst by confessing to the Feds of her illegal entry. It wasn't until the spring of 1963 that she finally contacted a lawyer to advise her. He developed a plan with the government that called for Aunt Mary to return to Canada, and establish residence for three months. At the end of this period, she could apply for alien status and return to Chicago. Then she could reestablish residence—same apartment on the north side—and finally apply for naturalization.

*

There was only one rite of passage left for me on Thursday, February 18, 1959 at 8:52 AM when I reached the legal age of 21. Whereas, yesterday on the 17th and up to the early morning on the 18th, I was just "Hughie Boy" or "kiddo", or better yet, "young man", now I was to be known as "man", "Mister", "Sir".

I had passed the first rite of manhood in Chicago 10 years earlier when I lit and smoked my first cigarette in the underground sidewalk clubhouse. In the years afterward, I moved from sneakin' a smoke in the alley, to smoking at home and flicking the ashes into the ashtray on the front room drum table.

Then I graduated from puffin' on Lucky Strikes to inhaling Winstons—the filter was saving my lungs, the tobacco company said. I even tried cigars at weddings or when a baby was born.

I had no trouble hurdling the second rite of maleness, playin' sports. I was proficient in football, basketball, bowling, and the annual love of my life, baseball. I could run, throw and catch the pigskin, dribble the basketball down the court, hit the softball hard and far, and compete to win the game. And although I had usually suffered rejection at being picked last or "left out" for the softball game as a kid, everyone agreed that by the age of 21, I not only could play these games, but also talk about sports. "He shudda bunted instead of swingin' away," I second-guessed the White Sox manager after the batter failed to advance the runner on first.

Just recently, I had overcome the third rite of male maturity. I had learned the hard way with a nasty bump on my forehead, to always eat well before going to a party. Then I took the advice of a veteran Chi-Annie who said, "Always count." He admonished me, wagging his right index finger in front of my face.

"One drink—mixed of course. Sip, pause, talk, sip, dance. Then maybe after a half-hour, a second drink—still mixed. Talk again, laugh, dance, sip instead of drinkin'. Walk to the toilet. Have some chips or popcorn. More dancin'. A little sweat—that's good! Gets rid of the poison. And no straight stuff! Don't put any whiskey in yer mouth that's so powerful it causes barroom floors to leap up and hit yuh in the face. Okay! After an hour or so, maybe a third drink, but that's the limit. Three's yer lucky number. And make sure it's got lotsa ice and Seven-Up. Ya wanna really nurse this one. Remember! Remember! Ya wanna be around at the end of the night to take that girl with the brown eyes, you've been dancin' with, home. Got it?

Three minutes of lost innocence and two bucks took care of the fourth rite. It was late one cool, June evening in 1958 when an older Chi-Annie and I drove to 14th St., east of Jew town. He knew the street and the old, frame house in the middle of the block with the red light in the window.

But there was still one rite of passage I had not conquered. One acquisition that would gain the respect of my peers, the pride of my father, and the interest of the opposite sex.

No, it wasn't a job or career. I had been workin' since the age of nine, fifth grade all the way thru high school, and now at the Santa Fe. There was no glory or great sense of manhood in me with work, even though my father had taught me that "an honest man gets his hands dirty at work." The manual labor on the docks and subsequent savings for college were all directed to getting a job where I *didn't* get my hands dirty.

And it certainly wasn't a gun that I needed to be called a man. My father took me hunting for pheasant one Saturday when I was eight years old. We were walking thru a corn field south of Chicago, as he explained to me about gun safety. I watched as he showed me how to carry the 12-gauge shotgun with the double-barrels disengaged from the gun stock and triggers.

All of a sudden, our noise spooked a pheasant to fly up in front of us. I looked with wide eyes as Daddy grabbed the double barrels with his left hand, locked them in place with the stock, raised the loaded shotgun, and pulled one trigger, "BAM", then the second, "BAM." But it was too late! The pheasant flew up and away, still alive.

The shotgun blasts scared me, and the thought of killing a brightly, colored bird with a long, pointed tail and ringed-neck, turned me off too. Besides, what was there to eat on a pheasant anyway.

I had no trouble at all with the BB gun Daddy got for my brother and me for Christmas when I was nine. "No birds," he warned us when we were practicing with it in the back yard against a cardboard target.

One day, Patrick and I spotted a rat crawling on the old wood Daddy had stored between the porch joists under Grandma Bosak's back porch. We quickly blocked one end of the porch joist space with a wide piece of wood. Then we ran to the other end with the gun. We could see that the rat was confused now because he didn't know which way to crawl, with one end blocked and Pat and I at the other.

"PUNF" went the gun when my brother fired at the rat. "Darn it, I missed 'em," he said to me.

"Lemme try," I said, grabbing the gun and cocking it. I looked down the 15 feet of old wood that was like a tunnel, and spotted that rat lookin' at me. I aimed by closing the left eye, sighting the barrel with my right. Then I slowly squeezed the trigger and held the gun firmly.

"PUNF"

"I hit 'em," I yelled to Pat.

My brother looked into the tunnel and could see the rat bleeding from the body and starting to crawl away from us toward the blocked end.

"PUNF" came the sound again. 'You dirty rat, take that," Pat was yellin'. He cocked the BB gun again and fired. "PUNF" And again he cocked, "PUNF" Again, "PUNF" BeeBees were flyin' all over that tunnel of death.

None of the Chi-Annies ever talked much about having a pistol, or rifle, shotgun, or even goin' huntin'. It just wasn't part of being a man, as far as I could see. Even the older guys who had been in the Army never had much to say about guns.

However, one Saturday afternoon, a bunch of us were takin' it easy at the Club, watchin' a White Sox daygame against the Orioles. Paul Richards, the manager of the GOGO SOX in the early '50s was now the skipper of the Baltimore team. As usual, the Sox were chasing the Yankees for first place that summer.

Into the Club walked Jimmy, one of the older neighborhood guys who liked guns. He came over to show us the new, aluminum '38 caliber handgun he had just got that week. The bunch of us stood around the front room as he was tossin' it from one hand to another. Then he took it in his right hand, put his finger on the trigger, and started pointing the gun towards us, wheelin' in a circle, making a prolonged "Whee" sound.

When Jimmy came to me, he stopped, smiled devilishly, said something like "Russian Roulette", and started to pull the trigger.

I yelled "NO", but it was too late.

"Click" I heard, mingled with my terror of staring at the barrel of that gun.

He laughed at me, and said, "Don't worry, there's no bullets in it. See." He pulled the bullet chamber down. Sitting in the top slot, with its firing cap exposed, next up in the barrel was a lone bullet.

Naw, my final rite of passage had nothing to do with guns, no matter which end of the barrel I was on. And it had nothing to do with the violence and victory of a fist-fight. By the late '50s, boxing had lost much of its glamour and toughness. Besides, I had already proved myself with the fists in a one-round tiff against another Jimmy four years earlier, after being "egged on" by the guys.

Like most things American, there were choices if I crawled and clawed my way up to the last plateau of masculinity. I had to decide. Decide between makes, models, colors, standard or whitewall tires. "Are you a Ford man, a Chevy guy, or maybe a classy Chrysler gent? 2-doors. 4-doors. Hey, how about a nice convertible! Black with chrome is really tough-lookin'. Classy! Stay away from red or yellow. White always shows the dirt and grease from the street. And lissen! Get the stick on the steerin' column. There's nuttin in yer way when yer parked at the Lake. Ya know whud I mean?"

With the connection of my girlfriend, Little Judy with the brown eyes and dark hair whose Uncle had a Mercury dealership in the northwest suburbs, and the advice of my father who had been kickin' tires since the '20s, I finally bought a '51 Chevy. It had a fantastic black paint job, flashy chrome, whitewalls, and a sweep-back 2-door styling. And the stick was on the column. Looked just like the Batmobile. *What a sharp car!*

I was now ready to conquer the world, my passage to manhood complete. I even got my father to call me Hughie instead of Hughie Boy.

*

By September of 1959, the White Sox were well on their way to the American League pennant, after a forty-year drought. I was heading back to college to study engineering at Illinois Institute of Technology. Once again,

I had saved enough money for tuition from my railroad job, this time at the Santa Fe, and I could count on limited expenses since I was living at home. The only other big expense was insurance for the "Batmobile".

My classes in Mechanical Engineering were in Machinery Hall, a tall, old red stone & brick building at 33rd and Federal. It was part of the set of red buildings at that corner which were originally Armour Institute in the 1920s. They now stood in stark contrast to the low, black, modern, steel Hermann Hall and the other modular classroom structures designed by Mies van der Rowe and Skidmore, Owens and Merrill. The campus had spread north to 31st and east to Michigan Ave. by 1959.

Shortly after I began classes, I noticed an article in the Technology News, the student newspaper.

> Coach Ed Glancy's baseball squad needs pitching help desperately. The 1960 baseball season will start with a fall tryout session to be held early in the semester.

I couldn't believe what I was reading. The I.I.T. team needs pitchin' *That's me! And tryouts soon. That's me again! My chance has come. Now where's my glove?* The old, black one I used when I played last summer at Harrison Park in the city, sandlot Mexican League. I pitched a little there, mostly in relief, not enough to be a force on the team. But, I did get the nickname of *"El Gringo."*

The tryouts were held in the old gym/fieldhouse on 32nd & Dearborn, one late afternoon in November. About 30 guys were there, playing catch, fielding grounders, loosening up. When Coach Glancy called for the pitchers and catchers to move to one side of the gym, I joined this smaller group. I looked around and saw nine or ten players standing, waiting for the Coach's instructions. I didn't know anyone there, although a few "veterans" from last year's team were talking to each other.

After 10 minutes of warming up and pitching to a catcher under the watchful eyes of Glancy, each tryout pitcher was excused. When it was my turn, I took the half windup on every pitch, pivoted, and followed thru, with my glove up, ready to field a batted ball. I kept the pitches low, around the knees, and didn't throw real fast, concentrating instead on control. And, I wasn't fooling around with any curve balls.

In less than a week, I found out that I had made the first cut and would be invited to spring tryouts. Coach Glancy liked my "mechanics", my movement and rhythm, and especially control. I could hardly believe that I had a chance to play college baseball after missing it in high school. Secretly, I always felt I could play ball if I had the opportunity. Here I was, in the center field shadows of nearby Comiskey Park, pounding that black glove and oiling it for the coming season.

My days were spent in Math and Science classes and German that fall semester, commuting the mile and a half from my home to campus in my "new" car. I didn't have a part-time job, so studying time was plentiful both at school and at home in the remodeled basement. The basement was usually quiet at night except when Daddy decided to sharpen his hand saws with a file while I was trying to do Advanced Algebra. When I complained that I couldn't concentrate with the screeching sounds coming from metal on metal, he just smiled and said he'd be finished soon.

To overcome the cold, basement floor in late fall and winter, I built a 3-inch platform out of spare wood Daddy had been saving. Onto the platform were my desk with just enough room for the chair. Next to me, for heat, was the old, oil stove.

The full load of course work proved to be good for me, challenging, but not overbearing. And the professors were fine. I had fun in German with Herr Richter, the bantam professor from Deutschland, whose vocation in life was pounding *Der-Die-Das* into our American heads. Teaching us the difference between masculine, feminine, and neuter nouns in German was his favorite. He would stand at the chalkboard and write *Der Mann*—m., *Die Frau*—f., *Das Kind*—n., He'd always make us recite these three nouns as examples of the three genders. Then he'd say, with a twinkle in his eyes, "You know, the Germans are very smart. They know about life. They know what God had in mind. The German word for God is *Gott, der* Gott—Masculine. But the German word for 'devil' is *Teufel*. And it's *Die Teufel*. A feminine noun!"

My social life was on the weekends, going out with Little Judy, the younger sister of one of the girls I had met in the Sunday bowling league. There wasn't much available at I.I.T. during the weekends, so we pretty much did the pizza, movies, parking routines, with an occasional family party.

At Christmas break, I was able to get a job sorting mail at the Main Post Office on Canal St. I could work as many hours as I wanted from December 15th to Christmas Eve. Some days I'd be there for 12 hours, working the morning and afternoon shifts. The money was good, just what I needed to stay full-time at school.

*

The music of Broadway was so much a part of American life. Popular show tunes were played on the radio and sung on TV to the delight of fans across the country. One such tune was "Everything's Coming up Roses" This bouncy, positive song seemed to have the perfect words and sounds to get the country moving again.

Ethel Merman, as the stage-mother of Gypsy Rose Lee, ushered in the decade of the'60s on Broadway with this upbeat, positive tune written by Styne and Sondheim. White Sox fans were smiling because the popular Minnie Minoso was returning to the South Side of Chicago to play left field, after a December trade with the Cleveland Indians. At the Rose Bowl on January 1st, the Huskies from the University of Washington paraded past Wisconsin's Badgers, 44-6. And to no one's surprise, to the genuine pleasure of many, Senator John F Kennedy stepped before the microphones at a press conference Saturday, January 2nd, and stated what his supporters wanted to hear;

> I am announcing today my candidacy
> for the Presidency of the United States . . . .

Again, I felt a surge of pride as I saw his announcement on TV. His words and confident manner stirred me in a subtle way as he finished the announcement with;

> I can win the nomination and election.

Right away, the newspapers said he was one of the favorites, along with Sen. Hubert Humphrey and Sen. Stuart Symington, with Sen. Lyndon Johnson waiting in the wings, and Adlai Stevenson characteristically undecided. I knew deep down that I'd follow Kennedy's progress with the spring Primaries and the summer Convention. Already I was feeling good that John Kennedy would get the nomination, and then I would gladly cast my first vote for President of the United States.

*

My first semester report card from I.I.T. showed a smattering of B's and C's, and one A. I felt good sharing this with Mommy and Daddy. And, tuition money was holding up for the spring semester—tuition for the whole year was $800. I was fortunate to get a job on the truck docks at 30th and Halsted during the two-week semester break. (I didn't know anyone at school who could afford the beaches at Ft.Lauderdale, where the girls are). I had to lie to the dock foreman though and say that I wasn't in college and *was* looking for full-time work.

As soon as the second semester began, I was invited to a wedding, my brother Jake's. He and Judy—the attractive blond—decided to get married early because Jake was facing the draft. So, they exchanged vows on February 27th at Nativity Church on 37th and Lowe. A huge wedding reception was held that night at the Knights of Columbus Hall on 31st, attesting to the popularity of the bride and groom.

By early March, the I.I.T. basketball season had ended and their Coach, Ed Glancy, could now conduct the spring tryouts for baseball. After showing lots of control again in these tryouts, using more speed with my pitches, and mixing in a few curveballs, Glancy liked what he saw and picked me to be one of his pitchers for the 1960 season.

Practices started on Tuesday, March 15th, and continued for four weeks. Opening Day was scheduled for Tuesday, April 12th at 3:00 PM vs. Chicago Teachers College. We would be opening at home, at the brand new Tech Field at 31st and Dearborn.

Before that first game, Coach Glancy told us that last year's team had an 0 and 14 record. "1959 was a frustrating season," he said. "Lotsa power, but no pitchin'." But now he had high expectations, especially because the team as a whole looked good, pitchin' and hittin'.

We rewarded Coach by starting the season with two wins, the soggy opener against Chicago Teachers 10-6, and the second game victory over North Park College, 6-5.

In that North Park game, at their field on the north side of Chicago, I was called on to relieve Ed Fandel, who had pitched the first six innings. We were ahead by one run when I came to the mound. *Was I nervous?* You bet, but still with control of my fast ball, keeping it low, and using a wide curve ball when I had two strikes on a batter, I was able to get their three hitters on ground balls. The Tech victory was saved!

Wow! I felt great as I ran off the pitcher's mound after the last putout was made by Bob Hilvers, our big first baseman. I was on top of the world when the guys patted me on the back in the dugout. Fandel came over and added, "Thanks for the relief."

Coach Glancy really made me smile when he came up to me in the locker room, slapped me lightly on the back, and said, "Nice pitchin' kiddee."

My pitching career suffered a setback a week later, though, when the Tech team traveled to Aurora College for our third game. Glancy picked me to start the game. We had to drive to Aurora ourselves, and since I had a car, three teammates came with me. I should have known this was not going to be my day because half-way to the town of Aurora, on a stretch of new expressway west of Chicago, the engine on my '51 Chevy blew a radiator hose. I was so busy talking to my teammates I didn't realize it until I happened to glance at the engine heat gauge. By the time I stopped the car, the engine was completely out of water, and smoking.

After everything cooled down, we taped the old hose as best we could, found some water in a nearby ditch, and hurried to make that game at Aurora College. I was really nervous now, not only because I had to pitch, but also worrying if this old clunker would now get us to the ball field in time. Fortunately, I hadn't blown the engine. But it sounded like a machine gun, with the rings in the cylinders and the valve heads chattering loudly as we drove into the town. People on the sidewalks would turn their heads to us as we drove by, wondering what was making all that racket.

Even though I started off with a five-run lead in the first inning, both our defense and my lack of good speed with the fastball against the better hitters, led to a four-run first for Aurora. I lasted until the fourth inning and then gave way to Dave McGuire with our team behind. Coach Glancy had seen enough of me after I misplayed a comebacker with men on second and third. By the end of the game, we were on the short end of a 14-10 score. *Sadly, my baseball dream bubble and my '51 Chevy burst on the same day!*

Throughout that season, I continued to pitch relief, having some success and some failure. A lack of stamina seemed to keep me from being effective over five or six innings. I just didn't have the body size to throw hard for that stretch. My curve ball was fair, easily tipped off to the hitters I faced by my side-arm delivery. And the drop ball I experimented with, wasn't dropping in actual game. It was flyin'outta the park!

Even though I came face-to-face with the reality that I was a fair pitcher, I still enjoyed the game of baseball. It was such a great feeling to be part of a team, to practice together, joke around, needle one another, feel the tension of competition, and taste the sweetness of victory. Our Techhawk team won nine games and lost six in the 1960 season, a very pleasant improvement from the year before.

*

Mag and Buck were the first in the family to leave the old neighborhood of Bridgeport. After three years of marriage, and two kids, Susan and Tommy, and living in the first floor flat of our house, they bought a new, tri-level home in Glendale Heights. It was unfinished, so some of the family, myself included, would drive the 30 miles to the far, western suburbs to spackle and paint walls and ceilings on the weekends.

In between these visits, after the spring baseball season had finished, and final exams were over, I was working on the Batmobile, replacing the engine that had melted down with a rehabbed one from "Monkey" Wards. I was getting my hands dirty (actually greasy) with the mechanical car work, and actually enjoying it. Once more, it was good to handle tools, pay attention to car parts, figure out how the carburetor and distributor work, and keep track of what was taken off the old engine and from where. Those parts hadda go back on the "new" engine someplace.

The culmination of the engine overhaul occurred one early, June afternoon in Daddy's garage. I turned the ignition key to see if the new engine and overhauled head would run. They ran, coughing, sputtering and choking as the cylinders misfired. Daddy said, "It's probably the carburetor. Take it off and check the valves inside."

Sure enough, he was right. The needle valve was upside down—my fault. Tryin' again, she fired like a race car engine, purrin' so smoothly. Now to get back on the road!

That June of '60, my brother Jake was drafted and sent to boot camp in the Army. My younger brother, Fred, graduated from DeLaSalle Institute, and was accepted at the University of Illinois at Chicago, Navy Pier, as we called the school. And Maureen, the youngest, became the last of six LeVoys to graduate from St.Anthony de Padua School. Subsequently, she became the third LeVoy girl to attend St.Patrick's Girls High School, following Mag and Kate.

I closed my first year in Mechanical Engineering at I.I.T. with a 2.68 grade point average. The course work was not challenging me so far, and I found my interest in the major field kinda lagging. Although I understood and liked the Math couses—Descriptive Geometry, Trigonometry, Algebra, Analytic Geometry, and Calculus—the courses in Mechanics, Dynamics, Statics and Production Methods did not "grab" me, or lead me to imagine a career in engineering. *Something was missing!* I had more fun speaking German in Herr Richter's classes, messing up *Der—Die—Das* with every noun. *Was ist los? Bist du ein Dummkopf?*

Summer came and that meant work. I wasn't taking any courses, and needed to make enough for the fall semester's tuition, which went up to $475. Returning to the Santa Fe Railroad, I was able to get a job as a fireman at their switching yards on the south west side of Chicago. My duties consisted of sitting in the switch engine, looking out the window, and relaying switching signals from the switchmen on the ground who were down the line of boxcars. Without a doubt, it was the most boring job I ever had, especially when the hours I would be called for work were usually midnight to 8 AM. Every one of those nights that summer was a battle to stay awake to see what was ahead of us on the tracks. My eyes were needed because the engineer was on the other side of the cab and could only see on his side of the switch engine.

*

"Hey kids, ya wanna be a Sox player. Have ya got a glove and a pair of gym shoes. Then come over to Sox Park tomorrow for a tryout. That's right, a tryout! Bill Veeck promises that the Sox will look at your talents. Who knows! Maybe you're the next Nellie Fox, or Early Wynn." It was Jack Brickhouse, the Sox announcer, advertising another one of Bill Veeck's promotions.

"Tryouts at Sox Park? Just bring my glove? Was this real?"

I decided to call Clare Krusinski, one of the teammates from I.I.T. He had heard the promotion and didn't know whether to believe it or not. He had always wanted to play pro ball as a shortstop. He was a good fielder who could hit also.

The next morning, I told Mommy and Daddy where I was going—White Sox Park. They both laughed at me for believing this promo by Veeck.

Daddy said, "It's just another Veeck stunt to get publicity, like the exploding scoreboard in centerfield. Remember, you have to work tonight."

I had to agree with him because with all the trades Veeck had made after the Sox won the pennant in '59, but lost the World Series to the Dodgers in six games, the Sox of 1960 were *not* in first place. Maybe this was a diversion from the fact that the Sox were not contenders this year.

But, my desire to play ball, and the romance of walking on the hallowed ground of the professional playing field at the age of 22, propelled me forward to 35th and Shields.

I couldn't believe the crowd of kids outside the main gates. Thousands of teenagers and young men with their gloves, White Sox hats, and some with their own bats. *Did I stand a chance with all this competition?*

Once we were let into the park, an announcement was made over the Public Address that all pitchers and catchers were to report to the centerfield bullpen. Infielders had to go to the first and third base lines, and outfielders to left field.

My first step on the field brought back memories of running along the left field wall to steal that batting practice ball when I was 10. Pat Seerey had scared me with his growl, but then hoisted me up to my buddies, with the ball in my hand. Now I was a young man who had permission, in fact, was invited to not only walk on this field, but actually perform my baseball skills. Wow!

Once the pitchers walked across the outfield to the bullpen, we had to fill out a card with personal information. Then we stood in a line, waiting to pitch to Ray Berres, the White Sox pitching coach. While waiting, I noticed the guys ahead of me were given 10 pitches each. That's all. *I better be on target when my turn comes.*

Finally, it was me on the rubber. I looked at Berres 60 feet away, took my comfortable half-windup, rotated on the rubber with my right foot, kicked off that same rubber pad embedded in the ground, and delivered a nice, low pitch on the inside corner of the plate in front of him.

My other 9 pitches were just as smooth, and low, over the plate. Berres yelled, "Good job" after my tenth pitch. Then he nodded to his assistant who was by me and the rubber.

"Gimme your card, kid. Berres likes your pitchin'. You make the first cut. Go over to the right field stands and grab a seat. We'll call your name when it's time for the second tryout," the assistant told me.

I was elated. Berres likes me. I'm in the runnin'. Maybe this is for real, not just a gimmick like the scoreboard above my head here in centerfield.

I ran, not walked across right field to the stands, carrying my glove and bag of lunch. There were some guys already sitting there, waiting I suppose, just like me. I was so excited, I tripped over one of the short steps in the box seats aisle as I made my way up to the right field wall and the foul pole.

I sat down in the second row near a couple of guys. They had big smiles on their face like me. When I looked around I could see a few more prospective pitchers joining us in the stands. It was time for some food, even though it was only 11 AM on the scoreboard clock. With the crowd of guys trying out for pitcher, it'd be an hour, at least, before the second round. I could relax a little, eat my sandwich, and look around at the other guys trying out in the infield. Maybe I'd see Clare at shortstop.

The sun was shining. The temperature was in the 70's. I was in my "second home". I had visions of standing on the mound with a Sox uniform, winding up to face that fearsome Yankee hitter, Mickey Mantle. All I had to do was sit and wait for that "call" to strut down to the bullpen. "Hugh LeVoy. Please report to the centerfield bullpen," I imagined hearing, as though it was just a matter of time.

Forty years later, it's the year 2000, and I'm still sitting and waiting for that White Sox call!

*

Recall with me the words of Isaiah:
They that wait upon the Lord shall
renew their strength; they shall
mount up with wings as eagles; they
shall run and not be weary.

As we face the coming challenge, we
too shall wait upon the Lord, and ask
that he renew our strength. Then we
shall be equal to the test. Then we

> shall not be weary. And then we
> shall prevail.

I watched and listened intently as John F Kennedy somberly and prayerfully finished his Acceptance of the Democratic Party Nomination for President. It was a hot night on July 15th, and I was supposed to be sleeping, getting rest for the midnight shift at the railroad. But I wanted to see and hear him talk after he had won enough votes on the first ballot at the Convention, with Wyoming putting him over the top the night before.

Kennedy looked tan and youthful, but tired at the Coliseum in Los Angeles. There was a stridency in his voice, an urgency, a thrust, as he pounded the air with his right hand. Throughout the first half of his speech he kept calling for change;

> . . . . it's time for change . . . . the world is
> changing . . . . changing face of the future
> . . . . a change—a slippage—in our intellectual
> and moral strength . . . . today there can be
> no status quo.

And following these phrases, he moved me to silent agreement at the end;

> . . . . we stand today on the edge of a New Frontier
> . . . . But I tell you the New Frontier is here I
> am asking each of you to be pioneers on that
> New Frontier . . . . My call is to the young at
> heart . . . . Give me your help, your hand,
> your voice, your vote.

I heard John Kennedy's "call" that summer night, his dramatic, pleading voice. *Awakenings stirred within me, subtle thoughts about getting involved, faint feelings of guilt that I was not helping others, energies surfacing to do something. It was clear that the persona and pleas of this man on the screen were getting to me personally. I was changing.*

Was I one of the "young at heart?" Did I need to look at a greater role in life than engineering? Was this the beginning of a new frontier for me?

A new experience greeted me when I returned to I.I.T. for the fall of '60. Fraternities! I was "rushed" by a couple of Houses and finally picked Theta Xi. I decided to join them rather than the Delts because the Brothers had very little pretence about frat life, were lukewarm toward the academic world, liked to drink beer, but mostly because one of my baseball teammates, Bob Keller, was an officer in the House.

Little Judy had broken up with me in August, mostly because of my immaturity. I was too interested in "wrestling matches" instead of conversation and light romance. Again, I performed badly, and this time I was tossed out of the ring.

The only real social life at I.I.T. was with the Greeks. There were about seven male fraternities and a couple of sororities. Besides parties at the frat house, and dances, there also were interfraternity sports events, choral competition, and the annual drama contest.

Course work was challenging, especially Calculus, but the most interesting class was Economics. Our professor was totally captivated by the Nixon—Kennedy campaigns. Part of every class became an analysis of the two candidates. And then, after the first televised debate on Monday, September 26th in Chicago, we spent the entire period giving our opinions as to who had won. Even the prof, a moderate Republican, had to admit that Kennedy's stance and phrase, "I think it's time America started movin' again," could not be matched by Nixon. There was a lot of talk among us in that classroom how healthy, knowledgeable and poised Kennedy appeared in contrast to the pale and "me too" Nixon.

A week before the November election, two professors had a debate of their own on campus, one supporting Nixon, and his opponent supporting Kennedy. That was followed by a mock election. To no one's surprise, Nixon edged out Kennedy by 26 votes out of 928 cast. We all got a sense, however, that the real election would be close, very close. The national polls kept saying the same thing. A Toss Up!

*

When Mag and Buck moved out of our first floor flat at the house on 28th Place in May of '60, my younger sister, Kate, and her fiancé, Don Fumarolo, started to rehab the place in anticipation of their coming fall wedding. Once again, the walls started crumblin' and the dust went flyin'. And similar to the floor above, the massive arch between the front room and dining room was demolished to open the two, small rooms to one large one. Sure enough, my father was called upon to cut the final stud that was holding up . . . . er, holding up . . . . uh, nothing, except my mother upstairs, on her knees praying the Rosary that the 2nd floor wouldn't collapse into the 1st.

Kate met Donny thru her girlfriends from St.Pat's. They all lived in the Italian neighborhood called Taylor Street, just south of the Loop and west of Halsted St. Donny was a thin, likeable guy of 21, who was eager to learn remodeling, willing to get his hands dirty, and not afraid to wield a crowbar.

My father accepted him into the family after Donny asked for Kate's hand. But privately, Daddy complained to me, "How in the hell is he ever going to nail two boards together when he's swinging the hammer with his left hand?"

Fall turned to winter on Saturday, November 5th, as light snow started falling in the morning of their wedding day. The scene was the altar at St. Anthony's Church. My father and mother were in the first pew again, on the bride's side of the main aisle, looking on as their second daughter was formally leaving them—only to move downstairs. Mommy was beaming, proudly wearing the mink stole around her shoulders that she always coveted for weddings. Mag and Buck "stood up" for the wedding as bridesmaid and groomsman. Jake was not there, serving in Germany with the Army. Standing next to me in the family pew was my little brother Fred—who was now six feet tall—and attending college. And on the other side was Maureen, who had just begun St. Pat's Girls High School.

During the wedding reception at the Berwyn Eagles Hall, I searched for and found my cousin Cissy and her husband Tommy Howe among the 250 guests. I was dying to talk to him about the big, torchlight parade that Mayor Daley had staged the night before for Kennedy. Tommy had to work at this huge campaign event because he was a Water Dept. plumber and ward politician. The article in Saturday's paper talked of "Searchlights, fireworks, ward workers—the works." But I couldn't get downtown to actually see my candidate and the hoopla.

When I finally met Tommy at the bar, I blurted out, "Did ya get to see Kennedy? What does he look like? He's really got a great tan?"

Tommy sensed my eagerness for anything of a personal nature that he could relate to me about seeing Kennedy in the open limo coming down Madison St., heading to the Chicago Stadium. "Oh yeah! Kennedy was smiling and waving his right hand to the crowd. He looked great. When the motorcade got close to me, Kennedy looked at me and shouted, 'Hi Tommy. How's Sissy and the kids?'

"Really," I said incredulously, while Tommy was grinning from ear to ear. Slowly, the joke settled into my head, and I patted him on the back for his subtle humor.

Three days later, on Tuesday, the 8th of November, I woke early, dressed, ate some breakfast, grabbed my books and headed for Mark Sheridan School on 27th and Wallace. The campaign signs were up on the schoolyard fence and parkway as I turned the corner of 27th and Normal, KENNEDY—JOHNSON, KENNEDY FOR PRESIDENT—LEADERSHIP FOR THE 60's. I smiled as I walked past them, knowing I was going to help him get elected.

The polling place in the basement of the school was unusually busy, much more so than the Primary election that was held in April. I waited patiently, observing the democratic process being implemented by election judges that I knew from the neighborhood. The Democratic precinct captain was smiling, thanking me for coming to vote.

Shortly, it was my turn to walk into the voting machine, and pull the red handle in the middle to close the curtains. I felt strange to be all alone, inside, in front of all those little levers with names above them. I could hear the judges and observers talking outside. *Some tension started to creep into me. What should I do? Should I vote the straight Democratic ticket by flipping just one lever, or go thru each office and flip the levers. If I spend too much time in here, the precinct captain will think that I'm splitting my ballot. He wouldn't like that, and neither would Mayor Daley, his boss, The Boss. I could feel the captain's eyes staring at my curtain, wondering what's taking so long.*

But I just had to read each office and flip the levers of my choice, no matter how long it took, beginning with the first one with Kennedy-Johnson printed above the lever. That first flip for President gave me such a feeling of pride in my hero and participation in the democratic process. I was making history in this little cubicle with the touch of a finger.

After what seemed to be an hour, I turned the big lever to the right to register my vote and open the curtain. Back to the real world now.

I felt good all day at I.I.T., knowing that I had voted for Kennedy, somewhat confident that he would pull out a victory. It was the same feeling I had in 1959 when the White Sox would go into the last of the 9th inning, tied 4-4. I just knew they would find that leadoff walk, followed by a sacrifice bunt, and then a bloop single to left field that brought home the winning run. All the fans in the stands would be cheering and happy as they headed home with another triumph.

During election night I was *not* prepared for the uncertainty I heard on TV. The early returns from the eastern states looked good for Kennedy. And the projections for voter turnout were pushing a record of 69 million voters—a sure sign of a Democratic victory. But then Huntley-Brinkley predicted a "cliff-hanger", and by 10 PM the commentators were wondering if Kennedy could possibly get 269 electoral votes. Ohio went to Nixon, California was a toss-up—Nixon won the Golden State eventually by 35,000 out of six ½ million votes cast. Texas was still out, Michigan was close, and surprisingly, so was Illinois. The big lead that the Democrats had in Chicago was slowly being whittled down by Republican counties downstate, as the hour approached midnight.

Mommy came into the front room in her nightgown and told me to go to bed because I was keeping everybody awake with the TV—even though it had been turned down to barely audible. She and Daddy had gone to bed at 11:00, a full half hour after their usual time because of the election coverage. She knew that I was riveted to the TV and wouldn't shut it off on my own. She also knew that I'd stay up all night, just like I did with a good book.

But she and Daddy had to get up early the next day, and I had school. So, I reluctantly pressed the button and watched the light on the screen shrink into the center and disappear. Now, the big question in my not-so-tired head was whether I could get to sleep with the drama going across the country. *Would I toss 'n turn most of the night, imagining all kinds of vote return scenarios?* Could Kennedy win without *me* watching the results? As a kid, I used to believe it was good luck for the Sox if I was listening to their game. I could silently root and send my will power for a base hit thru the radio all the way to Nellie Fox, who was batting with the bases loaded. But in bed, I couldn't send any vote power to the polling stations.

The next morning I woke with a start at 8 AM. I could hear the radio in the kitchen, and my mother with the dishes. Like a bolt, I jumped outta bed and hurried to the kitchen. As soon as she saw me, Mommy smiled, and said, "Well, Himself did it."

I cheered, grinned and gave her a hug. "He won! Kennedy won!" I shouted.

The announcer on the radio was going thru the numbers for Illinois. It sounded like Kennedy had won by a real close margin, "Razor thin," the announcer said.

"Kennedy is President," I spoke to myself. "Unbelievable," as I punched the air with my right fist. What a triumph for Kennedy and his family! A starving Kennedy immigrant from famine-filled Ireland started an American Irish family 112 years ago in Boston, and now, in 1960, the great-grandson has been elected to the highest office in the land. From peasant to President. From thatched cottage to the White House. And from powerless, tenant farmer under John Bull's tyranny to the most powerful person in the free world. The American Dream! What opportunities for progress the United States had provided in those four generations.

This was a victory for Kennedy's ideals, his challenge to "get this country movin' again," his concern for minorities and the unemployed. This election was a triumph for religious freedom over intolerance, for now a Catholic was elected President. It was a success for democratic discussion as shown in the televised debates, the first in history. And finally, for me, a young man of 22, who was developing ideas and ideals of my own, concerns for others, a sense of democracy, and a more mature understanding of "call", the victory of John F. Kennedy was a clear sign to me that the connection I was making with his spirit was genuine and fulfilling.

*

The prospects for continuing my studies full-time at I.I.T. began to look dim at Christmas time. I looked over my bank account and it showed that I didn't have enough money for tuition, books, and expenses, even though I was working at the Post Office for the holiday season.

What should I do? Get a full-time job and go to I.I.T. nights? Give up school completely and try to get a job as an apprentice pipe fitter or sheet metal worker? Maybe my career and future was full of dirty hands and a perpetual sore back. This "kiddee" just couldn't escape manual labor no matter how much Math I knew.

My solution turned out to be at I.I.T. I had noticed a couple of times when I went to German class that the COOP Program had an office in the same, old building on 34th and Federal. After an inquiry at this office in early January, within a week I was interviewing at various Chicago-area companies who hired engineering students part-time. Students could get on-the-job training and experience in their field of study, with a salary, for a semester, and then attend I.I.T. full-time the following semester, using the pay for tuition, books, etc. A Coop student could follow this schedule for two years, alternating between school and work.

By the third week of January, I was now commuting with the "Batmobile" to Vapor Corporation, in the near, northwestern suburb of Niles. Vapor manufactured steam boilers, and had a large staff of engineers, many of whom were mechanical.

My role at Vapor would be to learn the manufacturing processes for producing boilers, the design of each mechanical system, the quality control of the machine work and production, and research for the development of more efficient heat-generating designs. I was assigned to work in these various departments for six-week periods to gain the experience and expertise that each phase offered to a prospective engineer.

This move to the Coop Program helped me to get hands-on experience for future engineering work. It gave me opportunities to talk to and interact with professionals. And most importantly, the salary gave me enough funds for full-time study at I.I.T. the following semester. It seemed as though I had the best of both worlds, work and study.

*

Let the word go forth from this time and place,
to friend and foe alike, that the torch has been
passed to a new generation of Americans, . . .

Little puffs of vaporized breath burst from his mouth as he finished each phrase of his Inaugural Address. The cold air was the remnant from an unusual snowstorm that fell on Washington the night before. The sun was shining however, brightening the right side of his face as he stood at the rostrum just east of the Capitol. No top coat. No hat. Just the tux with tails, and his full head of hair to keep him warm. His voice was high, with his right hand characteristically tapping the air to punctuate his points. I kept hearing tones of melancholy, longing, as though he was invoking the spirits of his ancestors, and more than three centuries of American leadership in this historic Address.

With raised voice, jaw set forward, looking directly at his audience, which was both in front of him and throughout the United States on TV, pointing straight ahead to leave no doubt as to whom he was speaking, President John Fitzgerald Kennedy issued the challenge that eloquently stated his "call" to service;

> And so my fellow Americans; ask not what
> your country can do for you—ask what you
> can do for your country.

And he followed that challenge with a broader summons;

> My fellow citizens of the world; ask not what
> America will do for you, but what together
> we can do for the freedom of man.

I heard those "calls" as I watched the Inaugural Address. *Silently I began to ask myself; What should I be doing? Where do I go to respond to this personal plea from my hero?*

Less than two months later, on March 9th, President Kennedy announced the formation of the Peace Corps with an Executive Order. 500 to 1000 young American volunteers would be trained and then sent forth to undeveloped countries that had requested help. They would be teachers, doctors, nurses, agricultural agents, carpenters, technicians, and others—all who wanted to respond to Kennedy's "ask not" with their idealism and concern for people worldwide.

While the work at Vapor Corporation was worthwhile, and the coursework at I.I.T. a test of my intellectual abilities, there was this nagging feeling that I should be doing something else. Kennedy's "calls" had stirred me and were leading me away from engineering, although he had made a campaign issue of the space race that had accelerated with the Russian launching of Sputnik in 1958.

I felt a greater awareness of discrimination with the publicity surrounding the civil rights movement. I was much more sensitive to poverty, both in this country with campaign coverage of impoverished areas, as well as in foreign countries with news coverage of places to be served by the Peace Corps Volunteers.

There always had been awareness in our family to poverty abroad, what with my mother's contributions to help her brothers in Ireland, both our prayers at Catholic school for the poor people in mission countries, and on the light side, my father's admonition at the supper table—"Eat those turnips. Just think of the starving kids in China."

And our family subscribed to the Maryknoll Magazine, which covered, in clear, color photographs, the work of the Maryknoll missionaries in places like Peru, Japan, The Phillipines, Tanganyika, and other places. There was very little doubt that I was captivated by the pictures of these young men, priests and brothers, teaching a class of young, native children in a thatched hut with no walls and a dirt floor.

By the beginning of winter, 1961, I was seriously discerning a change in career. Although the work and study in engineering had been worthwhile, and I was successful in both areas, something was missing for me. Perhaps mechanical engineering was too clear, too concrete, easy to see and measure, bolts, machines, heat, etc. Somehow the word "theoretical" started germinating in me, as well as ideals and concerns. There seemed to be a growing need to abstract, to think deeper perhaps.

"Mini-calls" to consider religious life were popping up too, long been latent, but now surfacing for me to ponder. In front of me also was the whole area of politics and public service, made so attractive, inviting, and rewarding as I followed the daily announcements and decisions of President Kennedy.

I continued to devour newspaper articles about Kennedy's work and that of his administration, grimacing at the embarrassing defeat at the Bay of Pigs in December of '61—with the subsequent second-guessing by the press that Kennedy was not up to being President—and silently cheering in April of '62 as he forced the Big Steel companies to rescind a price increase of six dollars a ton, after he had persuaded the Steel Unions to settle for a 3% wage guideline.

I marveled at Kennedy's grasp of issues and details when I was able to catch a Presidential news conference on TV. It seemed that he knew everything about each reporter's question, and delivered it calmly, sometimes with a touch of self-deprecation that brought smiles to the assembled reporters.

But there also appeared to be stiffness in Kennedy's back, as he stood at the Presidential podium, hardly moving his upper body, as though his chronic back problems were giving him pain. And now I could see the lines in his face from stress, and the tiredness in his eyes.

I was feeling the anxiety of doubt between what I was studying, and what I really should be doing. It seemed as though the possibilities were enormous, but I couldn't find one path to follow. Was there a course for me? A road to follow? Was something out there that I could latch onto if only I could identify it? I was wandering, loaded with a bundle of energy and extremely mixed emotions.

On top of all this was guilt. The whole process of "call" always carried tones of discomfort because I wasn't responding. I wasn't heeding the summons—I had heard so much of in grammar and high school—to give up everything and follow in the footsteps of Jesus. Since seventh grade, when Father Laske started talking to me about the minor seminary at Quigley, I was always uncomfortable with the feeling that God wanted me to be a priest. *But I kept rejecting Him. How do I push away God's call from my consciousness? If the thought is in my mind, then there must be some substance.*

I finally decided to switch majors from Mechanical Engineering to Physics in January of 1962. Again, I felt that something more theoretical, thought provoking, futuristic, is what would both challenge me intellectually and meet the demands of my growing spirituality. Continued study in Math attracted me also, since it was one of my strong academic areas. Math was the tool that physicists use to develop their theories to explain nature.

The change to Physics meant that I had to quit the Coop Program at Vapor Corporation because they only hired engineers, not physicists. I had been thrifty though, saving enough money for two semesters of study. So, in late January, I began my first full-time course work in Physics at I.I.T.

Ironically, it almost never happened that I would study Physics. World events and Presidential decisions about Vietnam in the fall and winter of 1961 almost determined a temporary career for me—soldier in the Army. On December 15, 1961 President Kennedy communicated to South Vietnam President Ngo Dinh Diem that the United States would increase the size of its military assistance mission to 2000 men, made up of combat support units—air and helicopter—military advisors and instructors, and green-hatted Special Forces to train and lead the South Vietnamese in anti-guerilla warfare. But most importantly for me, Kennedy ordered the Defense Department to be prepared for the usage of combat troops.

In the January 6th mail, I received a letter of Summons to Report for Physical Examination prior to induction into the Army. I had ten days to get ready for the exam and likely draft into the service. At least I thought I was healthy enough to serve.

For the last two years of attending college, I had received student deferments. I was surprised by the draft notice because I thought that I was getting old—soon to be 24 in February—and also because I was studying in a scientific field which was highly prized by the U.S. Government with the space race on with Russia.

Mommy was sitting at the kitchen table having her afternoon cup of tea when I showed her the notice. She became slightly agitated because she had heard the news about the possible U.S. military build-up in Vietnam to counter both the North Vietnamese forces as well as the terrorist Viet Cong in the South Vietnam countryside. She had the feeling right away that if I went, I would see action. This obviously worried her. She was frightened too because Jake was serving his two-year stint in the Army, stationed in Germany.

And my brother Fred, who was 20 years old, had to worry about being drafted. He was in college at the University of Illinois—Navy Pier—studying aeronautical engineering. There was the distinct possibility that all three of Mommy's sons would be in uniform by the middle of 1962.

When Daddy came home from work that night, I told him of my draft notice. He looked surprised too, figuring I'd be able to study Physics at I.I.T. until I graduated. (Both Mommy and Daddy really couldn't figure why I would leave the Coop Program in engineering to study this highbrow field of Physics.)

"I'm going to report for the draft exam next week," I said to both of them at the table. "I won't try and get out of it, even if it means going to some Southeast Asian country to fight. If that's what Kennedy wants, then I'll do it." This was my first response to his "ask not."

Perhaps the paperwork from I.I.T. was late, or maybe the local draft board had enough guys. Or just maybe it was my switch to Physics. Whatever was the reason, I received another letter from the Draft Board two days before I had to report. It said that I was granted a 2S deferment to continue studies at I.I.T. I didn't have to report on Friday, January 16th for the physical examination. Talk about timing!

I earned a B-average the first semester in my new major. The study was difficult, especially the lab work. Courses like Electricity and Magnetism and Kinetic Theory were theoretical, especially with the Advanced Calculus that I had to know to solve the problems. And while I did well, there was still a cold feeling about my future, a lack of real zest or commitment for my career.

My membership in Theta Xi Fraternity continued because this provided the only social life on campus. There were opportunities to meet and date girls, as well as go to Old Town or Rush Street for a Friday night of drinking and socializing. (I even got into a fistfight with a "hotshot" who tried to butt in with a blonde I was talking to at a popular bar. Unfortunately, I only lasted one round because he had a better left-hand jab and outweighed me by twenty pounds.)

Summer meant work and this time in '62 I found a job at a trucking outfit near Archer & Cicero Avenues, repairing and painting freight trailers. This turned out to be a hot, messy job, with sloppy paint all over me each day as I worked in the hot sun. But I needed the money for the next semester at I.I.T. I hadn't heard from the Draft Board since January, so I assumed I wouldn't be called as long as I stayed in school.

Physics classes and study continued in September, but so did the thoughts of service to people as a priest. By now, I had pretty well absorbed the spirit of Kennedy's "calls", the idealism of the Peace Corps, and the sense of mission in work such as the Maryknoll Missionaries. I felt, developing within me, a sensitivity to poverty that I would see in Chicago first hand, or catch on TV with local news and documentaries from other cities or countries. Those same thoughts I had a year ago about, "I should be there. I should be helping those people," were being refined as I concentrated more and more on serving.

It was becoming obvious to me that I wouldn't continue at I.I.T. and graduate in Physics. By January of '63, I still had a B-average in course work, but had one more full year plus to get a bachelor's degree. *It didn't seem to be where I was however. I didn't have the "drive." I needed something that called for dedication, sacrifice, and life-rewarding work. Something that would challenge me totally and give me a sense that I was responding not only to a "call" but also to a "need" within the lives of others. How could I pass those people by, and continue with studies in Physics and Math?*

Much to the disappointment of my parents, I told them that I was leaving I.I.T. I shared my feelings about a career in Physics, and my growing desire to serve others. I let them know I had thoughts of the priesthood, but also ideas of government service. Kennedy had raised the level of respect for public and political work, with both his rhetoric as well as his personal charisma. Like many a man with a hero, I found myself wanting to be just like him. Cool, intelligent, good-looking, and most importantly, raising ideals and putting them into action. HE was who I really wanted to be.

I had a friend from the neighborhood, Bill Green, who was working in City Government, and had been active politically for quite awhile because his uncle was Mayor Richard J. Daley. We met for lunch and I told him my thoughts, my inner feelings about career, my struggle to find a life where I could serve others. I was concentrating on public service and the priesthood. Could he offer some advice or give me a picture of his experience in government.

Bill was realistic about public service, especially at the level of the City of Chicago. The pay was not high, the hours were good, there were plenty of opportunities to be of service, and dedicated people didn't necessarily have to be involved in ward and city politics.

In early January of 1963, I decided to follow two paths. Give the City of Chicago a try with a job, and begin inquiries with the Maryknoll Fathers about the missions to see if I really had a "call." After a visit to Matt Danaher, the 11th Ward and City Patronage Chief, with my precinct captain, explaining to him that I was interested in seeing if there was a career in City Government for me. I was given a clerk's job at the Department of Boiler Inspections, starting in February. This was a low-level job, handling inspection reports rather than meeting the public. But it was a start!

Questions about my "call" to the missions led me to Father Quinn Weitzel, a Maryknoll priest, who was in charge of recruitment for the Chicago area. Conferences with him at the Maryknoll House on Astor St. on Chicago's Gold Coast, helped me to express my "calls" to service, and desires to help those who were living in poverty. I gradually developed confidence in my search for missionary work as I explained my family background, work experience, education, and current thoughts that were leading me to serve in the missions. It seemed, after two sessions with Father Weitzel, that I was definitely headed to request admission to Maryknoll. At least, within me the path seemed to be good, as though I was headed in the right direction.

Father Weitzel cautioned however that there were trials, pressures and loneliness that beset a missionary in the field, no matter whether it be in Africa or Asia or South America. While the pictures in the Maryknoll magazine are attractive and inviting, the reality of the work in the field is difficult, having been too much for many a person, no matter the strength of his vocation and need to serve.

It was at this point that I noticed the greyness in his face, slight touches of sadness in his eyes, as though he was talking about limitations that affected men he knew, or perhaps even himself. I sensed that he was not happy living in a mansion and doing recruiting, instead of pastoral work in a remote village of Tanganyika.

Days at the City Boiler Inspection Dept. proved to be boring and nowhere near fulfilling to serve people. Shuffling inspection reports on paper and transferring the dates of inspection to index cards wore on me. Constantly I would look at the clock to see if it was time for break, or lunch, or going home. There were no human issues in this office except the complaints of middle-aged men and women who felt stuck in patronage positions.

"If you're serious about applying to the Maryknoll Missions, you will have to take a battery of tests and an interview with Father Eugene Kennedy, in the Maryknoll Minor Seminary in Glen Ellyn," Father Weitzel told me in April. "Father Kennedy has developed instruments that identify characteristics in a prospective seminarian that help to determine whether the candidate will be successful in missionary work, Father Weitzel continued.

At this point, April of 1963, at the age of 25, thirteen years after Father Laske first approached me to consider Quigley Preparatory Seminary, I was ready to apply to Maryknoll. I had spoken to my parents earlier and told them of my strong interest in Maryknoll, and my decision to spend my life in service to others. *Although this decision was a long time in coming, I felt good that I had reached this point. I had to act upon my feelings, these innermost yearnings to help others.* And, there wasn't a girl in my life, having struck out twice before. I figured that I wouldn't get another chance to hit in the game of romance.

The next week I met Father Kennedy at the Minor Seminary in Glen Ellyn. The campus was large, well laid out, with lots of grounds for walking and prayer—and sports. The halls were bristling with energetic, young men heading to and from classes. *I sensed and saw the enthusiasm in their faces, energy that I knew was directed toward preparation for mission work. This was the spirit I was looking for, the zest, the desire to prepare for a tough life of service. Here seemed to be the team I wanted to join.*

Father Kennedy's partially bald head glistened from the lights above his head as he briefly interviewed me in his small office on the first floor, prior to taking a battery of tests to determine suitability for the missions. I talked to him about the experience I had with Maryknoll through reading the monthly magazine. I told him of the praying I had done these last twelve months to give me a sign for the right direction. I emphasized my need to serve others. And, I related to him the "calls" I had received in grammar school, high school, and now in college. The vocation to the priesthood kept coming back to me, as though it was always lying below the surface of my consciousness.

"Father Kennedy believes that you have a vocation to the priesthood," Father Weitzel told me the next week at our conference in the mansion on Astor St. "He feels, however, that your calling should be to the diocesan priesthood instead of the missions," Weitzel went on.

"Was this decision based upon the battery of tests I took?" I responded, surprised by what I had just heard. "Did he see something that is a problem?

Father Weitzel sighed, looked greyer in his face than at other meetings, and went through a long monologue of the difficulties, pressures, and dangers that are part of the daily life of a missionary in a foreign country. Maryknoll only takes those young men whom they feel have a personality and spirituality that can sustain them in the field for long periods of time. Months and years without family or friends. Endless days without modern conveniences, living a rudimentary life. He finished with, "Father Kennedy and I think that you can better serve God in the priesthood here in Chicago."

I should have seen the signs and signals I had been getting all along from Father Weitzel. He was never enthusiastic about my inquiries and pursuit of Maryknoll. I always thought that his cool response was part of his quiet personality and somewhat sad demeanor. He never patted me on the back and said, "Let's go for it." He never told me that I had the ideals and desire for mission work. And there was concern he raised about my age, now that I had just turned 25. Maybe I was too old to be trained!

I left the mansion very disappointed, and the gray skies of a cloudy April day didn't help. The image I had in my mind for six months of speaking Spanish and working in a mountain village of Peru, not only spreading the work of Christ, but also ministering to the needs of the people, was quite clear. But now it would have to be erased because I couldn't be a missionary. I would not be training for another continent.

After walking briskly the block it took to reach my car, my thoughts recalled, "you can better serve God . . . in Chicago." Maybe my call was here instead of overseas. Maybe I could expend my zeal in the inner city where there was certainly plenty of poverty that came in all colors. Although it felt like I was forced to choose second fiddle, perhaps this is what God wanted for me, a life of care to the needy in my hometown.

The process to apply for the priesthood in Chicago took a couple of months. To begin was the interview with Father Norbert Randolph, my pastor at St.Anthony de Padua Parish. His letter of recommendation to Monsignor Eugene Lyons, the rector of the Diocesan Seminary in Niles followed our meeting at the parish.

Next, I had an interview and application with Father Ed Breen, the Vice-Rector and Curriculum Director at Niles Seminary, just northwest of Chicago. He reviewed my educational accomplishments, especially the college credits. And finally, in the middle of June, I received the decision from Monsignor Lyons and Father Breen, inviting me to enroll at Niles to study for the priesthood.

I had mixed feelings about entering the diocesan seminary. On the one hand, this was an excellent opportunity to study for the priesthood and eventually serve the people of Chicago. But, on the other, it wasn't answering my call to the missions. It didn't feel right, like getting the consolation instead of the prize. Would I really be happy staying here, near home, instead of heading off to Africa or Asia or South America?

Part of the requirements to enroll at Niles Seminary was a refresher course in Latin. *Amo-amas-amat, amamus-amatis-amant.* I love;you love;he, she, or it loves; we love;you love;they love. So, in early July of 1963 I packed a bag and headed north to the Benet Latin School at St.Benedict Abbey to study Latin. The Benedictine Order had the Abbey, which was situated in the countryside just over the Wisconsin border, near the Adlai Stevenson estate in Libertyville, Illinois.

My first experiences with religious life at the Abbey were like scenes from the Middle Ages. Meals were eaten in silence, with spiritual readings being read by the monks. Prayer was held according to the Divine Office, six times a day in the chapel. There was *Matins* and *Terse* in the morning along with Mass, *Sect* at noon, *None* in the middle of the afternoon and *Vespers* and *Compline* at night. Each prayer period involved chanting of the Latin verses from the breviary in the monk's choir behind the altar. Latin classes met three times a day, morning and afternoon. And finally, study and spiritual reading were mandatory after supper. Of course, all of these activities were accomplished by me while wearing the long, black seminarian cassock.

We had opportunity for some recreation and mingling after meals and in the late afternoon. I found chances to talk to the other students in the Latin class, as well as some of the monks. One student, Michael Flaherty, had also been turned down by Maryknoll. He hoped to be accepted however, once his Latin proficiency improved.

The six weeks at the Abbey seemed to be a light introduction to seminary life. There was no stress for spiritual growth or Latin competence. I felt at times like I was in summer camp, with walks around the Abbey and alongside the corn fields being the big event of the day. I did begin to sense the spirituality of the monks as I observed them in choir for the Divine Office and at daily Mass. (I always had trouble controlling my smiles at choir, however, because the Abbot chanted the introductory Latin response in a clear falsetto voice)

My thoughts invariably settled on this monastic way of life as I participated each day. But I couldn't relate to the monks' need to live in a rustic community, wearing a brown robe and sash. Somehow, it seemed as though time had stopped for them. They definitely chose to get away from society in order to live a holy life. *I had this call, this urge to get movin', to relate to people, poor people. I just couldn't see myself chanting half the day for the rest of my life.*

During my stay at the Abbey, it was nice to get letters from Mommy and Daddy, Maureen, Jake, and my godmother, Beatrice Curley. They reinforced my decision to study for the priesthood with their words of support. Father Randolph stopped at home to see my parents and inquire as to my progress in Latin. Even Rudy Guzik, my philosopher friend from I.I.T., wrote to keep in touch and urge me on.

The only "being" that wasn't happy with my new career was our dog at home, Queenie. After I left home in July for the Abbey, it took her two weeks to realize I wasn't in the front bedroom each morning for her to wake me. I suppose I should have told her that she didn't have to "call" me out of bed anymore.

And I'd get the latest news about my White Sox from Daddy. The '63 team was young and exciting. They had a good combo of pitching, speed and hitting, what with rookie Gary Peters pitching and the hitting of rookie Pete Ward and veteran Floyd Robinson. Maybe they'd overcome those damn

Yankees this year, just like in '59. I suppose that I should say "darn Yankees" now that I am in the seminary.

*

"Life is Worth Living," Father McMahon announced, with a flourish, to our Religion class at Niles Seminary as he swooped into the classroom from the hall. He swept the crimson cape in a half circle to emphasize the color against his black cassock. Cheers and applause from the 2nd year class greeted his entry.

And for just a second or two, I stared at him from my seat in the middle row. "He looks just like Bishop Sheen," I thought to myself. "He even sounds like the Bishop."

Father McMahon treated each of his classes at Niles to one grand entrance a semester. He thoroughly enjoyed playing Fulton J. Sheen, the Catholic Bishop star of TV in the 50's. Now, here it was, September of '63 and Father McMahon was keeping Bishop Sheen's image alive even though he was no longer on TV.

One of Bishop's er . . . I mean Father McMahon's first announcement to our class had to do with his family history. He stated, quite authoritatively that the McMahons were in the Book of Genesis. There was a pause in the class. Father McMahon stood in front of us, waiting. Finally, a cooperative student raised his hand and asked, "OK Father. Where does it mention your family in the Book of Genesis?

"Why, young man, I'm sure that you remember Chapter 1, Verse 26. And I quote; 'God said, Let us McMahon.'

Father McMahon stood in front of us with a cat-eaten grin, again waiting. There was silence in that room as the words from the Bible settled in. All of a sudden the play on words, the similarity in sound, the joke was realized. First came guffaws, then laughter, followed by our cheers and polite applause. The Biblical celebrity took two humble bows amidst the applause. This Irishman was now claiming origins back to the Israelites as well as special creation by God Himself. Who are we to question such a holy man?

The light atmosphere I was exposed to in Religion class was found elsewhere in other classrooms, dormitories, halls and grounds. I learned quickly that very few priests on the faculty were referred to as Father or Reverend by seminarians in their own conversations. The Rector was Lyons, not Monsignor. The priest in charge of Finance was known as Schmid, not Father. And many priests had nicknames. It took me a couple of weeks to figure out who "Jock", "Elmer Fudd", "Hern", "Matty", "Phlebes", and "Boris" referred to in our conversations. And of course, how could I ever forget Winters, the "humble" Old Testament scholar who introduced me to family history writing.

Being six or seven years older than my classmates, and a newcomer to seminarians who had been together since first year high school, I was surprised at the familiarity between seminarians and priests. At first I wondered if this recognition showed some disrespect. But I slowly began to realize that familiarity was the operative word to describe the whole atmosphere on the 2nd year class side of the seminary. These guys were used to each other. They had most of these priests already in previous classes. And most importantly, my classmates were *not* going to elevate the priests to a pedestal when they knew exactly where and how many warts each priest had.

Meals were a continuation of the frivolity, quips, needling, puns and word games. There was no mandatory silence like St. Benedict's Abbey. Instead, there might be a lengthy, detailed discussion or sharing of opinions and scenes from the latest James Bond movie. "Did you see how Bond (always pronounced with the English "o", BAUND) skied down that hill in 'Goldfinger' to escape his assasins?"

Each afternoon, after the day's classes, we had opportunities for recreation. A tournament was set up for flag football—we called it touch football in Chicago. Each dorm on both the 1st and 2nd year halls put together a team of 12-15 players, 6 for offense and 6 for defense.

Since I had stature among my classmates in the dorm due to my age and ability to throw a pass—thanks to practice with that Bears football when I was young—I was given the position as quarterback. We had a couple of fleet receivers in Tom McAuliffe and John Byrnes, and a tough, all-hands short yardage receiver in Jim (Skuts) Skonicki. Our defense was led by Wendell (Bucky) Sebastian, who rushed, and Julian (T) D'Esposito who played defensive back.

After the first two games against other dorms, it was clear that our dorm had a very good football team. Our offense could score touchdowns regularly, and the defense kept shutting down the opponents. I was passing the ball so well to our receivers that one of the 1st year seminarians, Rick Guerin, started calling me, "Fran Tarkenton" after the great Minnesota Viking quarterback of the '60s.

Dorm life was laid out with individual metal cubicles, 8 feet wide, 8 feet long, and 8 feet high, consisting of a bed, closet, desk and chair. There was no ceiling on the cubicle, so if all the guys in a dorm stood on their chairs and started singing *Tantum Ergo*, the choir would number 20 and they'd all be smiling at each other. What it really meant is that each seminarian's cough or sneeze during study time and the night, was heard by everyone in the dorm.

Or, as I can readily attest since it was opposite to my cubicle, whenever a fire truck would leave the firehouse down the street on Touhy Avenue and head south on Harlem Avenue, Tom Nangle would slide his chair out very abruptly, run from his cubicle opposite mine to the window just next to my room, open the bottom window fully, climb up on the radiator pipes, and "Ooh" and "Aah" as the clamoring fire trucks drove by. (I bet he'd make a great Chaplain for the Chicago Fire Department)

Intellectual life popped up regularly with both course work and discussion groups. There seemed to be quite a bit of interest in Shakespeare among my class, as led by Father Flaherty. And of course the talk of the halls usually settled on the latest quip, or quiz from Father Winters' Old Testament class.

My attempt at language research, however, met with silent rejection by my classmates. The story started in New Testament Greek when Father Mahoney made the remark that Greek was more laconic than Latin, and certainly much briefer than English. Since we were working with a textbook that had Greek on one side of the page and Latin on the other, it was fairly easy to select a verse in both languages, then count syllables to see which is briefer.

That night, during study hours, I took out the English New Testament. I opened the Book blindly and put my right index finger down on the page randomly. Next, I counted the syllables in that verse. Then I turned to the Latin-Greek texts, found the same verse, and counted syllables. To my surprise, English was the most laconic, then Greek, and lastly, Latin. I selected two more verses randomly, and counted in the three languages. Again, English was briefest.

Before New Testament class the next day, I shared this "research" with Father Mahoney. He had no trouble taking back his statement from yesterday. But when he exuberantly shared these results with my classmates, he was met with disdain and silence. Their unspoken message seemed to be, "Who cares which language is most succinct! We're not interested in Greek or Latin."

The reason I had enrolled in Niles Seminary, the call I thought I was answering, was not being met with increased spirituality on my part though. Sure there was daily Mass and meditation each morning, prayers at noon, Compline and Points for Meditation at night, as well as special liturgies. *But I didn't feel a sense of connection with God which I thought should be part of religious life. No matter how hard I concentrated during morning meditation, there was no deep connection to Jesus that I felt or experienced. He was "out there" somewhere instead of in my person, in me. The intimacy with Jesus that priests would convey as so important for spirituality was not with me. Jesus was not close. I kept calling Him, but there was no response.*

We did have an opportunity to serve inner-city kids as tutors, and I volunteered, along with 25 other seminarians. One night a week, we'd bus down to St. Malachy Parish on Chicago's near west side, at Washington St. near Western Avenue. For quite a few weeks, I worked with Otis, an African-American kid about nine years old. He said that he needed help in Math and Reading.

It was fulfilling for me to provide homework help to Otis. But interestingly, his innocent gesture one night has stayed in my mind. It was a warm night and I was tutoring in a short sleeve shirt. My arms were in front of Otis. As he responded to my homework questions, he kept looking at the blonde hair on my arms. Finally, he took his right index finger and ran it down my forearm, from elbow to hand. "Man, that's nice. I wish I had hair like that on my arms."

The first two months at Niles rolled by nicely. As the cool days and chilly nights of November strode in, the smokers found it a little more challenging to be outside from 9:15-9:30 each night for the break before Compline. Even Monsignor Lyons, our regular visitor to the evening break, started to dress warmly, although he had a hot cigarette in his lips.

The flag football tourney ended—our dorm was the seminary champs. We turned to basketball and handball in the gym after school. The other late-vocation fellow, Joe Gits, and I teamed up as doubles partners for the handball tourney.

Meals continued to be the social events of the day, especially lunch. There was such a buzz to the refectory at lunch as everybody was energized from a morning of classes and then the brief walk between buildings. We all knew that there would be a great lunch prepared by the Sisters from Mexico. They always had a wonderful meal ready for us.

I was lucky in November because I was assigned to the table at the front where all the lunchroom managers sat. This was known as the table with all the laughs. No other collection of guys had more fun and were more entertaining than the quartet of John Manz, Tony Talarico, Ralph Yale and Jim Wilson. Even though they had major responsibilities as far as supervising each tables's work crew, there was time for jokes, banter, laughter, and a little horseplay.

*

It was Friday, the end of the week. The sun was shining brightly even though it was the 3rd week in November. We had my favorite breakfast at the refectory this morning, corn bread with lotsa butter and syrup. I never could settle for one piece, so when the platter was empty, I sent it back with our table hopper for more. Now if only the coffee could be as good as the corn bread.

At the beginning of my second class, New Testament Greek, Father Mahoney handed back our mid-term tests. *Hagios ho theos.* God is holy. I passed with flying colors.

I was settling into seminary life at Niles. The routine was consistent. The food great. Sports after classes. Companionship. Laughs—would you believe that one of my dorm mates was swigging SCOPE because it had alcohol listed on the label. Spirituality in a bottle. Increase your HOPE with SCOPE!

Everyone was looking forward to our trip home for Thanksgiving. As much as we enjoyed the atmosphere in the seminary, we quietly awaited Wednesday of next week, the 27th, to ride home to our families. We hoped to see friends and neighbors also,

So, lunch that day, the 22nd, was full of laughs again. Everyone was unwinding from a heavy week of classes, study, tests and prayer. Cliff Craelius was the hopper at our table. It seemed as though every trip he made for food was met with jibes and comments. And we were at the table with the refectory managers.

I had to leave early, at 12:30, to prepare some papers for the first class in the afternoon with Father Ahern. As I left the refectory, another seminarian, a first-year student, joined me in the short walk to the back door of the dorm building. "Let's play two," I joked with the freshman, imitating the famous remark by Ernie Banks when he stepped out of the Chicago Cubs dugout on a bright, sunny day. Ernie loved to play those doubleheaders.

Just as we made it to the dorm door, Mike Michelini came bursting thru the door. "President Kennedy's been shot," he yelled at us.

"Yah sure. Tell me another story, Mike," I told him as I reached for the door knob.

"I'm not kidding. He's been shot," pleaded Mike.

From the open door I could hear the seminary radio. I stepped in with the freshman.

"President Kennedy has been shot in Dallas. He's been rushed to Parkland Hospital along with Vice President Johnson. We have no word on his condition at this time. I repeat . . ."

I stood in the doorway listening, not believing what I was hearing. I was stunned as though what I was hearing was a nightmare I had experienced before. The President was shot? Assasination!

The radio announcer continued with the same message. "President Kennedy has been shot . . ."

Slowly I moved to walk up the short flight of stairs to the main floor. By now, the other seminarians were entering from the refectory, joking at first, but not prepared for the shocking news from the radio. Their happy mood changed so quickly to silence, immobility, incomprehension.

Suddenly, the radio switched off and Monsignor Lyons came on the public address. His voice was shaking, sorrowful, full of incomprehension also. But he did tell us to get our books and materials for afternoon classes and report to those classes. He advised the teachers to let the students sit and absorb the shocking news in class and feel free to be silent, meditative at this time.

Like zombies, we walked to our cubicles, got our books and materials, and dragged ourselves to class. The news broadcast continued with announcements that the President was in surgery with a bullet wound in the head. Vice President Johnson was seen holding his chest as he walked into Parkland Memorial Hospital. We could hear the gravity in the announcer's voice. *I began to fear the worse.*

No one said anything in Father Ahern's class. Many of the seminarians buried their heads with their arms on the desks. I just stared straight ahead, still trying to absorb the sudden shock. I kept praying that the President's head wound was superficial, even though the dread in the announcer's voice seemed to be saying otherwise. For some reason I kept waiting for those horrible words.

And then they came. "President Kennedy is dead. He was pronounced dead at 1:00 PM by the surgeons at Parkland Memorial."

We looked at each other with moist eyes, incomprehensible stares, and very sad faces. How could this happen? Our hero, who was so much alive and in our minds and hearts since 1960, is now dead! We stared hopelessly, silently, not knowing what to do next. One of our own had been taken from us, so quickly and decisively.

I grieved in silence. I couldn't find tears or words. This death was such a loss that I sealed my feelings and sorrow in the cocoon of my mind and body. I tried to reach out but I couldn't connect with others. This killing was so shattering. Where would I go now?

The rest of Friday was a blur. All of us somehow stumbled thru the rest of the afternoon. There was a prayer service in chapel. Afterwards we spent time in solitary walks on the grounds. Dinner was lifeless, with hardly any conversation or eating. So much had been stolen from us, our innocence wounded. Evening Compline was somber. We needed no points for meditation to write in our notebooks for the morning. The sudden, tragic death of John F. Kennedy was the only event occupying our minds, hearts and souls this 22nd of November evening.

On Saturday, we had a chance to call our folks to talk about the assassination. Mommy and Daddy were so sad, both for the President's family and the country, but also for me. They remembered how I followed JFK thru the 1960 campaign and afterwards with his Presidency. They also knew quite well that he was my hero.

Grief turned to silence, with anger creeping into me. I felt a tremendous loss of innocence as I reflected on Kennedy's death. *It was as though my life had stopped with his sudden death. What was worthwhile had been taken. What was good had been stolen.* The time of Camelot was lost forever. And nothing was there for replacement.

Why bother now with hope. Idealism was smashed with those bullets. I could do nothing now except breath. Like Camus' stranger, I was sitting alone on the beach, wondering where there was meaning now. Was anything of value left? Would I ever care again? Dare to have a hero? Cold reality was all I felt. No warmth! No hope! No sense of the future!

I will not bother again with ideals. I will not stretch my imagination, climb the mountain, or dream the impossible. My hero was coldly killed by a high powered bullet, just as easy as hitting the target on a rifle range. There would be no more heroes to follow. Only people living their lives and affecting me none.

As the weekend enfolded, with TV images of Oswald's killing by Jack Ruby, I began to write. And watching the somber, stately funeral with the President's coffin, the riderless horse, John John's salute, and the eternal flame, my soul quieted. There was refuge and solace in the seminary silence. The words of my tears and feelings came slowly at first, but gradually were formed on the sheet. One line led to another, until I had paid my tribute to John Fitzgerald Kennedy.

HIMSELF

So dead hung the great Senate room,
reflecting the spirit of the nation he served.
Absent are its historic voices.
only present the pale, November dusk.

Our man is gone.

So still the jabbing right hand
joining with "we've gotta get moving"
Forever gone, the slow and easy smile,
the fragile pause and quiet confidence.

Our man is gone.

So old the young now feel; so very old.
No more the unbounded joy,

for even he was not safe.
Youthful vigah has left; caution reigns.

Our man is gone.

So quiet out of the shadows she came,
past desks of New York, Jersey and on.
No life in her face either,
just pain, remorse, regret.

Our man is gone.

So clearly she knew him best,
bringing forth a single red rose,
lying straight and lean on his old desk,
fresh and full of life.

7

MARG'RET FLANAGAN LEVOY

Sure, I love the dear silver that shines in your hair,
And the brow that's all furrowed and wrinkled with care.
I kiss the dear fingers so toilworn for me.
Oh, God bless you and keep you, Mother Machree.

Anonymous

Mommy had been slipping for over 3 years now, suffering her first stroke in early 1960. My sister Mag, who was living downstairs from us with her husband Buck, and the two children, Susan and Tommy, heard something drop that morning. Shortly afterwards, when Maureen came down to her apartment to watch the two kids, Mag feared something had happened. Sure enough, when she entered Mommy and Daddy's bedroom, she saw Mommy's drooped mouth and misshapen right hand. Mag also saw the deep, grave concern on Daddy's face.

I was shocked when Daddy woke me that morning and told me Mommy had a stroke. Even though I knew as well as my brothers and sisters that her health was fragile because of the rheumatic fever she had in Ireland, as well as St. Vitus Dance, it still was difficult to look at her in the bed, with so much fear and confusion in her eyes. I sensed immediately that Mommy was starting to give in to mortality as her weak body found it hard to continue.

After medical care, hospitalization, and rest, Mommy recovered. She was able to return to the chores of the home, especially with help from Maureen, Fred, Kate, myself, Mag and Daddy. Our brother Jake was now married and living nearby in the Bridgeport neighborhood.

Mommy continued to have trouble with her right arm, as I dramatically found out one suppertime. I came into the kitchen and saw her trying to cut slices of the homemade white bread she had baked earlier. There just wasn't any strength in her hand and arm to cut thru the thick crust. Extra pressure was needed to get the knife blade past the hard, brown crust into the soft white bread, and Mommy didn't have anything extra.

Dejectedly, she let the knife fall down next to the bread. She turned to me with a depressing look and sigh. She was giving up.

"I'll cut the bread, Mom," I told her, touching her left shoulder, squeezing slightly. She looked tired, resigned, defeated, as though part of life had already left her. The smile that was on her face before the stroke was now gone. Her eyes lacked depth, understanding, intensity in what she was doing or saying.

I wanted so much to give her back the strength she once had. The strength that spoke forcefully to me when I messed up as a kid, didn't get the chore done, or whined about oatmeal. And the strength that swung the stick across my back when words wouldn't do. I didn't know whether to cry or hug her to show my care and concern. How could I tell her, "I'm sorry for you, Mom. It hurts me to see you so weak. I wish you could be like you were before, with a sparkle in your eyes." *But those words didn't come. I didn't say what I was feeling.*

Mommy turned, head down, to grab the big spoon on the stove to stir the simmering vegetable soup. At least she could do that, her sigh told me. Our moment was broken. Instead of expressing my care and concern to her, instead of letting her know my sorrow, I grabbed the bread knife and began slicing.

Long before her illness, Mommy made it clear that she would be in this world with us long enough to see all of her children graduate from high school. We'd usually laugh at her remark and change her future wish to "all the kids married", or until she had grandchildren and great-grandchildren. Her self-imposed limit on life seemed so far away. We didn't accept her wish as sincere.

The finality of Mommy's wish, predicting her death, was too hard for us to accept when she was healthy, taking care of a house, raising six children. But now, with her stroke, (vascular accident is the term used by doctors, according to Daddy) we began to look at the prophecy as a sincere wish by her to leave a legacy. Some sort of achievement for an Irish peasant girl who barely had six years of formal education in far-off Loughglynn. Even with the weakness in her body, there was this determination in her to see every one of the six children walk across the stage to receive their diplomas.

We saw this determination once before with Mommy, before her stroke. In the spring of 1955, both Kate and I were to graduate in June, she from

St.Anthony's Grammar School and me from De La Salle Institute. Mommy came to Mag with a proposal. "Mag, we can't afford two graduation parties this June for Hughie Boy and Kate. Do ye think I can work at Woolworths to make a little bit o' money?"

Mag was astonished at this. She had heard God knows how many times from Daddy that "a woman's place is in the home." This was his gospel about marriage—the husband brings home the bacon and the wife is there to cook it. His badge of honor and self-worth partly came from the fact that Mommy had *never* been sent to work outside the home, like some of the neighbors' wives and close friends. Even though we barely made ends meet throughout the 40's and 50's, Daddy held firm to his stance that Mommy stayed home, took care of the kids and the home. His pride (and stubbornness) would not allow it.

"How can you possibly work at Woolworths without him knowing?" Mag questioned Mommy.

"I'll leave the house after Kate and Fred and Maureen have their lunch and go back to school. Then I'll take the Racine Downtown bus to Woolworths and work from 1:30 to 4. I'll be back before your father gets home from the Railroad at 5," Mommy answered. And if he does find out I went downtown, I'll tell him I had to go to the Federal Building for something to do with my citizenship."

It worked! Mommy was employed as a hot peanut sales woman at the same Woolworths on State Street where Mag was for two afternoons a week. She worked a total of two months, clearing $150. Secretly the earnings were deposited in her bedroom bank, ready cash for the June graduation parties.

Everyone in the family knew of Mommy's brief career outside the home, except . . . . Yes, Daddy! "Mums the word," we would remind each other to maintain the secrecy, shuddering to imagine the magnitude of his volcanic eruption if he did discover. Fortunately, he never did find out about her transgression of his authority, even when Mommy's W-2 tax forms came in the mail the following January. Thank God she found them in the mail first.

"What'll I do? Yer father does all the taxes. He'll know I went to work when he sees these," Mommy panicked.

Kate and Mag and I looked at her, wondering what to answer to calm her somewhat. There seemed to be no way out. Finally, Mag said decisively, "Give me the tax forms." Taking them from Mommy's shaking hand, Mag proceeded to tear them into four pieces and deposit them into the garbage can. The IRS never came calling!

1961 and '62 saw gradual weakening in Mommy's body. She needed more rest each afternoon. Some of her chores were picked up by Fred and Maureen and I. One of my tasks was to do laundry in the basement every Monday. I liked to watch the agitation of the clothes, soap and water in the machine.

But, more than once, I came close to getting my fingers caught in the ringer on the old Maytag. I found an appreciation for the clothes washing work and risks that Mommy faced every Monday for all those years.

Mommy insisted, however, to cook the meals. We continued to see the variety of meals just like the days of our youth—meatloaf to pasta, soup to chili.

And then she had another setback late in 1962. Once again, she suffered damage to her mouth, and a loss of strength. She recovered quicker this time than the first stroke, bouncing back from bed within two weeks. She was making a valiant effort to continue her place as wife, mother, and homemaker.

I became more discouraged, finding out from Daddy that strokes come in two or threes, with the final one resulting in death. I'd look at Mommy stirring the rice on the stove for rice pudding and I'd imagine her leaving us. She seemed to have half-a-life, with the other half stolen by these vascular accidents. I felt so pessimistic about her health that I could only help her with chores rather than talk to her about her feelings.

By the time I entered Niles Seminary in September of '63, only Maureen was at home. Fred was studying aeronautical engineering at the University of Illinois at Champaign. She began her senior year at St. Pats Girls High School, the third sister hoping to graduate from St.Pats. Mag and Kate had preceded her in attendance and completion at the old school downtown.

Mommy was happy that I had finally settled on a career, after the changes from Engineering to Physics and from that to the Priesthood. I did make her think twice as to whether I had a serious call the night Daddy and she and I went to Lawrence Beyer's wedding reception. I was wearing the traditional black suit with white shirt and dark tie. When the band starting cranking up for the fast music, my toes started tapping, just like they did at the teen dances in the early '50s. Pretty soon, I was asking Rita Beyers, Lawrence's sister, to dance. It was a fast jitterbug. Soon we were flying around the floor, keeping pace with the band.

Well, did I get the daggers from Mommy when I returned to our table. Her stare was asking the question, "Well now, what kind of seminarian would be out on the dance floor twirling a girl around like . . . ? That's not the behavior I want to see from my future priest."

Mommy wrote regularly as I started my studies and life in the seminary. Her writing appeared weak and she complained in one letter about the cramps in her right hand. She'd faithfully end her letters with, "God be with you always," and lots of + + + for kisses. The envelope was addressed by Daddy, with his distinctively clear writing. Even from afar, I could tell that she was struggling, just making it from one day to the next

Our first year at Niles Seminary finished quietly the last week of May with mixed expectations. On the one hand, I had done well in my course work, getting "B's" overall. Spiritually, I was not succeeding, for the intensity I prayed for in chapel and walking the grounds during meditation was not happening. But, the camaraderie amongst my classmates was certainly inspiring, especially at sports, breaks and meal times. Even though I was seven years older than them, I fit in well, especially in athletics and social time.

The news from Mundelein, the major seminary in northern Illinois, and the next home for our ordination class of '70, was not good. The old seminary administration of Monsignor Mal Foley and Father Ed Fitzgerald had not changed, or improved for many years. Instead of adopting the aggiornamento of the 2nd Vatican Council in Rome, which had started in 1962, the powers-to-be at Mundelein were retrenching to hold back the tide of change. Our class and the class ahead of us, which had been at Niles in '62-'63, were now the tide.

Our seminary year ended just in time for me to attend Maureen's graduation from St. Pats the first week of June. She was the last, the caboose as Mommy and Daddy called her. When we sat down to a dinner of baked ham and mashed potatoes after the ceremonies, Kate and Don and their first baby, Angela, just born in May, came upstairs to join us.

There was a tired look of satisfaction on Mommy's face that evening. Not only had she enough energy to cook a great dinner, but now she silently patted herself on the the back for celebrating her last child's high school graduation. She had survived long enough to appreciate America's gift to its children, Education. (Little did we know that she had a mini-stroke, or TIA—Transient Ischemic Attack—three days before the graduation, requiring a visit to her doctor.

The following Monday night, I began my summer job at B & B Motor Freight on west 31st St. Once again, I was working on the freight docks, handling cartons and crates. And one more time, I had to leave the house at 10:30 PM to catch the late-night buses to work. This time, it was necessary to catch three separate buses to reach the docks by midnight.

Standing on the corner of Archer & Halsted each night at 10:30 reminded me so much of my first freight dock job at the Wabash RR in 1955. I was always the only person waiting, a lonely traveler intent on making a buck to pay for the seminary training.

The tuition at St.Mary of the Lake Seminary for the coming year, 1964-65, would be $600. Plus I had to purchase supplies, books, and a zimora, the great, woolen, black overcoat that had survived many a winter at Mundelein. These coats were indestructible (some said that they were made in the Middle Ages by Irish monks) and were usually purchased from other seminarians who either left the seminary or went on to ordination and the priesthood.

In either case, the seller no longer needed this antique article of apparel, instead surviving Chicago's winters with a heavy jacket or a modern raincoat or overcoat.

Even though scholarships were available to needy seminarians to cover part of the tuition, I felt it was important to work, especially since I was physically able, and also my parents didn't have money to pay the tuition. Similar to my other freight jobs, the physical exertion of lifting and handling freight challenged both my psyche and body to get the job done. I felt a quiet satisfaction each morning at 8 AM as I was punching out, knowing that I had completed a night's labor in the dimly lit trailers of B & B Freight.

It was Saturday, the 13th of June. Mommy was feeling good. Maureen's graduation was over. Now she saw Maureen off each morning during the week to work at Hyland Electric, the same supply house where Kate was working. So good was Mommy feeling that she announced at noon that she was going to bake an apple pie to complement tonight's dinner. She was hoping to have a festive meal for Daddy and I, Maureen, Kate and Don, little Susan, her first grandchild who was spending the weekend with us, and baby Angela, her latest grandchild.

We tried to dissuade Mommy from baking on a warm June day, but she insisted, probably feeling renewed in spirit, now that all of her children were graduated. All were either married, or single and working, or in college. She had reached her goal.

No one of us were going to pass up a tasty meal with such a great dessert, so we let her have her wish, but helped to cut the apples and roll the crust.

By the time dinner came, there was a good amount of heat in the kitchen from the gas oven. Even with the wall fan exhaust running, and the kitchen window open full, there was a warmth that felt uncomfortable. Daddy suggested that we eat in the dining room because there was a little breeze from the living room windows. And besides, Mommy's dinner and dessert deserved a formal setting.

For the second time in a week, we were eating together in a festive mood. Mommy was enjoying the compliments, even though the labor and heat from the kitchen had taken its toll. Her face seemed more tired than usual, and she picked at her plate of food.

When the dishes were done, Kate and Don went downstairs with Angela. Maureen went out with her friends for the evening. Daddy and I decided to sit out on the first floor back porch. And Mommy and little Susan got comfortable in the living room love seat to watch TV. Coming up was one of Mommy's favorites, *The Lawrence Welk Show.*

Daddy and I settled in to our chairs on the back porch just outside the door to Kate and Don's flat. He asked me about the B & B freight work, wondering whether it was like the Wabash. I said that the work was much the same, except there were no characters like Mike Judge and the others I found on the Railroad.

The sun was partly down as we looked southwest, across the alley to 29th St and Normal. Pretty soon our conversation turned to the White Sox. They were in first place, but had to face the Yankees and the Orioles this month. Daddy wasn't confident their young team could compete. Nellie Fox and Sherm Lollar had been traded before the season, and Little Looie Aparicio had already gone to the Orioles the year before. The Sox youth movement was now in the hands of Pete Ward at 3rd, Don Buford at 2nd, and Ron Hansen at short.

All of a sudden we heard the upstairs screen door open with a bang. "Grandma's sick. Hurry. Grandma's sick," Susan was yelling down to us from the back porch.

Daddy and I ran from our chairs up the stairs, two at a time. Susan was at the top of the stairs. "Something's wrong with Grandma," she kept pleading.

We hurried into the living room. I could hear the bouncy strains of the Lawrence Welk band coming from the TV in the living room. I also could hear Mommy's labored breathing as though she was trying to catch as much air as possible.

She was lying back against the love seat with her head to the side with her arm stiffly held straight down her side. "Marg'ret. Marg'ret." Daddy called to her. Her eyes were closed. She didn't respond, all the while struggling with deep, nasal and mouth breaths.

"O my God," my father said. "It's serious this time. I'll put her in the front bed. Call the Fire Department ambulance."

All our fears for Mommy were somehow being shown to us with her unconsciousness and labored breathing. I knew this was very serious, very bad for her.

I ran to the dining room phone and quickly dialed the Fire number. In the meantime, Daddy had managed to carry Mommy into the front bedroom. He kept calling her, "Marg'ret. Marg'ret," but she wasn't responding, just lying there gasping for air.

By this time Kate had come up from downstairs. She was crying, holding Mommy's hands in hers.

The ambulance came in ten minutes and I flagged them down outside. Dusk had set in so they had trouble finding our address. Two firemen ran up the front stairs with me. Daddy greeted them, leading them into the bedroom to Mommy.

They realized immediately that Mommy needed to get to a hospital. But they hesitated! "You know, Mr.LeVoy, we're not supposed to transport ill patients from homes. That's the job of a private ambulance service," the fireman in charge said softly.

"Listen," Daddy answered in a desperate voice, "I have three brothers on the Fire Department. One was killed in the line of duty in 1951. You gotta take my wife to the hospital. I don't know of another ambulance. This is an emergency. She can't wait."

There was a pause as the firemen looked at each other, then at Daddy and me. I could sense their indecision. "Get the stretcher ready," the Lieutenant again spoke softly. "We'll take her over to Mercy."

By the time Mommy was strapped in and carried down the steep front stairs to the ambulance, neighbors had clustered nearby. They were silent or spoke in hushed voices as Mommy was nestled into the rear of the vehicle.

"Call Mag and Jake and Fred, Hughie Boy. I'm going with your mother to Mercy. Pray for her. Kate, tell Maureen when she comes home," he nervously directed the two of us as we stood on the top of the stairs.

I could see the shock again in his face as the porch light shone on him. The darkness of evening was settling.

Then he hugged Kate and grabbed my left shoulder with his powerful left hand and squeezed me. His contact seemed to say that we could handle the shock of Mommy's attack. "I'll call from the hospital," were his parting words while he started to descend the stairs.

Slowly the ambulance pulled away from the curb, flashing its red lights, and starting the ominous siren. I could see Mommy on the stretcher inside with the paramedic ministering to her.

Prayers for her came easy to me, but I couldn't get past the dread I felt when we first saw her on that love seat. It was, God forbid, like the finality of her life was here, in our living room. I somehow had no sense that she would revive, or worse yet, recover from this struggling for air. She was leaving us, my heart was feeling, my instincts were telling me.

The dreaded call from Daddy came at 2 AM, Sunday morning. Mommy had died shortly before in the emergency room. She fought until the end, he said. But eventually there was no strength to continue. Her labored breathing stopped. God took her rather than have her struggle unconsciously in a hospital bed. Mercifully, her labors ended on a Sunday, the day of the Lord, the day of rest.

Throughout the periods of mourning, Mommy's wake and funeral, I felt a tremendous pressure that seemed to have no outlet for my sorrow. *No tears were coming, no sobs, just a stoic presence to the multitude of family, friends, neighbors, and seminarian classmates. The strain of all these conversations, the Requiem Mass, and Mommy's burial forced me within myself, rather than expressing genuine sorrow. The tears were in my eyes, but would not flow.* The Irish have a saying, "Bitter the tears that fall but more bitter the tears that fall not."

I kept saying to myself that I may not cry now, but will feel the pain of her loss every day of my life. She will not be mourned and forgotten, I prayed, asking God to bring her to reward with Him in heaven.

Guilt engulfed me each day now when I thought of the difficulties I gave her. The lack of care and concern I'd display with her, getting bogged down with my own inner conflicts, personal struggles. Many a time I was stubborn or moody, silently demanding attention from her and Daddy. More than once I was abrupt with her instead of being gentle, taking advantage of my youth and schooling and not understanding her and her fragile health. *What would I give now to return to those moments in our life together so that I could speak kindly and gently to Mommy.*

I have often thought of her since her passing, continuing to marvel at the days she was granted by our Creator. After all, she was just a peasant girl from a small farm in Western Ireland. Born and raised without shoes, she received her first pair when it was time to leave that farm and travel across the ocean to America. Spending her youth in a damp, deprived cottage near Loughglynn, she survived rheumatic fever and St. Vitus Dance to emerge in Chicago as a blossoming young woman. And struggling thru six nominal years of education at the Irish school near the crossroads, she went on in the United States to become a citizen, work outside the home, and maintain the finances of a family of eight.

Perhaps that is why she pleaded in her prayers each afternoon that God take her only after all the six children graduate from high school. What kind of determination must she have summoned to demand that each of us must complete our education, and then be ready for life's work.

But, without a doubt, all of her children are in awe with her hidden strength to not only carry and deliver six children, but also raise them with Daddy to be caring, successful young men and women. Our faith would be sorely tested if we had to face the life-threatening medical conditions that Mommy did to bring forth God's creations. Only the personal grace from Jesus, with the intervention of Mary, His Mother, enabled Mommy to accept her risky role as bearer of children.

Mommy is truly a heroine. Not in the sense of a woman who made newsworthy achievements in spite of overwhelming odds, or rescued a child from a burning home, or flew solo across the Atlantic. No, her heroism is much humbler. It's made up of countless hours of prayer, along with years of simple, direct care for Daddy and their children. It's made up of daily attention to the tasks of being a housewife, the drudgery of cooking, cleaning, and correcting. No doubt, her heroism ultimately resulted from clear, strong values that she passed on to us, her children.

Unfortunately, because the six of us took so much from the strength and reserves in Mommy's body, she failed to reach the age when she and Daddy could retire, relax, and tend to less chores, housekeeping, and finances. Her early passing can only be understood with our belief that she has ascended to the heavenly reward she most clearly merited.

On St.Patrick's Day nights, when the crowd would start to settle into their chairs having sung out the great Irish songs, and warmth and melancholy, started to creep into each one's heart, the tenor bard would softly say, almost in a whisper, "And now it's time to sing one for me dear mother, Mother Machree.

> *There's a spot in my heart which no colleen may own.*
> *There's a depth in my soul never sounded or known.*
> *There's a place in my memory, my life, that you fill.*
> *No other can take it, no one ever will.*
>
> *Sure, I love the dear silver that shines in your hair,*
> *And the brow that's all furrowed and wrinkled with care.*
> *I kiss the dear fingers so toilworn for me.*
> *Oh, God bless you and keep you, Mother Machree.*

CLASS OF NINETEEN HUNDRED AND SEVENTY
FIRST PHILOSOPHY (B)
1964 - 1965

Fourth
Row: John   Thomas William John   Frederick John   Thomas
            Parker   Job   Brennan Hillenbrand Konopasek Byrne   Lavery

Third   John   Patrick Thomas Eugene Michael Thomas Ronald Thomas Paul   William Thomas
Row: Blaszak Lyons   Nangle Nowak   Plesko Fitzgerald Mass   Dever   Kramer Sieck   Winikates

Second Anthony William Hugh   Thomas   Michael Louis   John   James   Joseph   James
Row: Talarico Veith LeVoy Franzman Kelly   Cameli Janega Czerwionka Sullivan Geisler

    Francis Corby   Donald Pokorni

First   Michael William Thomas John   Paul   James   James   Joseph John   Robert   Nicholas
Row: Mack Donnelly Hickey Jacobsen Russo Furey Crowley Lits Doyle Baranowski Zangara

    John McKeever

The Lady from Loughglynn, c.1930

8

LEE DUNWORTH

You searched the mountains overhead,
the waters and the stars.
And with a falcon's razor eye,
You wandered thru the air.
Looking, looking for a little dove
Your wandering heart could love.

Pat O'Hayer, 1966, "For a Friend Who Wandered Many Years"

A bright yellow and red canopy of fall colors greeted me as I made my way down the leafy path in the woods near the Seminary Philosophy Dorm. The afternoon sun peeked thru gaps in the treetops, casting spotlight beams on patches of the forest floor. This serene beauty overcame my advance on the path just as I reached the ravine that separated me from my destination. I was alone. All was quiet except the rustling leaves.

After pausing on the edge, I asked, "Why did you make these woods?" to the God who was somewhere both beyond this Creation and yet somehow within this beautiful autumn scene. "Were these woods put here for me to stand alone, and think? Think of You?"

I stood still, quiet, reflective. The presence of God seemed near. He was inviting me. Slowly I surrendered to the peace around me. It drifted down from the canopy, penetrating my skin, loosening my hold on time. *All I had to do was let go!*

My contemplation was interrupted by a distant, "thud", the familiar sound of a foot meeting a ball. My thoughts now returned to my destination, the football field on the other side of the ravine. It was afternoon rec time for the seminarians at Mundelein.

Mundelein Seminary, the major seminary of the Catholic Archdiocese of Chicago, was all that it was advertised to be. 840 acres of woods, St. Mary's Lake, scenic roads, and the perfectly placed, symmetrical seminary buildings. The Philosophy, Theology, Chapel, and other buildings were in colonial red brick, with broad columns in front of each edifice. These buildings were raised from the road, sitting on higher ground, adding stature to their presence, giving the visitor a glimpse of grandness.

In the center of campus was Our Lady's statue, sitting on top of a 50' column, exactly at the intersection of the Philosophy and Theology sides of campus, directly in line with the Chapel of the Immaculate Conception on one end, and the huge, multi-level promontory that took that same visitor out to the stately, southern view of the calm waters of the Lake.

This truly is a place to encounter God, in all of his natural and man-made structures. The roughness and pristine look of the forest contrasted so clearly with the exact placement and construction of the multiple buildings, the quaint bridges with post lights, and the curving roads. It was as though the complete plan by William George Cardinal Mundelein and his architects in 1920 was manifesting that God and man together, can create a place of beauty and order, a natural and yet controlled environment that would inspire young men to leave the world (Chicago is 40 miles to the south) and reach for holiness while training for the priesthood.

Within this sylvan setting, I found the Church's structured daily life. My day began in silence, meditation in chapel on the previous evening's points for meditation. Mass followed, not quite the new Liturgy approved by the 2nd Vatican Council.

Our Grand Silence ended at breakfast in the separate Refectory Building, a short walk from the Philosophy Dorm. Morning classes began soon after breakfast and lasted until noon prayers. Again, lunch at the Refectory followed by social time, mail, and then the afternoon classes. Rec time followed classes in the late afternoon, with football being the fall competitive sport.

Evenings were comprised of dinner, social time with a walk around the lake, study for 2 hours, and finally, Compline and Points. Our heads were on the pillow by 10 PM. The Magnum Silentium engulfed the Seminary.

"Did you hear that Fitz told Kenny that he didn't have a vocation. And that he should decide to leave the Seminary," John Gubbins, from the Class of '69, the Class ahead of mine, was telling me the latest gossip on our walk down the lane one night.

"What did Kenny say to Fitz?" I asked John. (Fitz was the nickname for Father Ed Fitzgerald, the slight, aging Philosophy Dean)

"Kenny told Fitz, 'With all due respect, Father, you don't know much about my vocation. I intend to become a priest,'" John answered my question.

I could imagine Fitz's shock as his analysis of Kenny's vocation was thwarted. Fitz had been Dean for over 20 years and was used to his decisions being obeyed, especially since his approval was needed for a seminarian to continue studying. He was the gatekeeper, the inquisitor, the hatchet-man. And he delivered all these life-decisions with such a faint, slightly falsetto voice that the hearer would swear that Fitz was going to cry if he was countenanced.

The dynamics of this conflict, however, were really beyond Fitz and Kenny. The conflict was even beyond the Rector, Monsignor Malachy Foley (Mal to everyone in the Archdiocese). The real battle was in Rome at the Second Vatican Council. And it was all about windows. Windows in the Church that should be opened as Pope John XXIII had stated in opening the Council. "Aggiornamento" is what he called for, an updating of the Roman Catholic Church, a meeting between the Church and the modern world.

But there were powerful, entrenched Bishops and Cardinals, led by Cardinal Ottaviano, the head of the Curia, who tried to close and lock every window that John XXIII opened. These men didn't want the fresh air that came thru open windows. They believed that the traditional atmosphere that we Catholics had breathed for centuries was needed for salvation. "Who knows what heresies are floating in this 'fresh' air."

Even though John XXIII and Cardinal Ottaviano were short, stocky men, with no agility for running through the Vatican opening or shutting windows, the Pope had a mysterious ally. Most of the hierarchy and laity who were bent upon reform of the Church in the early '60s, quietly believed it was the work of the Holy Spirit. Just as at Pentecost, the Spirit came in the form of wind, this time to Rome to rattle and blow open those apertures of freedom and fresh air, the windows of the Church.

And just as the Catholic laity were yearning for changes in the Church, like the recently passed Constitution of the Sacred Liturgy by the Vatican Council, which now required Mass in the native language, the ordination classes of '69 and '70 were pushing Fitz for greater freedom, more participation in the secular world they would soon minister to and serve. Was Mundelein's curriculum and life of spirituality just more stale air that needed to be blown out by strong breezes? Did the future priests of the 70's need a "fresh" mind that was not bound by tradition?

It was late October, with a light drizzle starting at midday. This particular afternoon, the football game was against First Theology on their field behind the Theology Dorm. I didn't stop in the woods to absorb God's presence this day. My mind was focused on the game at hand. What a difference an autumn day makes when there is no sun to brighten the tree tops and cast rays into the forest. No thoughts of the magnificence of Creation today.

From the beginning, the two teams were evenly matched. Each of us managed only a touchdown in the first half. Part of everyone's problem was the slick field that wouldn't allow sneakers to dig in for stops and starts, jogs and cuts. The smarter players slowed down, making sure of their footing before changing direction. It seemed as though we were all playing in slow motion, afraid to slip and fall.

Late in the third quarter, First Theology had long yardage to make a first down. Their quarterback had a good arm, and let fly with a perfect 30-yard spiral pass towards me, playing defensive back. I could see his intended receiver gliding toward me and positioning his arms to make the catch. As the ball arced down in its spiral, I covered the short distance to the ball, and leaped in front of the receiver to intercept the pass.

Yeah! I had it in my hands. My momentum carried me forward in mid-air. But when I hit the ground, with my wet, tennis shoes, I felt a sickening slide in my right knee. The sensation was of my lower leg slipping backwards on the wet grass while my upper leg moved forward, tearing the knee apart.

"Dammit. Dammit," I cursed as I lay on the ground grabbing my right knee. The ball had long since fallen out of my hands, definitely not the interception I was trying to make. I resorted to pounding the wet grass, escalating my curses.

Mike Kelly, the other defensive back on our team came running up. "Are you hurt?" he frantically asked.

I kept working my fists into the ground, seemingly oblivious to him and the receiver standing above me.

"Are you hurt," Mike again asked, "Physically? . . . . Morally?"

Besides the hurt to my knee, there was the huge pain to my ego, my pride. I had never suffered a serious injury in all the athletic contests and physical work situations I had confronted. Football, baseball, basketball, running, tackling, handling freight, ladders, wheelbarrows, nothing ever caused an injury like this. *My inner self had always said that I was indestructible, capable of leaping high for a thrown football, catching it, and safely landing on my toes, ready to run with the ball.*

But now, the inner regulator which monitored my body told me very clearly that I had seriously injured my right knee. Injured to the point of being carried off the field, dragging behind a useless right leg.

To be exact, my injury was a torn ACL, anterior cruciate ligament. The diagnosis was made by a visiting doctor at the Seminary infirmary. "Yes," he said, "the knee would heal in time. No, I couldn't play football and expect to run, jump, twist, turn on that same knee. Most athletes have the knee ligament sewn back, but as long as I wasn't an athlete, it wasn't necessary, especially if I couldn't afford the operation."

So now I was wounded, both physically, and just as important, psychologically. Not quite the vigorous young man I was before jumping for that interception. The slight limp I still had after a week, and puffiness around the knee kept telling me that I wasn't able to do all the things I had done before.

I noticed again that the spiritual intensity I prayed for was not developing. Each evening's meditation points by one of the priests was clearly heard and digested by me, as well as written in my notebook. But, when morning came and I read my notes, a level of communion with God was not reached. *Why couldn't I contact Him?*

There were times when I squeezed my hands, intensified my silent prayers, but still no sense of touching or talking to Jesus would reach me. *Why wasn't I moving to a deeper level?* It seemed as though all of my attempts at intensity led only to tension, to stress.

Father Shields, my spiritual advisor, did not seem to help. He was a thin man with an obsessive blink in his left eye, and an obvious nervous manner that resulted in stuttering. He even talked fast, blurting out his comments instead of measuring his words, and adding some feeling. I tried to explain to him my intense path to spirituality. He listened, provided advice, but just didn't connect with me as Father Matty Hoffman had done at Niles the previous year. I somehow felt that Father Shields had more inner struggles of his own as manifested by his occasional stutter and frequent blinks.

By the middle of January, the seminary pot of soup was boiling. Fitz had enough with these seminarians. A pizza party had been the fuse that lit his fire (or ire). *The seminarians in the Philosophy House had to be told to stop questioning, stop discussing, and get on with the virtue of obedience. They had to understand that the authority of the Church is what carried Holy Mother Church through nearly two millenniums. Milleniums filled with apostacy, heresy, reformation and schisms. But through all of this history, the primacy of the Pope, the authority of the Bishops provided the glue, the bonds that held the Church together.*

Fitz began his points for meditation to us in Latin. "Should we pray *Gloria in excelsis mihi* instead of *Gloria in excelsis Dei.*" He paused, and then added "Laudamus me, or Laudamus Te. Are you seminarians self-centered instead of Christ-centered?"

"I may be without feeling, as you criticize me, "Fitz continued in his characteristic high, pleading voice. "But I believe and pray that the solution to our conflict is in one word, *Fiat.*

He let that Latin word hang in the air, by now, the compressing, tense air of the Philosophy Chapel. Then he added *Fiat's* translation, "Let it be done."

Every one was intent now on Fitz's words. It was clear that he was agitated, upset, at his limit of patience, or possibly understanding. His pauses gave me sufficient time to take notes as well as absorb his emotion.

"I'm going to tell you an allegory, the Allegory of the Boats. All of us, seminarians, theologians, deacons, faculty, administration, even the Rector are to go to the seashore. Boats are waiting. The sky is dark. We are told to get into the boats, sit down, and grab the oar by our place. We are *not* told where we are going. Don't ask the destination! Just sit down and row. Don't stand! Don't question! It is mysterious for all of us. But if we are to survive, we must pray. We must ask for help, "Lord, we perish. Give us what you want.""

Fitz had reached the dramatic moment of his allegory. We could feel the sag in his voice, sensing that his passion had peaked. Exhaustion was slowly taking over. He paused again, head down at the lectern, trying to catch his breath.

Slowly, he raised his head for one last admonition. "Obey . . . . Just, . . . just obey," he gasped weakly, his high voice pleading to be heard.

Then he left the lectern and walked down the center aisle to his prie dieu at the rear of the chapel. I watched as he knelt down, his face more ashen then usual, his shoulders stooped low from this emotional confrontation with us.

As the allegory and its message of obedience filtered into our minds and spirits, anger followed. Fitz's message clearly told us to quit questioning, forget about change. *Just obey. Get in the boat. Sit down and row.* But his call to authority surely was anathema to the spirit developing in our two ordination classes. It was a flagrant demand of suppression. *Be quiet! Shut up!* is what we heard.

While the atmosphere in the Phil House was tense, the Aula, or classroom building usually was light and cheery for me. The first class each morning and afternoon was taught by a pint-sized, bouncy Jesuit named Tommy Byrne. Tommy's voice always appeared to be phlegmatic because his nose and throat sounded as though they were full of phlegm. Maybe he smoked too much.

Tommy's contribution to my overall level of wisdom was embodied in two Latin words, *Res sunt*, "Things are." It was Tommy's task to instill into our heads that all philosophical thought must begin with reality, hence, Things are . . . in the world. This is where Aristotle began his musings, his starting point, contrary to Plato's realm of ideas that had philosophy beginning with one's thoughts.

While the greater part of each morning class was filled with examination of Thomas Aquinas' development of philosophical theses based upon Aristotle, it was Tommy's afternoon performances in our class after lunch that made our day.

"Wow, was there a good Bozo Circus today. You should have seen Frazier Thomas and Bozo dance around the stage. Bozo had lotsa tricks up his sleeve on Channel 9." Standing in front of us, moving his arms in toward his waist, and then outward, like a kid at his 5th birthday party, smiling broadly with a twinkle in his eyes, was our erudite, classicly trained professor, the Reverend Thomas Byrnes, a.k.a. Tommy.

Our class got such a kick out of Tommy's mid-day performances that we'd ask about the Circus if Tommy had somehow forgotten to give us his report. "C'mon Father, tell us what Bozo did today." What is ironic is that Tommy's report each day was the only TV exposure we had. No television viewing was allowed in the Philosophy Dorm or Social Room. The Administration did permit us to watch the World Series in October in the Auditorium during our afternoon rec time.

Late in the afternoon, three times a week our class assembled in the large, auditorium classroom on the 2nd floor of the Aula. It was time for Church History. Our professor was Fitz. As we settled into our seats and set out new notebooks, Fitz opened an old, leather valise at the podium on the small stage.

All of a sudden, I could hear gasps and murmurings mixed with slight chuckling. In full view were a sheaf of papers in Fitz's hands, decidedly yellow from age, bent at the edges from many handlings, and broadcasting the message to those in the audience that here were the Professor's notes that had withstood the tests of time.

It took no great amount of thought to surmise that Fitz had made no changes in his class resources since the initial writing of his notes in the 1940's. Apparently Church History stopped with Pope Pius XII.

What further teaching need we hear that change was *not* a virtue here in Mundelein. What clearer message need we receive that tradition is fixed, that history cannot be altered, or better understood with recent research.

The tension surrounding me, the daily Magnum Silentium, lack of television or radio, and but one visitor's day a semester started to wear on me by December. Room visits to other seminarian friends were prohibited, just as walks around the almost 3-mile Lake roads with the same friends more than once a week were frowned upon. The caveat that we heard from the Administration read—NO PARTICULAR FRIENDSHIPS.

"Don't get too close to another seminarian," was the clear message, even though clerical wisdom consistently taught that a priest's best friends should be other priests.

I found myself writing depressing notes and deadly questions during Compline and meditation each night and morning. *How do I encounter the drabness of seminary life? Is this life for me? What are the joys, the hard points here? Where can I find strength? Am I progressing spiritually? If only I could pray harder, my relationship with God would be better. I need to be intense! I must strive for perfection!*

And on another, brighter morning, I wrote, *Who really loves me? Family? Friends? Relatives? God? I have this deep desire to be loved, a hunger to be wanted as well as a need to love. Can I, as a future priest, find fulfillment in a life that prohibits a wife and children? Will I be able to continue on this path of celibacy?*

On a gray, wet day, my meditation was about: *It's tough to be old, to be sick or crippled, or lonely, unable to move around or do things. How does a person think when they are like this? What do they look forward to? Do they ever consider suicide? How much suffering must they go through?*

My right knee continued to wobble whenever I ran or played handball, or some pickup game in basketball. It seemed to be a sign of my shaky vocation, as I limped through Christmas and the New Year. I was surprised at the lack of strength in my knee to pivot or stop quickly, always accompanied by an internal vulnerability as the joint began to slide slightly. Even walking around the Lake on snow and ice presented some touchy moments if I slipped with my right foot and felt the slide in the knee.

My 1st semester grades of straight B's brightened the horizon somewhat as I prepared for the continued study of Philosophy and pursuit of perfection. But the stress I had experienced since coming to Mundelein increased each day as the opportunities each afternoon for vigorous physical exercise, which always had been my outlet to relieve tension, were now limited.

Study, prayer, and introspection became my daily regimen. I was turning within myself. My meditation notes were not filled with the points from the priest, but rather personal examinations. *If I am going to find fulfillment in life, I really need to become deeper with others.* And, *I want to integrate all of my actions so that I will be conscious of a unity in my life.*

In April, I finally realized that this tension should be seriously addressed with a conference with Father McDonough, one of the excellent advisors at Niles. Much of his counseling helped priest candidates to discern whether to continue. When we met at Mundelein, he saw right away that perhaps the seminarian life, the vocation to the priesthood was not possible for me. Maybe I needed to be in a less structured, less spiritual atmosphere in order to grow. Certainly, he advised, my pursuit of perfection was harming me more than helping. Most likely, my "call" to serve others was genuine, but could be met in other ways such as education, or medicine, maybe social work.

There was no doubt, he emphasized, that I had a vocation. The question was Where? Doing what? Serving whom?

A few days after meeting with McDonough, we heard the sad news that Cardinal Meyer, the Archbishop of Chicago died from complications of brain surgery. He had been one of the progressive leaders in Rome during the Vatican Council. He had even been mentioned as a possible successor to John XXIII in the Conclave that elected Pope Paul VI in July of 1963, just two years earlier.

My personal thoughts and concerns were put on hold as the Seminary prepared for and received the burial of Albert Gregory Cardinal Meyer on a cool, sunny day in April. As the hearse passed by the Philosophy House with seminarians standing as an honor guard, I was caught up in the grandness of the event, the sheer volume of vehicles following the hearse, as well as the tremendous loss of such a gifted man, a man of many talents whose leadership was so greatly needed now in the Vatican deliberations.

By the middle of April, I was leaving too, leaving the Seminary world for a return to home in Chicago. Monsignor Foley and Father Fitzgerald agreed with Father McDonough that I should leave religious life. It would be better for me to pursue my call to serve others in lay life. And it would be wise to make this transition as soon as possible. My psyche needed a different environment.

When I did get home, I felt a great sense of failure, though. So much had I wanted to move forward, so much did I hunger for the respect of family and friends. How could I go on now that I was 27 years old, without a career, a goal, a sense of identity. Where do I start? What can I do?

> *But mountainside grew sharp with thorns*
> *The waters hard with ice,*
> *And stars had struck their brazen fires*
> *Too high above your face;*
> *Heavy years were piling up,*
> *Your days were soon to stop*

Pat O'Hayer

It seemed as though hunger had been my motivation all thru my life. Hunger to tap that nickel on the pew and get attention from Daddy, hunger to play softball on the street with the older guys, hunger for a better house to live in, hunger for an education beyond high school, hunger for friends, and maybe one special friend. Finally, perhaps a fatal quest, *hunger for perfection*, oneness with God.

My brothers and sisters were surprised at my return home, and Daddy was disappointed. He always had a sense of pride with my priestly vocation, well aware that Catholic popular belief held that parents of a priest were guaranteed a place in heaven. I must have disappointed him very much, with these attempts at education and future careers, always ending in failure. *I was going nowhere!*

Maybe it was time to end this constant tension and inability to succeed. Maybe I should just quit trying and resort to a feeble-minded job, 8 to 4:30. Then I'd fall into drinking to forget my failure just like my Grandfather Hugh, and Uncle Stephan. A life of loneliness, dissipation, and avoidance would be easier than these struggles for fulfillment. *Why bother trying. I probably wasn't meant to get anywhere, anyway.*

Or quicker yet, instead of this dreary life of mediocrity and alcoholism, perhaps I should finish myself now, and avoid days and years of self-pity and guilt. How can I take one step forward now when this proverbial rock has pushed me back against the hard place. *I couldn't move forward! Was the end near?*

The embarrassment, frustration, and sense of failure caught up to me as I walked down Michigan Avenue in early May. I had just spent a frustrating hour answering questions from a psychologist, watching as he puffed lasciviously on a large, black cigar in his downtown office. Instead of listening to me and maintaining eye contact, he'd watch the cloud of smoke he had just expunged from his mouth, as it slowly drifted to the ceiling. He appeared to be enamored by his oral creation. I had the distinct feeling that he was more interested to see where that cloud was going than my future. *Was I like that smoke, just drifting away?*

His services were part of the transition plan for men who leave the diocesan seminary. His obvious goal was to guide me into another career or job with adjustment to lay life. But all he succeeded in doing was irritating me into anger because of his simple questions about my future and at the same time, his obvious, delightful puffing on the cigar. He seemed to have no awareness of my inner turmoil, the sense of failure and my fight for some kind of self-respect.

I had a tremendous urge to take that cigar out of his mouth, and smash it in his ashtray. On the way out, I'd say, "No thanks for your services."

The cool, fresh spring air of May diffused my anger somewhat. I decided to walk instead of going for the bus home. Perhaps I could walk the five miles home from downtown and be rid of tension. Maybe this brisk exercise would relieve me of that rock that was pushing against me.

At the first stop light, I could feel the pressure again. And the doubts. *Why not give in. Stop trying! You've had it. You're goin' nowhere. This rock, this hard place are too much for you.* I hesitated at the curb. The light was red.

No I won't give up! One way or another I'm goin' stop this rock from crushing me. Keep pushin' it until it moves. I don't care how long it takes, but

I'm gonna keep tryin'. I will not be backed down, becoming another lost soul. I will not be a failure! I will use the gifts that God has given me, no matter what it takes.

The light turned green. I took one step off that curb . . . and then another across Monroe Street. And another!

A day later the rock budged slightly. It seemed lighter now. I managed to slip away from its pressure long enough to get a job on the Wabash Railroad freight dock with my father. He was now working in the new, state-of-the-art freight center at 47th and Wallace, in the old Canaryville neighborhood, just south of Bridgeport.

Ten years after starting my full-time work at the old Wabash docks just south of downtown, I found myself returning to moving freight again in May of '65. Another reminder that I was not progressing in a career like other 27-year old men. *Would this be my work both now and the future? A future of smoking, booze, and gambling like some of the dock workers?*

While the rock would roll up on me at times, bringing self-doubts and depression, my father too was struggling. Struggling with pains in his chest. He kept saying it was congestion, but my fears said it was more serious. All of his adult life he smoked cigarettes, Camels to be exact, the strongest cigarette on the market. As long as I knew my father, he had a cough, consistently bringing up phlegm with his loud hacks and clearing of his throat.

Just recently he switched to cigars, somehow reasoning that they were better for him because he wasn't inhaling. But the coughing, phlegm and pain continued. His face was losing color, sleep was spotty, and he started to lose appetite. And he had no energy for bowling, his favorite recreation.

The guys at the freight office kept urging Daddy to see the doctor. They saw his color going gray too, his work slowing down, and his conversation minimal. I tried to persuade him to go to the doctor. I even told him that I'd drive. But there was a resistance he put up all thru the summer months that made me think that he didn't want to know the reason for his illness. It's as if he knew it was very serious and didn't want to face the doctor's diagnosis.

At a deeper level, I sensed Daddy's wish to die. Although he had somewhat adjusted to Mommy's death, and tried to keep up contacts with friends and family, there was now a clear feeling of loneliness in him. Somehow, he was telling us that he didn't want to continue living without her. Maybe he knew that this illness in his chest would progress to the point that he could lie down and pass on. His faith told him that he would see Mommy then.

The pressure rock kindly stayed a few feet away from me, not bothering to cast doubts to torment me. Living at home with Daddy, Fred, and Maureen enabled me to save money again from my dock wages. If I continued thru early September at the Wabash freight dock, I'd have enough to return to school. Once again, I'd be in classes, pursuing that elusive degree, the piece of paper that tells the civilized world that I'm ready for the challenges of a career. Maybe I could finish a degree in Philosophy in two semesters.

Daddy's condition slipped measurably by late August. He no longer could sleep with the constant pain. His coughing was both deep and painful. He had no appetite. In early September, he finally saw the doctor. Almost immediately, the doctor entered him to St.Bernard's Hospital for tests.

The lung biopsy confirmed what all of us feared. Both of his lungs were cancerous. Both were inoperable. His illness was terminal. He had perhaps three months to live.

We took the medical news stoically, probably because we knew how much he had smoked throughout his life. We also felt deep down that Daddy would be at peace after death since Mommy was gone from our home.

Fifteen months after Mommy succumbed to a stroke at home, Daddy breathed his last in the hospital on September 26th, 1965. He died somewhat peacefully, with Jake at his side. Like Mommy, he had but 58 years of life, much too young to not have enjoyed at least one month or one year of retirement.

Amazingly, I felt little pressure from the rock. The hard place was almost gone, replaced by the marble facade of Loyola University's Lewis Tower campus. What I did feel was a great relief that Daddy had not lingered for a long time. He had suffered enough over the last year of his life. Mercifully he was finally taken by God. He no longer had to fight pain and coughing, and loneliness.

I believe, through the hand of God that Daddy would move on now to his reward, life after death. He had been a caring husband, a strong father, and loving grandfather. He provided leadership to the community as a Big Brother, lector at church, Holy Name member, and a respected freight clerk at work.

Besides an unfulfilled retirement, Daddy never got the chance to build his dream house. After being his gopher on many jobs, and his listener about his youth and dreams, I knew how much he loved building. He always whistled when he worked as though he reached harmony with his hands and head as he measured, cut, and nailed. Invariably I'd smile when I heard those notes coming from his pursed lips. The simple melody told me that he was happy with his creation. *The new porch was strong, the stairs steady, the remodeling just so!* He was fulfilled.

Like with the loss of Mommy, my tears were all inside, kept there by me to insure they were real and not simply for the occasion. Daddy had tried all of his life to work, to lead, to support. I clearly felt his legacy, that desire to build, that sensitivity to listen, that almost universal drive to be respected. *How could I fail to call him my hero!*

*

Pat O'Hayer was sitting at the usual table in the Student Union on Monday morning. He was sipping a cup of Loyola's fresh coffee, with a cigarette sticking out of his right hand. As I approached, he brightened.

"There's Hugh, the sage of the South Side. Sit down. Sit down and tell me about your rendezvous with Bernadette," Pat chuckled. The emphases on *rendezvous* and *Bernadette* were pronounced.

"It was fine. We went to see a Bond flick," I answered, not too excitedly. "A drink and a sandwich afterwards. Bernie's very nice. It's too bad she's promised," I added.

"Yah, she told me she has a boyfriend in Colorado. Going to college, me thinks," Pat continued.

"And how did you do with Beth? Did she go out with you on the weekend?" I asked somewhat hesitantly.

Pat's smile faded quickly. His pink Irish face fell down to the coffee. Then a puff on the cigarette followed. "I walk the sands alone this afternoon," he whispered, his words fighting to get through the smoke.

I looked confused, "What."

'Oh, it's just the first line of a poem I'm working on. Something about the sea and its periphery, the sands." Pat went silent and drifted for a moment.

"Elizabeth?" I reluctantly asked.

"Yes." He paused. "My muse, you know."

Pat and I were attending Loyola's Lewis Towers campus on north Michigan Ave. for the fall semester of '65. He had gone to Quigley, the high school for prospective priests. But, he didn't pursue his vocation further, instead enrolling at Loyola to study for a degree in English. He spent a lot of time with verse, both his own as well as other poets. His favorite was William Butler Yeats, the early 20th century Irish romantic poet.

Pat not only had read and studied Yeats' writings, he consistently memorized poems, giving forth a quick recital of not only, "The Lake Isle of Innisfree", but also romantic verse like "No Second Troy" and "Down by the Salley Gardens." Pat constantly fell into poetic lines, especially if romance was the subject of conversation. He affectionately referred to Yeats with the moniker, "Willy B."

Pat had a kinship with Willy B. Both had suffered thru unrequited love. Yeats' fatal attraction was with Maud Gonne, the turn-of-the-century dramatic persona. I felt so keenly Pat's hopeless attention to Beth, reminding me so poignantly of Lucy; my emotional downfall from ten years earlier.

The bell rang for class changes. I glanced at the cafeteria clock. "I gotta go. My morning class in Philosophy of God meets in five minutes. And Catania's giving a quiz," I said quickly to Pat.

Resting by a forest pond
Hid from searching eyes
You meditated on the fates
Of hidden destinies:
Your mind, tired with scraping the deep,
Put on a heavy sleep.

Pat O'Hayer

My renewed career (at age 27) was in the study of Philosophy. That was the advice I received from the Dean at Loyola. He indicated that one year of full-time study, and a semester to study for Comps would earn a Bachelor Degree. I could then pursue professional work, probably teaching or social work. My personal rock and hard place were now history, along with the pursuit of perfection, that impossible goal of religious life. The only striving I need do was with the required textbook for each class.

October's cool and dry weather turned, as usual, to grey, wet days in November. The trees had long since lost their leaves, looking like skeletons against the sunless sky. They seemed so bare, lacking cover of leaves against the coming cold. Another Chicago winter was waiting to descend from Canada, roaring thru central Wisconsin, pent on chilling people, animals, and automobiles in its path.

This Friday evening was chilly, damp, and of course, dark. I debated about wearing the winter jacket or my raincoat. We were going to Old Town for some folk music and beer, and probably doing some walking. The jacket would be warmer but not as classy as the raincoat. *Yah . . . probably the raincoat!* More mature looking. Less bulky than the heavy coat. Easy to fold up when we're in that place, John Barleycorn.

Tom Lenkart was picking me up at 7:00 with the girls. This double-date was his idea. He was studying at Loyola also, having left Mundelein sometime in the summer. We had a special connection in the seminary, being pew partners with Albert Lewis at Niles, and then playing next to each other on the Mundelein softball team, he at 3rd and me at shortstop.

Tom was built like a ballplayer, tall, thin, with great hands, along with a sharp mind. And he had that gut desire to play hard and win. Just recently he must have started playing the guitar, because he wanted to hear the folk singers in Old Town tonight.

I was a little surprised when he mentioned double-dating a week ago, telling me that he was going somewhat steady with a girl from Evergreen Park on the far south west side. She was a junior at St.Xavier College. He assured me that his date could arrange for one of her classmates to join as my date.

What perked my attention to Tom's offer, strangely, was his girlfriend's name, Lee Dunworth. *That name sounds interesting. A girl named Lee. I'd like to meet this Lee!* I smiled. Maybe she's as good looking as Lee Remick, who starred in *Days of Wine and Roses* with Jack Lemmon. And who knows. Perhaps she's as smart as Lee Phillips, the newscaster from WBBM, Channel 2 Television.

I grabbed the tan raincoat when Tom rang the bell. No cap tonight for my head though.

"Did you have any trouble finding the place in the dark?" I asked Tom after I answered the door.

"Just that little jog in Canal Street was a little confusing. Your directions were easy to follow," he answered.

"Watch these steps," I cautioned. "When they're wet, you can slip and fall all the way down from the second floor. They're way too steep to casually walk down without a hand on the banister."

28th Place was empty as we began to cross to Tom's car. I could see a girl in the front seat. The inside dome light was on. *That must be Lee. Wow! Bright red hair!*

"Hello," the girl in the front said with a bright smile as I opened the rear door and stuck my head into the back seat. "I'm Lee Dunworth."

My attention stayed with her as I was about to say "Hello. I'm Hugh." Our eyes were fixed as though some spiritual bond had instantly connected us. I was not aware of Tom getting into the car, or the girl next to me in the back seat.

Finally, I broke this connection that held us together. Turning, I heard Lee saying, "This is my friend, Barb Janz."

I smiled. "Hi, I'm happy to meet you," extending my hand to clasp Barb's.

"Shall we leave the dome light on, so we can talk and see each other?" Tom asked after he got settled in the front seat.

"Very good, Tom." Lee said quickly.

I was aware that she was still turned to the back, right in line with my vision.

"So both of you are at St. Xav's?" I questioned them, again fixing my eyes and smile at Lee, after glancing at Barb. The attraction returned, pulling me even stronger to Lee's attention. *What a smile she has! Warmth! She's such an attractive girl! How can I talk to Barb, my date, with Lee turning toward me? And what about Tom?*

Our chemistry continued while we drove to Old Town, parked and walked to the pub, John Barleycorn. By now, Lee and I were discussing Philosophy, our common major. (Tom was an English major, and Barb in Science). That led to sharing stories of religious life (She had been in the convent for two years), and Tom joined us as we discussed the rigors of spirituality. Before long, all of us brought up our families, and again Lee and I found a link because we both were from large families, she being the oldest of 10.

At one point, after a few beers, I was keenly aware that Lee and I were monopolizing the conversation as well as our attention to each other. *I wondered if Tom was getting jealous, and whether Barb was bored. Were we too obvious? Too attentive to each other?*

As the evening progressed with visits to other pubs, listening to more folk singers, it was obvious to me (and probably Lee) that we shared an attraction to each other. There were clear, but unstated feelings between us. Our somewhat exclusive communication with one another confirmed silently that we needed to see each other again.

My foreboding returned, however, on the drive home. *How could I pursue Lee when one of my friends is dating her? Did I give her too much attention at the expense of my date for the evening, Barb?* As I stepped out of Tom's car at 28th Place, my emotions were jumbled. I didn't know what to feel.

The following Monday at Loyola, I ran into Pat in the 9th floor hall on the way to Modern Phil. Class.

"So, my friend, how was your double encounter in Old Town?" Pat queried, spacing his words and using nuance like a bard reading a poem. Today he looked even more so like Dylan Thomas, with a cigarette dangling from his lips.

"I've got a problem, Pat. A big one," I answered somewhat gravely. "I really like Tom's girlfriend, Lee Dunworth."

Pat took a puff from the cigarette and pushed the butt into the sand receptacle in between the elevators. 'This is serious, Hugh. Whether to honor friendship, or follow one's heart," he pronounced.

"I gotta run to class. See you in the Union at 10:30?" I asked quickly, moving down the hall.

"Yah," was Pat's answer.

All of Saturday and Sunday I had been thinking of Lee, and how to see her again. At the same time, I felt guilty with these thoughts which undermined Tom and his feelings for her. When he had first mentioned her to me, he told me about his affection for her. Now, I would be coming between the two of them.

When Pat and I finally got together after morning classes, he was understanding about my feelings for Lee. "Sounds like the girl of your dreams. A muse, and a philosopher combined. A pearl to be sought, and found. Need I urge you to follow the arrows coming from your heart?"

I smiled. I had been thinking during the morning classes, instead of taking the professors' notes. "I know what to do," I said slowly, with a sly grin. "I'll throw a party and invite Tom. Obviously, he'll accept and invite . . ."

"Lee," Pat exclaimed, finishing my sentence.

*

The end of December, 1965 saw the beginning of peace efforts by President Lyndon Johnson to end the Viet Nam war. He sent the Vice-President, Hubert Humphrey, to Yugoslavia to meet with Tito. Averill Harriman visited Paris to get support from DeGaulle. Ambassadors were dispatched to other countries to bring the US message to stop the hostilities in southeast Asia.

My efforts were beginning also as I approached the New Year, 1966. My goals were peaceful too, somehow connecting with Lee Dunworth and, at the same time, remaining friends with Tom Lenkart. My plan was to start tonight, December 31ˢᵗ, New Year's Eve. I had good reason to be confident in my plan because of a phone call three weeks ago.

"Hi Hugh, this is Lee . . . Lee Dunworth."

I could hardly believe who was on the other end. *Lee Dunworth! Calling me!*

"Uh . . . hello Lee. It's good to hear from you," I somehow answered.

"Tom invited me to your New Year's Eve party, and . . . I'm wondering if you are serving any food," she continued.

She's on the phone, asking me about food. Does she know how much I like her? "Er . . . yeah. I guess so. Maybe a ham and rye bread for sandwiches, "I volunteered. "Nothing real fancy."

"Well, I can make a pan of lasagna if you want something hot to serve," she added quickly. "We can heat up some Italian garlic bread too."

There was a pause. She was waiting for me to respond to her offer of lasagna, but I was marveling at the innocence of her phone call and offer. The wheels in my head were interpreting all kinds of interest on her part to help me with the party. *Was she really saying, "I like you too." Were all those smiles on the double date for real?*

I finally answered her, trying to be casual and grateful at the same time." That sounds great. Everybody likes lasagna with garlic bread. Thank you. You're so thoughtful to offer the food for the party. There'll probably be eight or ten people."

Our conversation slipped easily from food to Philosophy. I was reading (perhaps despairing over) Kierkegaard's *The Sickness Unto Death* for Modern Philosophy, and she was struggling thru Sartre's *Being and Nothingness*. We shared our challenges with the rigors of Philosophy, hoping to use it as a basis for further study in Psychology or Theology. We weren't too sure however that existentialism was all that it claimed to be, especially after plowing thru Camus, Kierkegaard and Sartre. What ever happened to Aristotle and "Things are?"

Lee's brief call about food for the party developed into an hour-long conversation. It finally ended with a yell in the background, "Lee. Get off the phone!" It was her mother, she apologized. But when we did hang up, it was again clear to me that both of us had an unexpressed need to talk to each other, to share academic pursuits, ultimately, to be with each other.

Tom brought his guitar to the party, and Lee her "innocent" lasagna, with the "guilty" garlic bread. While Tom entertained the guests in the living room (the same front room of my youth) Lee and I were together in the kitchen figuring out how to turn on the oven. We also assembled the dishes and silverware to set the dining room table. My date couldn't help because she was hobbling with a cast on her broken right leg.

My other accomplice, Pat O'Hayer, made sure that Tom kept playing songs to keep him occupied while Lee and I developed our unspoken relationship within the old kitchen I had spent 28 years of life. *Could this girl be the one with whom I would share cooking duties in the future? Was Lee acting out the old wives tale that said," the way to a man's heart is through his stomach"?*

Lee's lasagna received compliments from our, I mean, the guests. And her garlic bread came out of the oven crisp and tasty. Just enough seasoning! Sitting at the old, dining room table brought memories to me of my parents' parties, especially those at the holidays. Many a Thanksgiving and Christmas, Daddy would be sitting where I am now, carving the bird for Mommy and the six kids. *Was this current scene with Lee serving, a preview of meals to come?*

Chicago's entry to the New Year would not be complete without the countdown on TV from State & Randolph Streets. The eight of us were standing in the living room with our glasses of champagne, listening to the announcer, and counting "5,4,3,2,1 Happy New Year."

I turned to Lee, but she was grabbed by Tom for the New Year's kiss. So, I made my way to my date, and hugged her, wishing her a Happy New Year. After making the rounds with hand shakes and hugs, Lee was finally free.

Our smiles spoke after our eyes met. "Happy New Year," she whispered.

"Yes. Happy New Year. I hope . . ." I didn't have a chance to finish before we embraced.

> *And while asleep a magic dream*
> *Came dancing in your head;*
> *You dreamt a little silver dove*
> *Was circling over head*
> *Scanning for a place to light;*
> *She was a dazzling sight.*

Pat O'Hayer

The holidays ended. Classes were soon to start at Loyola. Gone was the leisure to read through the latest Theodore White book, *The Making of the President 1964*, the account of Lyndon Johnson's victory over Barry Goldwater. I marveled at both the breadth of White's coverage of the campaign as well as his depth. How well he gave us inside looks at the political maneuvering by both candidates.

Finally, summoning the grit to sit down one, cold January night and begin reading for class, I picked up the dreaded German philosopher, Georg Wilhelm Friedrich Hegel. I had some notes from the first class on him just before Christmas. Something about Hegel's dialectical reasoning. There'd be more discussion once we read Hegel and classes continued. But I had trouble getting started, partly because of the difficulty reading and digesting this German philosopher and his contradictions, but also because I had another philosopher on my mind and in my heart. Instead of contradictions, this latter philosopher presented conflicts that the New Year's Eve party only heightened.

The phone rang.

"Hello," I answered, wondering who was calling on such a frigid night.

"Hugh? This is Lee."

Lee, calling me! "Oh, hi, . . . uh, Happy New Year again." *It's her!*

"I'm . . . I'm sorry to call you. You're probably studying," she spoke nervously.

I slowly recovered from the initial surprise of her call. "Actually, you just rescued me from Hegel. You don't know how much I dread plowing thru his work.

"Maybe as much angst as I have with Immanuel Kant," she added, laughing lightly. Her voice was smoothing out, becoming less tense, softer, clearer.

So you *can't* understand Kant," I joked.

There was a slight chuckle and "Awgh" from Lee, following my pun. "Clever," she commented. "Maybe you should try eating a bagel when reading Hegel."

I laughed now, "Very good, Lee. That's worth 4 points."

"Out of 5? 10?" she quizzed me.

"Out of 5, of course. It's original, isn't it?"

The bond between us surfaced again, easing its ties to each other thru this electronic piece of communication. I felt a subtlety with Lee that invited light remarks between us, a kind of banter that kept reinforcing our pleasure to be talking to each other. A familiarity allowing us to move smoothly from one level to another, without introductory words. *I was feeling warm now on this freezing night.*

The reason I called you is because my mother needs her lasagna pan," Lee broke my reverie. "She needs to use it for casseroles," she added.

"Oh! That's right. It's still here. We didn't wash it on New Year's Eve, so you couldn't take it with." I paused, thinking. "Why don't I bring it to Loyola and give it to Tom when I go back on Monday?"

There was silence on the other end of our connection. I waited, not understanding her pause. *Did I say something wrong!*

"Well," she hesitated, "I told Tom that I didn't want to date him again." She said this slowly and clearly, as though she had been rehearsing it.

Now it was my turn to be silent. Her words were sinking in. *She's not dating Tom anymore. Then . . .*

"So then," I added slowly, "I should bring the lasagna dish out to you in Evergreen Park. Maybe we can go to a movie afterwards?" *I could hardly believe that one week after New Year's I was asking Lee to go out on a date.*

"I'd like that very much. I was hoping you'd ask. I enjoy talking to you, especially about our studies in philosophy."

And for the next hour, we discussed the curriculums at Loyola and St. Xavs, our tentative career goals, and our families. Lee had this dream to study Theology in Germany. I told her that I saw myself staying in Chicago to begin a career in teaching. When we reluctantly decided to say "Good Night" (another Dunworth was yelling for her to get off the phone) we agreed to meet the following Saturday night.

I sat on the phone chair for ten minutes, going over our conversation. *Need I fear anymore that she likes me. Breaking up with Tom, although she said they never really were going steady. And now! A chance to be together! Thank you, God!*

The movie we went to see for our first date was *The Spy Who Came in from the Cold.* I chose it because Richard Burton played the spy who finally decided he had enough espionage for one lifetime. He was ready to settle down with his co-spy, Claire Bloom. The "Cold" in the title, of course, was the Cold War between the United States and Russia.

Somehow the movie title struck a sympathetic chord with me as though I was leaving the cold too. Could that chord have something to do with the weather, since it was frigid January in Chicago. Snow, ice, and strong winds. Wind chills. Numb fingers, frozen feet, and a red face.

Or perhaps poetically, was I leaving the chilly world of single-life, moving into the warmth and tenderness of a loving relationship with Lee. Certainly our moments together already had ignited growing flames that might easily lead to a consuming fire. (One of the first discoveries we made about ourselves is that her name, "Lenore", comes from the Greek, "Helen", which means "flame." And, "Hugh", is an old Irish name that means "fire."

The semester ended toward the end of January. After exams, my grades were straight B's. Now I could face one more semester at Loyola, completing my course work. All that was needed for a Bachelor of Science degree then was preparation and completion of a Comprehensive exam in the fall of '66.

My plans also included the start of a teaching career. At a meeting with Sister Filibert, the principal of St. Anthony's Parish School, she indicated that there were anticipated openings in Grades 3, 5, and 7 for next September. No nuns were available to fill these vacancies, so she had to look to lay teachers. She advised me that I could begin teaching without a degree, as long as I received the degree the following January.

Lee and I continued to see each other, now on both Saturday nights and Wednesday evenings. Our affection, attention, and intimacy for each other increased to the point where we sensed a strong commitment to each other. A soulful feeling that we should consider the future together, beyond dating.

It was at the Theology Symposium, held at St. Xavier's John XXIII Institute that I saw firsthand the depth of Lee's wish to study in Germany. Assembled in the College auditorium over four days in early April were the world's foremost Catholic theologians, discussing and debating doctrine. There was the German Jesuit, Karl Rahner; the French Jesuit, Jean Danielou; the Dutch Dominican, Edward Schillebeeckx; the French Dominican Yves Congar; as well as the English Charles Davis, and the American Gerard Sloyan to name the headliners.

I could not see how I would compete with these learned priests/ theologians for the attention of Lee. Her romantic vision of study in Germany in Theology at Munich or Tubingen University seemed to burn brightly as she watched and listened to these scholars. The lure of study abroad played into her idealism also.

Easter Sunday passed quietly with the cool, early April weather. A growing need developed within me to talk seriously about our future together. I took Lee to Bruno's Restaurant near Little Company of Mary Hospital. This small place was our favorite Italian restaurant on 95th. It was dimly lit, as usual, with a sparse crowd for a Saturday evening. In the background we could hear the soft Italian music. Pervading the dining room was the ever-present smells of Italian food.

Dare I ask her now? Is this the right time? Naw, wait until dinner is finished. A little food, some Chianti. Sitting close, holding hands. Then pop the question!

By the end of our intimate meal, "Volare" was on the background music, by Dean Martin. I settled back into the booth, pushing the empty plate to the left. Lee was just finishing also.

"How was your steak," I asked, nonchalantly.

"Very good. A lot more tender than the "Dunworth steak" I get at home," She answered.

"Dunworth steak! What's that."

"Pot Roast! The meat that feeds ten kids, as long as you cook enough vegetables, and serve lots of milk," she declared decisively, like a well-seasoned mother.

I laughed, somewhat nervously, grabbing the wine glass for a sip of Chianti.

"Any coffee and dessert tonight," interrupted the waitress while she collected the dinner dishes and silverware.

I was edgy now, realizing that dessert and coffee would mean more interruptions to our table.

"No," I answered her. "We're going to enjoy the rest of the wine first." I raised my glass in a mock toast to the waitress. She seemed to sense our need for some privacy, especially since we were seated so close to each other in the corner booth. Our hands were touching.

"And how was the lasagna?" Lee asked after the waitress left. The tone of her query had an edge of challenge to it. She removed her hand from mine. *Be careful, I thought.*

"Very good. Moist. Excellent sauce."

"Oh! Better than mine?"

"Uh . . . definitely . . . uh, not! More like a 7 or 8 on a scale of 1 to 10."

Lee smiled. She put her left hand over my right. "And mine?"

"Without a doubt, a 9. And maybe with a better oven, your lasagna could easily become a 10," I added.

We were very close now, warmed by the food and wine, holding hands, our legs touching at the thighs. Our eyes were focused on each other. *Should I ask her now?*

"You know, I'd really like to have your lasagna every week. I mean . . . in our own kitchen, baked in your new oven. Our apartment. I think . . . I mean . . . Well, would you like. Uh. Will you marry me?"

Lee's eyes misted. Her face smiled brightly even though her emotions were checked. She squeezed my hand so hard and moved closer, pressing her leg against mine.

"Yes," she whispered, "I want to be your wife. I love you."

"I love you too. Very much. I want you to be my wife," I said softly.

We kissed lightly, smiled, squeezed hands. The bond between us never felt stronger.

"I know you want to study in Germany after you graduate, but I think your ministry would be better in Chicago, teaching in a Catholic high school. There are many kids whose faith would mean much more if they saw you in front of a Theology class, a young laywoman. I have a feeling that's where the future of this Church will be, with lay men and women, like us . . . . I really want you to stay here and marry me."

Lee's face turned serious from the hopes I had just expressed. "I guess you're right," she spoke softly. "Germany is a dream, probably unreal. Besides, I don't have any money to study there. Even with a scholarship, my parents would have to pay my living expenses. And with the ten kids, that's out of the question."

We lightly touched lips to seal our commitment, knowing within us that we would be together from now on.

I grabbed the Chianti bottle and poured into our glasses, pausing as the last drops slid from the bottle into Lee's glass. "Let's toast our love," I proclaimed, raising my glass and moving it and my arm to encircle her arm and glass. We were now locked together for this taste of wine, this union of two lovers.

After a small taste, Lee gazed at me. "I can still see your face on that first night, last November. From the moment we met, I felt drawn to you like a magnet. You were so handsome, wearing your tan, trench coat. Your smile was so engaging, I wanted to," she paused, "be with you!"

> *A gentle diamond in the air*
> *As she graced the waters round,*
> *But all at once the dream was ended*
> *By a whirring sound:*
> *A cloud-white dove had set her nest*
> *Upon your rising breast.*

Pat O'Hayer

"My name is Hughie," I was telling Lee's young sisters and brothers, as we sat in the Dunworth living room. "I have an Uncle Donald, and two brothers.

Brian was wondering. "Oh yeah, what are your brothers' names?"

"Why of course," I quickly answered. "Louie and Dewey," smiling and mocking seriousness at the same time.

Lee's mother, Jean, laughed, "Oh Hughie!"

Paul wasn't sure either, so he blurted out, "What do Louie and Dewey look like?"

"Just like me. When you see them, you'll say that were identical."

Franny, the second youngest had been inching toward me during the conversation. By now she was just to my left. It was her turn to question me, "Hughie, when will we meet Louie and Dewey?"

"Franny, I told them that I'm getting married to Lee. So, I'm going to bring them to the wedding especially to see you."

Franny beamed like a princess who had just been invited to the king's ball. She'd be meeting Louie and Dewey at the wedding.

The engagement dinner at the Dunworth house followed Bruno's engagement meal by only five days. So quickly, Lee and I had to present ourselves to her parents (and kids) to ask permission. Hopefully we would discuss our plans for the wedding, date, time, place, etc.

Soon after we were settled in the living room, with the meal warming in the oven and eight of the nine children (Michael was away at college) present and listening in the living room, I broached the subject with Lee's father.

"Lee and I care for each other very much. We feel that we should marry so that we can share our lives."

'How are you going to support her?" her Dad asked me. "I understand that you're still in college."

'Yes, I'm finishing at Loyola in June, and then in September I'll start teaching at St.Anthony's in Bridgeport, my home parish.

Lee's mother leaned forward in her chair to ask, "Well, Hughie, when do you and Lee intend to get married? You know she has another year to go at St. Xav's."

Lee had been edgy throughout, shifting in her chair next to mine, alternately squeezing my hand and holding it. "We were thinking . . . we kinda . . . we want to get married after my graduation. Probably in June of '67, fourteen months from now."

"What?" her father blurted out. "Fourteen months? He stammered, incredulous. Staring at me and motioning to Lee with his hands, "Take her now! We need the bed!"

Everyone laughed, repeating his phrase, "Take her now! We need the bed."

The hugs and kisses followed, and then dinner.

*

When all else fails, teach! When in doubt as to a career, start teaching. You're a philosopher. Follow the examples of Plato and Aristotle. Be a teacher! Don't worry about the pay. Do it for the kids. The schools need young men to be in those classrooms. What greater vocation than forming young minds.

I had received this latest "call" from Sister Filibert in March. She said that I'd be a good addition to the faculty at St.Anthony's. Since I had been in the seminary, she felt that I would do well teaching Religion. And she and the other nuns would help me with the secular subjects of Reading, Math, Science and Social Studies.

My salary would be $4800 for nine months, September to May. When I received the Bachelor's Degree in January of 1967, I'd move into another lane with higher pay. What's more, I could walk to work, a whole block from my house to the school where I had spent much of my youth.

I decided to answer Sister's call. It was time to begin a career of service, especially now that Lee and I were to be married. I had reached the point in my life when I had to commit myself. Engineering, physics, and religious life had been serious attempts at commitments. But each of those proved *not* to be my calling. My understanding and knowledge of myself had been limited at each of those former times. I was searching, trying to find God's plan.

One of Aristotle's wise sayings is *Gnothi seauton* in the Greek. "Know thyself" I had spent my young life trying various ways to understand who I am. I pursued the reading of other's lives, comparing them with me. I reflected quite a bit about the life experiences I had, and the heroes that caught my attention, leaving many values in their wake. And I had all those emotional and personal effects and lessons learned from the attempts at other paths.

*

By December of 1966, after four full months of teaching 5th Grade, (and 7th Grade Religion) handling daily record chores like attendance, grading papers, preparing lessons, assembling audio-visual materials, and teaching all the elementary subjects from Reading and Math to Art and Music (except Social Studies), I had an inner feeling, a satisfaction, Yes, a realization that I had found my calling. Even Sister's admonition, "Don't smile until Christmas" which was supposed to establish me as a strict teacher, to ease the rigors of classroom management (discipline), did not deter me or bring on dissatisfaction for my chosen field.

The daily acts of preparation and delivery of lessons consistently challenged my intelligence, and gave opportunities for personal expression. I was the holy man in Religion, the actor in Reading, the taskmaster in Math, and the humorist throughout the school day. ("All right, 5th Graders, for an extra five minutes of recess, 'Who's buried in Grant's Tomb? Or one Friday, I said, "This class has been working so hard all week, you can take the next two days off from school." There would follow an eruption of cheers, until the boy in the middle row said, "But the next two days are Saturday and Sunday.")

I developed bonds and affection between those 35 students and myself. We worked together on birthday parties, touch football at lunch, school liturgies once a week, as well as all those hours of instruction and assignments.

By the time May of 1967 came, I knew clearly that I was experiencing the fruits of God's call. The hours in the classroom were labors that brought daily fatigue, but much more importantly left me with an inner sense of fulfillment, a quiet awareness that my talents were expended each day to the fullest with these children. I was beginning to see now that God had brought me along so that I would teach. I would stand in front of youngsters and lead them from one level of knowledge to another.

I was getting to know myself quite well now, happy and humble with whom I saw.

*

As Lee and I approached our wedding date of June 17th, the weather was constantly on our minds. Especially so, because a week before our big day, an early thunderstorm hit the Chicago area. It started at 3:30 PM on Saturday afternoon just about the time a week later when our wedding would start.

Coming with the storm was a tornado that touched down in Oak Lawn, the neighboring suburb to Evergreen Park on the west. The roof of Oak Lawn High School was peeled back by the tornado Heavy rains left basements on the southwest side flooded.

The aftermath of this storm was a heat wave and high humidity. To our disappointment, the hot, muggy weather lasted all week. Lee and I redirected our prayers to cool off the heat and humidity, only to see the thunderstorms return on Friday, the day before our Matrimony. *And we wanted a June wedding!*

What could we do if the thunderstorms continued on Saturday? All of those bright yellow dresses Lee's mother had sewn for the bridesmaids and flower girls, as well as the beautiful hand-made wedding gown Lee was to wear. Could God spare us the discomfort and blotches of rain on our parade? Would we start our life together under an umbrella?

But, all good things come to those who are patient, and pray! The weather turned cooler over night. The sun was shining on Saturday morning. There was a predicted high of 80 and a low of 60. Showers were likely during the daytime, and winds out of the northeast from 12-20 m.p.h. No thunderstorms! No tornados!

By the time I started dressing into my white tux and dark slacks in the early afternoon, the sun was *still* shining brightly at Comiskey Park, a mile away. I couldn't keep the TV off as I got dressed, even on my wedding day, because the White Sox were in first place, and the Yankees were in town for a showdown, four-game series.

The breeze continued throughout the afternoon, but the skies stayed clear, full of sunshine, with an occasional white cloud floating.

By 2:45, the scene in front of Holy Redeemer Church was a sea of colorfully dressed people with little splashes of yellow, the bridesmaids wearing their bright wedding gowns. I was in the vestibule with Wayne Storrs, my best man, and Jake, my brother and groomsman.

Earlier I had shown Wayne and Jake the wedding bands that were made downtown for Lee and I. They really liked that we had engraved the quote, "TWO SHALL BECOME ONE", with two intersecting circles on the rings.

As the organ began the Pachelbel Canon, a light buzz from the guests arose as Peggy and Brian, Lee's sister and brother started down the aisle toward the altar. Peggy was wearing one of the bright yellow dresses and shoulder capes that Lee's mom, Jean, had spent countless hours making for her first daughter's wedding. On her head was a light, airy, yellow mini-veil. And Brian, her partner, was wearing the white jacket, black pants, black tie tux. They both had big smiles as they led the grand procession.

In regular succession from their starting point in the vestibule, came two more sisters, Mary Jo and then Carol, and their escorts, Brad and Brian Lemberg, Lee's cousins. Each couple was greeted by the same light buzz from the congregation. Next came Maureen, my sister, with Jake. Finally, Lee's sister and maid of honor, Gilmary with Wayne.

With the new liturgical practices from Vatican II, all the members of the wedding party and the priest processed into church from the vestibule. So now it was my turn to walk down the aisle. I had no fears or last minute hesitation that would lead to nervousness. I was calm, knowing that Lee and I had found a bond between us, and were ready to develop that connection with a life-long commitment. We realized, soon after meeting on that rainy night in November, that our initial attraction was genuine, and would last forever. *I needn't look any further, for I had found a treasure long-sought.*

The congregation buzz turned to "Oohs" and "Ahs" as the two flower girls, Franny and Gina, Lee's youngest sisters, and the ring bearer Paul, Lee's youngest brother, all moved slowly down the aisle toward the altar. Gina had just turned three, Franny was five, and Paul was now seven years old. Smiles were popping up all through the congregation as the trio passed.

The organ above changed keys to signal the bride's entrance. From my spot at the aisle, near the first pew, I could see Lee begin to move slowly with her father. Now there were just smiles from both sides of the aisle, sort of a sign of respect for the solemnity and radiance of the bride. As the bride and her father passed each row, the guests rose to add dignity and formality.

When Lee and her father reached my place at the head of the aisle, he turned to her and gave her his parting kiss. And then he hugged her gently.

Methodically he turned to me, reached out to shake my hand. But as he did so, I noticed a slight wink from his eye, and heard his whispered words, "It's about time!"

I smiled broadly, shaking his hand. As he left for the first pew to join Lee's mother, Lee moved slightly forward. She looked just beautiful in the white dress with a beaded shoulder cape. The mantilla on her head added just the right amount of white to her flowing red hair. *She had such a radiant smile. A true, happy bride!*

"You look beautiful," I said, reaching for her left hand. Our eyes met again, just like countless times in the past. "Shall we become one, now," I softly suggested.

"Yes," she answered. "Lead the way."

For a Friend Who Wandered
Many Years

You searched the mountains overhead,
The waters and the stars,
And with a falcon's razor eye
You wandered through the air
Looking, looking for a little dove
Your wandering heart could love.

But mountainsides grew sharp with thorns
The waters hard with ice,
And stars had struck their brazen fires
Too high above your face;
Heavy years were piling up,
Your days were soon to stop.

Resting by a forest pond
Hid from searching eyes
You meditated on the fates
Of hidden destinies:
Your mind, tired with scraping the deep,
Put on a heavy sleep.

And while asleep a magic dream
Came dancing in your head;
You dreamt a little silver dove
Was circling overhead
Scanning for a place to light;
She was a dazzling sight,

A gentle diamond in the air
As she graced the waters round,
But all at once the dream was ended
By a whirring sound;
A cloud-white dove had set her nest
Upon your rising breast.

R. O'Hayer

Lee's College Graduation, 1967
Hugh and Richard Dunworth

Lee's High School Graduation, 1962

Hugh and Lee- Wedding Shower, 1967
Jean Dunworth

Mr.& Mrs. Hugh LeVoy

The Wedding Party in the Dunworth Yard.

ACKNOWLEDGEMENTS

I am grateful for permission granted by Willard Jabusch for usage of words from the hymn "Whatsoever you do" in Chapter 5

I am grateful for permission granted by Major League Baseball for usage of World Series play-by-play in Chapter 1.

I am grateful to the Chicago White Sox for usage of the photo of Minnie Minoso

I am grateful to Pat O'Hayer for his gift of the poem, "For a Friend Who Wandered Many Years"